MEGHAN

A HOLLYWOOD PRINCESS

MEGHAN
A HOLLYWOOD PRINCESS

ANDREW MORTON

Michael O'Mara Books Limited

First published in Great Britain in 2018 by
Michael O'Mara Books Limited
9 Lion Yard
Tremadoc Road
London SW4 7NQ

A CIP catalogue record for this book is available from the British Library.

Papers used by Michael O'Mara Books Limited are natural, recyclable products
made from wood grown in sustainable forests. The manufacturing processes
conform to the environmental regulations of the country of origin.

ISBN: 978-1-78243-961-5 in hardback print format
ISBN: 978-1-78243-964-6 in trade paperback print format
ISBN: 978-1-78243-965-3 in e-book format
ISBN: 978-1-78929-004-2 in audio format

1 2 3 4 5 6 7 8 9 10

www.mombooks.com

Cover design by Claire Cater
Typeset by Ed Pickford

Printed and bound by CPI Group (UK) Ltd, Croydon, CR0 4YY

To my wife Carolyn and all our friends in Pasadena.

Contents

Acknowledgements

S ometimes it helps to be in the right place at the right time. My wife Carolyn is from Southern California, and for some of the year I live in Pasadena, a few miles north-east of downtown Los Angeles. When Meghan Markle's engagement to Prince Harry was announced, it was remarkable how many local people had stories about the *Suits* actress. Pasadena was truly Meghan Markle Central: Edmund Fry, owner of Rose Tree Cottage, a little slice of England in the town, served her tea; her old boyfriend, now a realtor, sold a house just across the street; parents sent their children to the school where Meghan has either studied or performed; local photographers had boxes of slides with unseen shots of the royal-in-waiting, and the Hippie Kitchen where she volunteered as a teenager was just a short drive away.

So, starting in Pasadena, I would like to thank my friend Dr Wendy Kohlhase for introducing me to the enthusiastic and helpful staff and administrators at Immaculate Heart High School. School President Maureen Diekmann and Callie Webb delved deep into the archives stored in the basement to discover all matters Markle while senior teachers Christine Knudsen and Maria Pollia added their insights with regard to their former pupil. My thanks, too, to photographer John Dlugolecki for uncovering a charming series of shots of Meghan as she blossomed into a beautiful young woman.

Gigi Perreau, a Hollywood child star herself and Immaculate Heart alumni, and Emmanuel Eulalia, director of drama at St Francis High School in La Cañada, described Meghan's emerging talent. Elizabeth and Dennys McCoy spoke warmly of the young Meghan, while the thoughts of Catherine Morris, Jeff Dietrich and the staff at the Hippie Kitchen, who work tirelessly to help those without a roof over their head, were much appreciated.

With regard to Meghan's complicated and extensive family tree, I would like to thank genealogists Elizabeth Banas, Gary Boyd Roberts and historian Christopher Wilson, as well as Professor Carmen Harris, University of South Carolina Upstate, who put the lives of her ancestors in context. Family members Tom Markle Junior, Roslyn Loveless and Noel Rasmussen all helped tease out her equally complicated upbringing, while several friends, including Leslie McDaniel and others who remain anonymous, added their perspective. Tameka Jacobs and Leyla Milani talked perceptively about the girl they knew from the *Deal or No Deal* days, while several members of the crew of *Suits,* who for professional reasons did not want to be named, also pitched in. My thanks, too, to Samantha Brett, author of *Game Changers*.

I would also like to thank Professor Prochaska and Trevor Phillips OBE, former chairman of the Equality and Human Rights Commission, for their views on her impact on the monarchy and the country. I have discussed this issue with other former members of the royal Household, who have understandably asked not to be named. Thanks, too, to those in the popular press and social media who have carefully followed Meghan's evolving life and career.

A huge thank you, too, to my researchers, Phil Dampier in London and the indefatigable Lisa Derrick in Los Angeles. Additionally, without the consummate professionalism of my editors Fiona Slater in London and Gretchen Young in New York, as well as the dedication of editorial assistant Katherine Stopa and copyeditor Nick Fawcett, we would never have got over the finish line.

Finally, a big shout-out to all my Pasadena friends, acquaintances and neighbours, whose thoughts, suggestions and advice energized this whole project.

Pasadena
March 2018

The Stars Were Aligned

I was aware of Rachel Meghan Markle long before Prince Harry was on the scene. In the legal drama *Suits* she exuded a charisma that made her stand out, stealing every scene she appeared in, while beyond her acting she was also making a mark for herself as a campaigner for gender equality. So when I heard that she was dating the Queen's grandson, I honestly felt no surprise, and when their relationship deepened, as a biographer, I found myself in the right place at the right time. My wife Carolyn is from Southern California and for some of the year we live in her hometown of Pasadena. It also happens to be Meghan Markle Central. Her old boyfriends, schoolfriends and teachers all live in the area. It is such a close-knit community that one day I was even stopped in my driveway by a neighbour and told to speak to a local storeowner who had a Meghan Markle memory to share. In a cynical and chaotic world, this is at its heart an old-fashioned story of local girl makes good. Of course, it is also much more than that, because when on 19 May 2018 Meghan Markle walks down the aisle at St George's Chapel in Windsor Castle she will be making history.

In the last important royal wedding for a generation, Prince Harry's glamorous bride will be the first bi-racial divorcee ever to marry a member of the British royal family. Their union, blessed by Her Majesty the Queen, will make the monarchy seem more inclusive and relevant in an ever-changing world.

During the service, the 800 guests at the grand affair might hear a low hum competing with the singing of the choir. It will be the sound of the Duke of Windsor, who gave up his throne in 1936 so that he could marry a twice-divorced American, spinning in his grave, located nearby at Frogmore, in the grounds of Windsor Castle.

He was prevented from making the love of his life his Queen because Wallis had two former husbands still living. The only time Wallis was admitted into Windsor Castle was in her coffin in April 1986 for her funeral service at St George's Chapel. In the 1950s, the Queen's younger sister Princess Margaret faced the same predicament, choosing duty before the love of her divorced paramour, Group Captain Peter Townsend.

If nothing else, the wedding of the second son of Prince Charles and the late Diana, Princess of Wales, shows how much and how far the royal family – and the British nation – have changed and evolved during the reign of Queen Elizabeth II. It is a union and an occasion redolent with symbolism.

Since the romantic traumas surrounding Edward VIII and Princess Margaret, the royal family, like the rest of the world, have accepted, albeit reluctantly, the fact that divorce no longer carries the social stigma it once did. Yet even in the early 1980s when Prince Charles was scouting the shires for a bride, the notion of a divorced American marrying into the royal family was unthinkable. Then, the priority was to find a white Anglo-Saxon Protestant aristocratic virgin.

He found one in the winsome shape of Lady Diana Spencer, and the constitutional catastrophe of their marriage – and rancorous divorce – has caused the older generation of royals and their supporters to take pause before commenting on the chosen companions of the younger members of the family. Nor was the parting of the future king and queen a unique occurrence inside the royal family. The Queen's sister Princess Margaret, her daughter Princess Anne and her beloved second son Prince Andrew divorced their marital partners. All were enveloped in varying degrees of scandal, most notoriously when Andrew's wife, the Duchess of York, known as Fergie, was photographed having her toes sucked by her so-called financial adviser next to a swimming pool in the south of France.

That Meghan divorced after a brief two-year union with a film producer has hardly raised an eyebrow, let alone created a constitutional crisis. After all, the future king, Prince Charles, is a divorcee who married his former mistress, Camilla Parker Bowles, also divorced, in April 2005 in a civil ceremony just over the road from St George's Chapel. All very modern. Divorce, race and a racy past – the House of Windsor now welcomes all comers. As Prince Harry succinctly put it during his and Meghan's engagement interview: 'all the stars were aligned'.

It is an observation that Harry's uncle, Prince Andrew, the Duke of York, may reflect upon as he watches Meghan Markle make her stately procession down the aisle. For Prince Andrew it was not just the stars but the decades that were out of alignment. Just thirty-six years ago the prince, a red rose between his teeth, ran down the gangway of his ship, HMS *Invincible*, to be greeted by his proud parents, the Queen and the Duke of Edinburgh.

Back then, he was the world's most eligible bachelor and a fully certified war hero, having risked his life during the Falklands conflict between Britain and Argentina which left more than nine hundred dead and thousands wounded.

A few weeks later, in October 1982, he secretly flew to the private Caribbean island of Mustique, where the Queen's sister, Princess Margaret, had a property, Les Jolies Eaux. He and his American girlfriend, Kathleen 'Koo' Stark, the daughter of Hollywood producer Wilbur Stark, had, according to first reports, flown under the assumed name of 'Mr and Mrs Cambridge'.

When she first arrived in London in 1975, Kathleen wanted to be an actress and starred in a tepidly erotic rite-of-passage movie entitled *Emily*, directed by arty aristocrat the Earl of Pembroke. As pictures were circulated of Koo in various stages of undress, hysteria gripped the mass media and even some members of Parliament.

Their romance continued long after their holiday and the early revelations about her film role. She met the Queen, and Princess Diana considered her the perfect match for Andrew. She told me, 'Sweet Koo adored him. She was terribly good to have around. Very gentle and looked after him . . . all her energies [were directed] to him. [They] suited each other so well.'

Yet the stigma of that movie, one of her first, poisoned her relationship with Andrew. With her being forevermore known as a 'porn actress' – nothing could be further from the truth – her love affair with Andrew was doomed. But for a fifth-rate movie,

Kathleen might have been the first American to marry into the royal family since Wallis Simpson.

By contrast, Meghan Markle has taken acting roles in which she has been filmed snorting cocaine, teaching housewives the art of striptease, and having sex in a storeroom. She appeared semi-naked in so many scenes in the long-running TV drama *Suits* that she complained that scriptwriters were deliberately crafting scenarios to show off her body.

(Meghan might note that while the palace have ordered her website, The Tig – which contained intelligent and well-written essays about gender equality and race – to be scrubbed from the World Wide Web, videos of her very unprincess-like behaviour remain for all to see.)

While Meghan is not the first mixed-race woman to marry into European royalty – that honour goes to Panamanian-born Angela Brown, now Princess Angela of the tiny but wealthy country of Liechtenstein – she is the first divorced bi-racial American to take her place in the House of Windsor.

Though race has aroused plenty of debate in her own country – inevitably, because of America's past as a nation practising slavery and segregation – race relations have been largely ignored in conjunction with the royal family.

Ironically, when the engagement was announced in November 2017, moviegoers were enjoying *Victoria and Abdul*, the story of Queen Victoria's friendship with an Indian attendant, Abdul Karim. His presence at Court excited so much animosity that when the queen died in 1901, her successor King Edward VII personally supervised his eviction and deportation back to India. Victoria's daughter Beatrice erased all references to

Karim in her mother's voluminous diaries. As historian Carolly Erickson observes in *Her Little Majesty*: 'For a dark-skinned Indian to be put very nearly on a level with the queen's white servants was all but intolerable, for him to eat at the same table with them, to share in their daily lives, was viewed as an outrage.'

Though the present queen does not, as author Penny Junor argues, recognize colour, only 6 per cent of the 1,100 people employed by the palace are from ethnic minorities and only around 30 are in senior positions. While this ethnic imbalance is also reflected in the senior ranks of the civil service, it has been argued that the royal family have missed an opportunity to take the lead on race.

It is a subject that Meghan has not shied away from discussing, and she will already be well aware that people of colour do not feature noticeably inside the palace. Perhaps it is an issue she may decide to involve herself in after she settles into royal life.

As Trevor Phillips, former head of the Equality and Human Rights Commission, notes, the way in which Meghan handles herself will send out an important message. 'It is a very big deal that she has talked of her pride in her ethnicity. For people of colour that will be seen as a very positive, modern approach and immensely welcome.'

Not only is Meghan part of the discussion about race in Britain, her racial background also informs attitudes in America, the bi-racial royal being considered part of the Loving Generation, the cohort that gets its name from the Virginia couple Richard and Mildred Loving, who were arrested in 1958 and put in jail for the crime of miscegenation. Until the 1967

Supreme Court judgment of *Loving vs Virginia*, inter-racial marriage was against the law in some states.

In the 1970s there were about 65,000 black-white married couples in the United States. By the 1980s, a little over a decade after the Loving ruling, that number had doubled to 120,000. A significant jump, but one has to keep in mind that the population was around 240 million at the time.

With a white Republican father and a black Democrat mother, Meghan has found herself at the centre of an active discussion about the place of mixed-race individuals in society. Thus Meghan's narrative is that of a woman trying not just to find herself as a woman but to define her place in a world where she is seen as neither black nor white.

Looking to the future, she will also have to define herself as part of the far smaller world of royalty.

Even though Meghan is very much her own woman, it is interesting that those who taught her, or knew her, spontaneously mention the 'D' word in the same breath as Meghan. Comparisons with Diana are inevitable; Meghan's secret solo visit in February 2018 to comfort the survivors of the Grenfell tower-block inferno in Kensington, West London, revives memories of Diana's trips to the homeless on London's South Bank.

Other similarities can be seen in her broader humanitarian work and popular, glamorous appeal. But at her core, Meghan is a very different person, possessing a balance and self-assurance that Diana, certainly in her early royal career, struggled to reach. She is a woman who is camera-ready, not camera-shy.

Long before Prince Harry was mentioned in conjunction with Meghan, her high school, Immaculate Heart in Los

Angeles, regularly screened the 2015 speech that she made at the United Nations Women conference on gender equality as inspiration for the current generation of female students.

It is said that to be an effective Congressperson or member of Parliament – or President – it is preferable to have enjoyed a successful career outside the political world so that when you walk into the chamber – or the White House – it is not so intimidating. This is where Meghan finds herself. She has arrived at the gates of the palace fully formed: a successful actor, a popular blogger and an acknowledged humanitarian.

She can boast a bloodline of slaves and kings, servants and swordsmen. Hers has been a remarkable journey, a journey that began where else but in the city of dreams, Los Angeles.

1

In Search of Wisdom

For years she was troubled by a nagging question at the back of her mind: where does my family come from, what is my history? For Rachel Meghan Markle – known as 'Bud' and 'Flower' by her family – it was an endlessly perplexing issue. The fact that her mother, Doria Ragland, was an African-American from Los Angeles and her father, Thomas Wayne Markle, was a white Pennsylvanian only added to the confusion. She felt she had to find her place, where she belonged, in both the black and the white world. In the hierarchy of colour that still defines so much about place and position in American society, she was light-skinned and therefore seen as 'whiter' than her black cousins. So, along with her perplexity came a fluidity, a readiness to view the world from different perspectives, from both sides.

She had listened wide-eyed as her Uncle Joseph had told and retold the story of the Raglands' cross-country drive from Cleveland, Ohio, to Los Angeles in a borrowed car when her mother Doria was a babe in arms. Their adventure turned nasty when they pulled into a one-horse town in Texas in the teeth of a blizzard. They were looking for a room for the night but soon realized they were not wanted in the redneck town. One guy pointed off into the snow and yelled, 'The highway is that way. Get going. You are not welcome here.'

While it may be family lore – the road from Cleveland to Los Angeles goes nowhere near the Lone Star state – for Meghan's uncle, then around seven or eight, it represented his first real experience of racism. He further recounted that during this journey the family were told to use the back door for 'coloureds' when they stopped at a diner. As Meghan was to learn, the history of her mother's family was one of exploitation, discrimination and injustice. Some of it she would experience first-hand, such as when she felt the rush of blood to her cheeks when someone in a parking lot used the 'N' word to her mother because she did not leave briskly enough. It was a word that her ancestors – slaves who worked on the cotton plantations of Georgia – would have heard on a daily basis.

It is no wonder that Meghan was left bewildered by her family tree. Tracing her family back through her mother's line is a difficult business. Prior to emancipation, evidence about the lives of black people in the South was inevitably scarce. There were few written records, and most information was passed on by word of mouth. What we do know is that for years the family were the property of a Methodist, William Ragland, whose family originated from Cornwall in the south-west of England, before emigrating to Virginia and then North Carolina.

Ragland lived in Chatham County, North Carolina, with his slaves before moving to the rural town of Jonesboro in Georgia where land was regularly given away by the authorities in lotteries to encourage settlement. Traditionally, slaves were only known by a first name, given to them by their owner, and on occasion they also took their owner's surname. The scanty records that are available show that the first 'black Ragland', that is to say Meghan's first documented Ragland ancestor, was born in Jonesboro in 1830. This was Richard Ragland, who married a woman named Mary. Though much of his life was spent in enforced servitude, at least his son, Stephen, who was born in 1848, lived to see the emancipation that came when the Union, the anti-slave northern states led by President Abraham Lincoln, triumphed over the pro-slave Confederacy in 1865. According to records unearthed by Massachusetts-based genealogist Elizabeth Banas, at the end of the war Stephen Ragland became a sharecropper. But this was merely slavery by another name, as the overwhelming majority of what he produced was taken by the white landowner in rent and other dues, leaving an average sharecropper such as Stephen Ragland constantly in debt.

Though freed at the end of the war in June 1865, it was not until the 1870 census that most former slaves were able to register a name for themselves officially. Stephen Ragland stuck with his former master's surname and his given name. Not quite as romantic as 'Wisdom', the name Meghan believes great-great-great-grandfather Ragland chose when he was given the chance to make a fresh start. As she wrote for *Elle* magazine in July 2015: 'Perhaps the closest thing connecting me to my ever-complex family tree, my longing to know where I come from, and the commonality that links me to my bloodline, is the choice that my great-great-great-grandfather made to start anew. He chose the last name Wisdom.'

Sadly, the professional genealogists and researchers who have carefully investigated her history point out that the records, albeit sketchy and contradictory, show that he kept his original name. They also indicate that his first wife was named Ellen Lemens and that the couple married on 18 August 1869 and went on to have four children: Ann (who was also known as Texas), Dora, Henry, and Jeremiah, born in either 1881 or 1882, who is Meghan's great-great-grandfather. Based on census and tax records it seems that for some years Stephen and Ellen continued to live around Jonesboro on the Ragland plantation where they had been slaves. In fact, when Lemuel Ragland died on 19 May 1870, Stephen Ragland was recorded in the census as working for Lemuel's widow Mary, then aged sixty. Other family members living in the vicinity, probably in the same plantation bunk-house or rough-hewn wooden shacks, included Vinny and Willy Ragland as well as Charles, Jack, Jerry, Mariah and Catherine Lemens.

After a time in Jonesboro, the town now famous as the setting for the epic novel about the American Civil War, *Gone with the Wind*, the family moved the short distance to Henry County, an agricultural district noted for its rich soil and premium cotton. Stephen and his sons, Henry and Jeremiah, worked the land as either sharecroppers or hired hands. However, beyond the cotton profits, Henry County also had a darker reputation, as a home of the Ku Klux Klan, which had risen in the area in the spring of 1866. The Klan's first action in the county was to lynch former slave Dave Fargason during a local conflict centring on educating black children. Stephen's son Henry Ragland was also later confronted by a gang of armed white men but managed to escape with his life. Local historian

R. H. Hankinson observes that, soon afterwards, the KKK was wound up in the area – although the threat of violence remained.

Indeed, the threat of violence as well as grinding poverty prompted many to migrate north or west in search of better prospects. Sometime after the turn of the century, Stephen Ragland's daughter Ann, her husband Cosby Smith, whom she married in 1892, together with their six children, decided to make the 3,000-mile journey to start a new life in Los Angeles in the days when oil and oranges were more important to the town's economy than making movies.

Their decision to move inspired Stephen's youngest child Jeremiah, his wife Claudie Ritchie, daughter of the wonderfully named Mattie Turnipseed, and their growing brood to leave Georgia as well. Around 1910, when Claudie was twenty-five, they made their way to Chattanooga in Tennessee in the hope of building a better life for themselves.

It is likely that neither Ann nor Jeremiah saw their father, Stephen Ragland, ever again even though he lived to the relatively ripe old age of seventy-eight, breathing his last in Paulding County, Georgia, on 31 October 1926.

By then, Jeremiah and Claudie had raised five children, though one died in childbirth. Claudie, who was officially designated in the census as a 'mulatto' or of mixed race, worked as a maid at Miller Bros department store, then the company's flagship. Her husband Jeremiah found casual jobs working in a barber shop and as a saloon porter before setting up his own tailoring business. At that time, black people were barred from well-paying jobs or obtaining loans. Self-employment was the only route for self-improvement.

Just as the women in the family raised the children, they also made more of their opportunities, as they became available. Jeremiah's daughter and Meghan's great aunt, Dora, was the first Ragland to go to college and the first to set herself up as a professional, becoming a schoolteacher. Her younger sister Lillie did even better. She studied at the University of California as a mature student before training as a realtor and setting up her own business in Los Angeles. She was so successful that she was listed in the African-American *Who's Who*.

Their brothers did not climb so high, one working as a waiter, while Meghan's great-grandfather Steve found employment as a presser in a cleaner's shop in downtown Chattanooga. As Meghan's uncle Joseph admits: 'Culturally our family did not have male figures.' Steve married Lois Russell, the daughter of a hotel porter, when she was fourteen or fifteen. In the census of 1930, the couple were recorded as living with their baby son, Alvin Azell, later Meghan's grandfather, as well as Lois's father James Russell and assorted nieces and roomers.

When Alvin was old enough he made his way to Cleveland, Ohio, in search of work. There he met Jeanette Johnson, the daughter of a bellboy and elevator operator at the five-star St Regis Hotel. Soon after the end of the Second World War, Johnson had married professional roller-skater Joseph Johnson, by whom she had two children, Joseph Junior and a daughter, Saundra. It was not long before Johnson, who travelled from town to town to show off his skills, skated out of her life, leaving Jeanette to raise their children on her own. Enter the smooth-talking, snappily dressed Alvin Ragland, who soon had Jeanette's heart beating a little faster.

They married and moved into a basement apartment in a three-storey building in Cleveland. Their first child, Doria, Meghan's mother, was born in September 1956 and it was soon afterwards that Alvin uprooted the family and embarked on that famous cross-country ride to begin a new life in Los Angeles, where their Ragland relations had settled. For a time he worked for his Aunt Lillie in real estate and then he opened his own bric-a-brac and antique store in downtown Los Angeles. However, by then his marriage was over and Jeanette was once again left holding the baby. He married for a second time on 6 May 1983, his wife Ava Burrows, a teacher, giving birth to their only son Joffrey a few months later.

By this time, Doria Ragland was all grown up and with a child of her own. Two years earlier she had given birth to her daughter, Rachel Meghan Markle, at 4.46 in the morning of 4 August 1981 in the West Park Hospital in Canoga Park in Los Angeles. Meghan's arrival would change the narrative of her family forever.

❖

The blooming of Meghan's family from picking cotton under the blazing sun to seeing one of their own taking her wedding vows to a royal prince under the camera lights is an extraordinary story of upward mobility. And what a sublime contrast it makes with the not so distant past. The last American to marry a member of the British royal family was Wallis Warfield Simpson, who hailed from Baltimore, Maryland. Though she was twice divorced with two husbands living, King Edward VIII insisted on marrying her despite overwhelming opposition from the Church, the government and the Empire, all of whom objected to a divorcee becoming royal consort. As a result, he abdicated the throne, marrying Wallis at a modest ceremony in a French chateau in June 1937. Billed as the royal romance of the century, the king giving up everything for the woman he loved.

Fast forward eighty years. While the Duke and Duchess of Windsor, as Edward and Wallis became, would have been delighted that the House of Windsor had embraced the reality of divorce, they would have been astonished that Prince Harry's bride was to be of mixed race. For Wallis's family, the Warfields, had built their various fortunes on the back of slave labour.

For their part they did consider themselves benign and enlightened masters, Wallis's third cousin, Edwin Warfield, who was elected forty-fifth governor of Maryland in 1903, giving several speeches on the topic of 'Slavery as I knew it'. However, Edwin's tolerance only went so far; in the election for governor he stood on a platform of white supremacy, believing that 'ill-educated blacks' should be denied the franchise.

While Wallis was brought up in relative poverty – she and her mother were the poor relations of the wealthy Warfield family – she enjoyed the services of a black nanny, butler and maids. They were part of her life, albeit as downstairs folk who never crossed a line of familiarity. Indeed, she once observed that the first time she shook the hand of a non-white person was when she and her husband, the Duke of Windsor, glad-handed the crowds in Nassau during his time as governor of the Bahamas in the Second World War. People of colour simply did not feature in the life of Wallis or her husband except to hold out a tray of drinks. She was from a class, an age and a region where, quite unselfconsciously, Wallis and her friends were nonchalantly racist. In letters and table talk, she casually used the 'N' word and other derogatory terms. When Wallis was born in 1896, Meghan's great-great-great-grandfather Stephen Ragland was scratching out a meagre living as a sharecropper. The very idea that a bi-racial woman would marry a prince of the realm in the august setting of St George's Chapel, the scene of numerous royal weddings including that of King Edward VII and more recently the Queen's third son, Prince Edward, would have been unthinkable.

But Meghan won't be the first to challenge that particular notion. In 2004, the daughter of a prince, Lady Davina Windsor, married sheep-shearer, surfer and father Garry 'Gazza' Lewis, a Maori, or New Zealand native, in a private ceremony at Kensington Palace. Now twenty-ninth in line to the throne, Lady Davina and her husband were invited to the wedding of Prince William and Kate Middleton and look set to be present at Harry and Meghan's nuptials. The royal family barely batted an eyelid at this union between the daughter of the Duke and Duchess of Gloucester and a member of New Zealand's second-largest ethnic grouping. Unsurprisingly, not all members of Britain's aristocracy are quite as welcoming. When the glamorous food writer Emma McQuiston, the bi-racial daughter of a Nigerian oil tycoon, married Viscount Weymouth, the heir to the famous Longleat estate, in 2013, his mother's reaction was: 'Are you sure about what you are doing to 400 years of bloodline?'

Ironically, Meghan herself is not such an outsider as some may think, and her European bloodline is far older than 400 years.

Popular interest in Meghan has perhaps inevitably largely rested on her family's history of slavery and how, through hard work and endeavour, her ancestors made a life for themselves in an unforgiving world; what is less familiar is that Meghan has, through her father's family, links to the royal families of Scotland, England and beyond. When she wrote, 'Being bi-racial paints a blurred line that is equal parts staggering and illuminating,' she never realized for a moment that the blood of kings as well as slaves ran through her veins.

For starters, it is possible to trace a direct line through twenty-five generations to Robert I of Scotland, perhaps the most colourful of all Scottish kings. Better known as Robert the Bruce, he is the legendary warrior who, as he hid in a cave to avoid capture by the English enemy, watched a spider trying to spin a web. The spider repeatedly tried and failed to swing itself up from a long thread, an echo of Bruce's own failure on the battlefield. He gave the spider one last chance. If it succeeded in swinging itself up, he would wage a final battle to liberate his country.

The spider triumphed, and so did Robert the Bruce, defeating the English at the bloody Battle of Bannockburn in 1314. He remained king until his death in 1329, acknowledged as one of the most successful and best-loved of all Scottish monarchs.

Such a fascinating connection to this distant world of kings comes through her father's family, the Markles, whose bloodline tells a story shared by so many – ancestors whose roots were in the Old World but who sailed west to seek a better life.

The Markles, who have their origins in Germany and Holland, lived in Pennsylvania for generations, working as farmers, lime burners, carpenters, miners, soldiers and, in the case of Meghan's great-grandfather, the giant Isaac 'Ike' Markle, as a fireman for the Pennsylvania Railroad Company. Ike's son Gordon Arnold, Meghan's grandfather, started his own filling-station business, worked in the shoe industry and wound up in an administrative position for the post office in the small town of Newport. In March 1941, just months before America entered the Second World War, he married Doris Mary Rita Sanders, who hailed from New Hampshire.

It is the lineage of Meghan's grandmother that can be traced directly to the Scottish royals and more. Through her ancestor Roger Shaw, Meghan's trickle of blue blood was ultimately transported to America. The son of a wine merchant and shipper in the City of London, Shaw sailed from Plymouth in the west of England to Massachusetts around 1637.

Like many other young men, Roger Shaw saw America as the land of promise and opportunity. Thanks to his father's influence, the authorities gave him licence 'to sell wine, and any sorts of hard liquor, to Christians and Indians, as his judgement deemed, on just and urgent occasions, and not otherwise'. In time he became a substantial landowner, farmer and acknowledged pillar of the community.

Through Shaw's family, who originated from Yorkshire in the north of England, we find the critical link to royalty. Locally they were well-respected landowners and it was the marriage in 1490 of one of the clan, James Shaw, to Christina Bruce, the heiress daughter of Sir David Bruce, 6th Baron of Clackmannan, a direct descendant of Robert the Bruce, that sealed the royal connection.

Going back down the generations, Doris can also boast another interesting connection to royalty, this time through her ancestor Mary Bird, who appeared in the household records for Windsor Castle in 1856 and probably worked as a maid. There is some satisfaction here in that, like some latter-day Cinderella, Mary's descendant will marry her own prince.

This, though, is not the only royal and English bond. Meghan is also descended from the English immigrant Christopher Hussey, who lived in the whaling island of Nantucket off the coast of Massachusetts, as well as the Reverend William Skipper, who landed in New England in 1639. The Reverend Skipper's bloodline is of particular note. His royal connections and subsequent links to the Markle family ensure that, according to Boston-based genealogist Gary Boyd Roberts, Meghan is a twenty-fourth-generation descendant of the medieval King Edward III. Born at Windsor Castle, he successfully ruled England for fifty years until his death in 1377.

Furthermore, according to Roberts, Meghan is distantly related to most European royal families thanks to her English kinswoman Margaret Kerdeston, who lived during the fifteenth century and was the paternal grandmother of Anne of Foix-Candale, Queen of Hungary and Bohemia. There are other, more tangential, royal links. Skipper's ancestors Sir Philip Wentworth and Mary Clifford have distant blood connections to the late Diana, Princess of Wales, and the Queen Mother. As a result of royal intermarriage, Prince Harry, according to Roberts, is descended from Margaret Kerdeston in more than 240 lines, making the prince and his bride very, very distant cousins.

As Gary Boyd Roberts observed of Meghan: 'Much of

American and English history is reflected in her diverse ancestry.'

Of course, many people with European ancestry can claim distant links to royalty, but for Meghan, such connections naturally gain new significance. Her mixed European and African-American heritage has constantly reminded her, especially when she was growing up, about her difference and distinction. It is something she has learned to acknowledge and embrace.

2

Growing Up Markle

rowing up Markle in the 1950s was like a chapter from *The Adventures of Tom Sawyer*. Young Tom Markle, Meghan's father, and his two older brothers, Mick and Fred, enjoyed an idyllic childhood in the small Pennsylvanian town of Newport where they lived in a modest clapboard house. The boys played on monkey vines in the woods at the end of their dirt road, went fishing for catfish in the Juniata River, and in summer picked blackberries, their mother, Doris, turning their trove into delicious pies and jams. As a teenager Tom earned his pin money literally, setting the pins in the local bowling alley. Or he would join his father Gordon, who worked in administration for the post office, watching his beloved Philadelphia Phillies score home runs on their black-and-white television.

By the time Tom graduated from Newport High School, his brother Mick had joined the United States Air Force where he worked in telecommunications, though some say he was eventually recruited into the Central Intelligence Agency. Brother Fred headed south, found religion, and eventually ended up becoming the Presiding Bishop of the Eastern Orthodox Catholic

Church in America, located in Sanford, Florida, where he is known as 'Bishop Dismas'.

Tom took a different attitude towards his future. After graduating, he left small-town Newport and drove to the Poconos, a mountainous resort area in north-eastern Pennsylvania. There he worked at a local theatre, learning the technical backstage side of the business and gaining valuable experience that gave him a step up the professional ladder. He then travelled to Chicago after getting a job as a lighting technician at WTTW, the local affiliate for the Public Broadcasting Service. He also worked at the Harper Playhouse operating alongside the new owners, Bruce and Judith Sagan, who wanted to give the Hyde Park district, also the home of a certain Barack Obama, a vibrant new cultural centre. He soon became the theatre's lighting director, working on the controversial musical *Hair*, dance shows and classic Russian dramas, as well as jazz and chamber-music concerts.

Tom worked hard and played hard, spending down-time with his student friends from the prestigious private college, the University of Chicago. During one rowdy party at the on-campus International House in 1963, Tom, then nineteen, met eighteen-year-old Roslyn Loveless, a student who worked as a secretary in the nearby Amtrak offices. Both tall – she is 5 feet 9 inches, he 6 feet 4 inches – and with similar red hair, the attraction was immediate, Roslyn being amused by his quirky sense of humour and 'light air'. They married the following year, their only daughter, Yvonne, born in November 1964 and their son, Tom Junior, two years later, in 1966. In those early years, life was a grind, Tom often working eighteen-hour days and Roslyn holding down a secretarial job herself while bringing up two children. It was a constant juggling act, Roslyn's mother Dorothy helping out when she could.

Despite the daily pressures, they still enjoyed a busy social life and had a fun circle of friends, Tom keeping everyone amused with his off-beat brand of humour. Roslyn remembers one time at a Greek restaurant where he pretended to have a parrot called Stanley, passing the imaginary parrot from one person to the next and imploring the waitresses not to stand on him. 'It was hilarious,' she recalls. When Yvonne and Tom Junior started to lose their milk teeth, he sent them long letters from two tooth fairies, Hector and Ethel, who described their lives and explained what would happen to the teeth. From time to time he'd take the children to work with him. It was a thrill, especially as at that time he was lighting the hugely popular puppet show, *Sesame Street*. A trip to Wrigley Field to watch the Chicago Cubs baseball team, driving his dad's car in the parking lot at WTTW, being lifted into the air on the studio lighting gantry, hunting for quarters on a stage filled with foggy dry ice: these were some of the good times Tom Junior treasures.

In his eyes, Tom Senior was the fun dad, the dad who played the best games and made you laugh the hardest – when he was around. Which, sadly, was not often. Childhood expectation was invariably tinged with disappointment. He was consumed by his work, the fruits of his labour coming in local Emmy nominations – and a fat pay cheque. The price he paid for such success was his marriage, the constant late nights, the boozy cast parties, and the endless distraction and fatigue taking their toll. One of Tom Junior's earliest memories is the sound of raised voices, slamming doors and angry words. At some point in the early 1970s, when the children were still in elementary school, the couple decided to go their separate ways.

For a time, Tom lived in Chicago and had the children at weekends. But it didn't last long. He had a dream and that dream was Hollywood. Sometime before their divorce in 1975, Tom left his estranged wife and children behind as he started his new life on the West Coast. The children would not see their father again for several years.

At the urging of her brother Richard, who lived in New Mexico, Roslyn and the children travelled to Albuquerque to make a new life. For a while it was a happy time. Uncle Richard was not his father, as far as Tom Junior was concerned, but at least he was around, teaching him to drive his VW Bug in a parking lot and showing him how to shoot. Plus, Richard and Roslyn got on well together. For the first time in their lives the children did not have to live with a rancorous atmosphere at home.

The downside was that, as the only redhead at his new school, Tom Junior found himself bullied and picked on by his new classmates. Fellow pupils would steal his lunch money, while others started fights. He used to dread going to school, often coming home with yet another black eye. Worse was to come. One night he went to see the movie *Smokey and the Bandit* with his mother and her new boyfriend, a martial arts expert called Patrick. They arrived back home to find a full-scale robbery in progress. When Patrick tackled the thieves he was shot in the stomach and the mouth, the bullets whistling past Tom Junior. Although Patrick survived, Tom Junior was traumatized.

Between bullying and burglary, Tom Junior decided to leave Albuquerque and go and live with his father, who was now enjoying life at the beachfront town of Santa Monica in Southern California. He arrived in time to enrol in high school.

Though he still idolized his father, there was one big fat fly in the ointment of his new life: his sister, Yvonne. She had moved there a few years earlier when she was fourteen. They had always fought like cat and dog; the sibling rivals from hell.

When the trio moved from Santa Monica to a large home on Providencia Street adjacent to the Woodland Hills country club, Tom Junior snagged the downstairs den as his bedroom. He was especially thrilled when a friend sold him a king-sized water-bed. His excitement turned to dismay when he sat on it shortly after taking delivery only to be soaked in water. Inspecting the evidence, he discovered several holes in the brand new bed. There was only one suspect. His sister Yvonne immediately admitted responsibility but argued that it was retribution, as she had wanted that room for herself. Another episode in a bitter, resentful dance between the siblings. As Tom Junior told me: 'If she didn't get what she wanted out of you she was your worst nightmare.'

Enter into this bickering dynamic the figure of Doria Ragland. Small, watchful, with liquid brown eyes and a jaunty Afro, this was the woman who had turned their father Tom into gooey mush. Before he ever brought her home, the children noticed a change in their father. He was more relaxed, frequently taking time off work, cheery and light-hearted. In short, he was happy. The couple had met on the set of ABC's drama *General Hospital* where she was training as a make-up artist and he was well established as the show's lighting director. In spite of the twelve-year age difference – Doria was closer in age to Yvonne than to her boyfriend – the couple very quickly fell for one another.

A graduate of Fairfax High School, Doria had seen her education badly affected by the 1971 San Fernando earthquake. The quake had destroyed nearby Los Angeles High School so the two schools doubled up, Doria studying from seven in the morning until noon and then pupils from LAHS taking over their classroom for the afternoon. In spite of the difficulties, she was a member of the Apex club, a class for academically advanced youngsters. After graduating from Fairfax, Doria sold jewellery, helped in Alvin's antique store, called 'Twas New, and tended a bric-a-brac stall at a Sunday flea market. She also worked as a travel agent. It was a way of obtaining cut-price air tickets so she could see the world on the cheap.

Not that Tom Junior took much notice of the new addition to the Providencia Street household. What with his skateboarding, go-karting and working for a florist, he barely missed a beat when Doria moved in. He was too busy enjoying himself with his new circle of friends.

As for Yvonne, it was indifference, not to say dislike, at first sight. She resented the fact that the new arrival was taking her father's focus away from her, eager that Tom Senior use his showbiz connections to get her work as a model or an actress. During her time in Albuquerque with her mother, she had modelled jewellery and wedding gowns. Now the truculent teenager was seeing dollar bills in the Hollywood sign. When her friends came over to the house she dismissed the presence of her father's African-American girlfriend, referring to her, according to her brother, as 'the maid'. By contrast, her best friend, now a successful realtor, doesn't recall Yvonne using that language and, even if she did, she ascribes it to her sour Chicago sense of humour. Nonetheless, Yvonne was not, as her mother recalls, a particularly tolerant young woman.

Doria's arrival also coincided with Yvonne embracing the dark tenets of black magic. Even as a little girl Yvonne had had a fascination with the macabre, once bringing into her bedroom a mouldering gravestone that she had found in the basement of their apartment block in Chicago. This time around, as her brother Tom recalls, she bought a copy of Anton LaVey's *Satanic Bible*, installed an altar in her bedroom, played with a Ouija board, burned black candles and dressed in the all-black uniform of the goth. It may have been no more than a rebellious teenage obsession, and her brother never witnessed her performing any satanic rituals, but he described to me how he was still disturbed by her 'weird' behaviour. She left the house when it was dark and rarely returned before dawn. One of Yvonne's friends remembers those years, describing how she and Yvonne would dress up and go out dancing, especially if a British band was in town. 'We put on our make-up and got all decked out,' she recalls. 'We were out having fun.' The ritual of boy meets girl, rather than anything satanic, was their aim.

Much of the back and forth between brother and sister was more taunting and teasing than witchcraft. On one occasion Yvonne came to the flower shop where Tom Junior worked part time, to borrow money from her brother. While he and his colleague Richard, a devout Christian Scientist, were dealing with customers, she picked up Richard's Holy Bible and drew a pentagram, the sign of the devil, on its pages with her red lipstick. Before leaving she wrote '666', the mark of the Beast, on another page. Young Tom had his revenge when he called home telling his sister that Richard was so traumatized by her desecration of his Bible that he had run into the road and been hit by a bus. His ruse had her racing back to the flower store to check on Richard's condition.

Certainly Doria could be forgiven for wondering what she had got herself into when faced with this bickering back-biting brood. It was one thing falling in love with a man twelve years her senior, quite another being thrown headlong into his fractious family with brother and sister continually squabbling. A strong personality with a level head on her shoulders, Doria brought a sense of family to the gloomy house.

When she arrived, everyone was used to going their own way. Tom Senior worked every hour of the day and night, Yvonne was out clubbing with her friends, while Tom Junior was smoking weed with his own crowd. She brought them together as a family, Doria seen as the cool hippie peacemaker. She soon became friendly with their near-neighbour Olga McDaniel, a former nightclub singer, Doria spending hours with her shooting the breeze. 'The best way I can describe Doria is that she was like a warm hug,' Olga's daughter told me. Her masterstroke was to take Tom Junior to the animal shelter and help him pick out a family dog, which he named Bo. The noisy new arrival, a golden retriever-beagle mix, soon ruled their five-bedroomed home in the leafy Valley suburb of Woodland Hills.

At Thanksgiving Doria invited the Markles to join the Ragland clan, including her mother Jeanette, her father Alvin, her half-brother Joseph and half-sister Saundra, for a true Southern feast of sweet potato pie, gumbo, ham hocks and beans. 'Good times,' recalls Tom Junior. 'When I first met them I was uneasy and nervous, but they were really warm and inclusive, the kind of family I had always wanted. They were happy-assed people with a real sense of family.'

That sense of family was formalized when, on 23 December 1979, Doria and Tom Senior were married at the Self-Realization Fellowship temple on Sunset Boulevard, just east of Hollywood. The venue was Doria's choice, the new bride adhering to the teachings of Yogananda, a Hindu yoga guru who arrived in Boston in 1920 and preached a philosophy of breathing and meditation as part of the yoga routine to help followers on their path to enlightenment. Hollywood stars such as Linda Evans and Mariel Hemingway, Apple founder Steve Jobs and ex-Beatle George Harrison all followed his teachings. But even in such an enlightened setting, mixed marriages were still uncommon.

Less than half a century before Tom and Doria's wedding, California had repealed anti-miscegenation laws that banned marriages between black and white people. However, it was not until 1967 that anti-miscegenation laws were declared un-Constitutional throughout the nation by the United States Supreme Court, with their landmark decision in *Loving vs Virginia*, their story since being dramatized in a Hollywood film starring Ruth Negga and Joel Edgerton.

In 1958, Richard and Mildred Loving, a white man and a black woman, were married in Washington DC. When they returned to their home in Virginia, they were arrested in their bedroom under the state's Racial Integrity Act. Judge Leon Bazile suspended their sentence on the condition that the Lovings leave Virginia and not return for twenty-five years. They appealed the judgment but Judge Bazile refused to reconsider his decision, writing, 'Almighty God created the races white, black, yellow, Malay, and red, and he placed them on separate continents, and but for the interference with his arrangement there would be no cause for such marriages. The fact that he separated the races shows that he did not intend for the races to mix.'

The Lovings, supported by the NAACP (National Association for the Advancement of Colored People) Legal Defense Fund, the Japanese American Citizens League and a coalition of Catholic bishops, then successfully appealed to the US Supreme Court, which wrote in their decision, 'Marriage is one of the "basic civil rights of man", fundamental to our very existence and survival ... Under our Constitution, the freedom to marry, or not marry, a person of another race resides with the individual and cannot be infringed by the State', condemning Virginia's anti-miscegenation law as 'designed to maintain White supremacy'. While this judgment decriminalized miscegenation, mixed-race couples were still looked upon with suspicion by many, confronted by casual racism and sometimes outright hostility.

On their big day, Tom Senior, wearing a sports coat and button-down shirt, and Doria, in a flowing white dress with baby's breath flowers in her hair, took their wedding vows in the presence of Brother Bhaktananda. He stressed that the merging of the couple was for the 'highest common good' and to achieve union with God. The children of followers of Self-Realization have a reputation as being open, inquisitive souls. So when Doria found herself pregnant just a year after tying the knot, she and Tom couldn't wait for the new arrival. Further good news came when Doria's pregnancy coincided with Tom's first nomination for a Daytime Emmy award for his design and lighting work on *General Hospital*; he would later be nominated a further eight times. Not bad for a man who was officially colour-blind. If 1980 was a good year, 1981 was going to be even better.

As the months ticked by and the summer thermometer inched upwards, Doria became impatient for the waiting to be over. With the daytime temperatures often in the mid-thirties, she was grateful that they had a 'swamp' evaporative cooler and that the rambling home was dark and shady. In his spare time, Tom Senior decorated the nursery, painting the walls and hanging Disney characters and angel pictures around the white painted cot. Finally, at 4.46 in the morning of 4 August 1981 at West Park Hospital in Canoga Park, obstetrician Malverse Martin announced that Doria and Tom were now the parents of a healthy baby girl. This latest addition to the sorority of 'Valley girls' was, as her mother noted, a Leo. Typical Leos are supposed to be 'Warm, action-oriented and driven by the desire to be loved and admired. They have an air of royalty about them. They love to be in the limelight, which is why many of them make a career in the performing arts.' Never has an astrological star sign been more accurate.

The arrival of Rachel Meghan Markle transformed her father's life. 'He was just so, so happy,' recalls Tom Junior. 'He spent every single minute he could with her. My dad was more in love with her than with anyone else in the world and that included Doria. She became his whole life, his little princess. He was just blown away by Meghan.'

Meghan's seventeen-year-old sister Yvonne just blew past the infant, more interested in clubbing and make-up than playing with a newborn. '"Babies, yuck, no thanks," that was our feeling,' recalls one of Yvonne's friends. She was a teenager having fun, and fun was certainly not babysitting for the new arrival. Not only was Yvonne indifferent to the baby, now nicknamed 'Flower' or 'Bud', she felt left out on the sidelines, her father utterly devoted to baby Rachel. Doubtless she recalled his frequent absences when she was growing up and felt somewhat jealous of the attention now focused on her baby half-sister.

It became an understandable source of friction that her father did not spend, in her eyes, as much time as she would have liked in using his contacts to fix her up with acting or modelling jobs. That said, sometime down the road he did get her a walk-on part on *General Hospital* and an episode in the drama *Matlock*, in which she was killed off before the first commercial break. It seems, though, that she never fully exploited these opportunities.

Not only did Tom spend every waking minute with his second daughter, but in his own quirky fashion he tried to impose a little discipline on the somewhat *laissez-faire* household in order to protect his little 'Flower'. Previously he had always said to his son that if he and his friends wanted to smoke weed they should do so only in the house, but this instruction changed with the arrival of the baby. Tom Junior told me that on one occasion he and his friends were smoking a spliff in the sitting room while Meghan was in the nursery crying. His father announced loudly that he was going upstairs to change her nappy. Shortly afterwards he appeared in the sitting room carrying a full nappy. He joined the boys on the sofa, took a spoon out of his pocket and started eating the 'contents'. Grossed out, the boys fled the house. Only later did he reveal that he had earlier substituted chocolate pudding into a fresh nappy. It was his way of stopping the boys from smoking weed when Meghan was around.

But that was about as far as discipline went. Their house was still generally party central, Doria's friends coming over, playing music, practising yoga, which Doria now taught, and barbecuing. From the outside it seemed to be one big happy family, Doria's relations, especially her mother Jeanette, babysitting for the recently wed couple. Even Tom Junior pitched in, to give Tom and Doria a break. For the most part, Tom and Doria seemed happy, but then their bickering started. As much as Tom loved Meghan, he loved his job too; he was still a workaholic and thought nothing of spending eighty or ninety hours a week on set. And in his eyes, it was paying off, Meghan proving to be his lucky charm. After two nominations, in 1982 he and his colleagues on *General Hospital* finally won a daytime Emmy for 'outstanding achievement in design excellence'.

But it all came at a price. Doria had not signed up for this, dealing with his children, raising her own, kick-starting a career and trying to run the family's cavernous house. And though it was not Tom's fault, they were also living in a predominantly white neighbourhood where, because of her dark skin and Meghan's light skin, people often thought Doria was the nanny. They often stopped her and asked, quite innocently, where the baby's mother lived. It was a petty humiliation that she could do without.

It seemed too that Tom was wedded to work more than he was wedded to her. It was a feeling that had been shared by his first wife, Roslyn. Gradually, the harsh words and the fighting became the norm rather than the exception, Tom Junior and Yvonne recognizing the all-too-familiar sounds of a relationship breaking down. According to family friends, Tom's constant criticism of Doria over matters small and large wore her down. There came a point where Doria decided that enough was enough and went back home to her mother, Jeanette. As a family friend observed: 'Doria is not a door mat, that much I know. She spoke up for herself, protected herself and her daughter fiercely. Her head was on straight. I trusted her judgement.'

The couple split up when their little 'Flower' was just two years old, but did not divorce for another five years. Tom would have custody of his daughter at weekends and drop her off on Sunday evenings. Then, as Meghan told writer Sam Kashner, the trio would sit and eat dinner off their knees as they watched *Jeopardy!* 'We were so close-knit,' she recalls, a memory perhaps seen through the forgiving prism of a child desperate for her parents to be united rather than accepting the bleak reality of a mother and father at odds. Others were not so sanguine, pointing to Tom's bewilderment, not to say bitterness, that Doria had given their union so little time to prove itself. By the time Meghan was old enough to appreciate *Jeopardy!* the couple were divorced and living separate lives.

❖

Founded in 1945 by Ruth Pease, Little Red School House is a Hollywood institution favoured for the sons and daughters of LA's showbiz elite. While parents rarely saw Johnny Depp, whose daughter attended the school, waiting outside the school gates, Flea, bassist for the Red Hot Chili Peppers, used to pick up his daughter after school in a spray-painted Mercedes Benz. Teaching – based around the four-stage programme of Swiss psychologist Jean Piaget – is eclectic, imaginative and expensive: $18,800 for kindergarten, rising to $22,700 for grade six at today's prices. As the school only chooses the brightest and the best, older children have to take an exam before they are considered for entry. In 1983 Doria, who was now training as a social worker, and Tom enrolled two-year-old Meghan in the crèche-cum-kindergarten at the exclusive school.

The set-up was convenient for all involved. Little Red School House was close to the ABC studios in Los Feliz where Tom worked, and a few minutes away from Doria's work and her new home just south of Hollywood. Meghan would stay in the school until she was eleven years old. While reading, writing and arithmetic were at the core of the school day, children could dip into a whole range of subjects, from Spanish to quantum physics. In summer, children worked in the community garden, and went on nature trails at Leo Carillo beach or nearby Griffith Park. After school Meghan would go on bike rides or jogging with her mother, who also encouraged Meghan's early interest in yoga. Her mother insisted that she help prepare the evening meal, a daily routine that Meghan credits with fostering her love of food and cooking.

At the same time the school's stage shows, watched by proud parents, encouraged Meghan's budding interest in the theatre.

When she was five, Meghan entertained the parents with a rendition of the song 'The Wheels on the Bus', and was later featured in *Bye Bye Birdie* and *West Side Story*. On Halloween, Meghan and her friend Ninaki 'Nikki' Priddy played two corpses discussing the size and comfort of their respective coffins. Another time, she shared the lead in an adaptation of *How the Grinch Stole Christmas*. Unfortunately, her co-star Elizabeth McCoy came down with stomach flu just hours before the show began, leaving Meghan desperately trying to memorize both parts. 'That was the worst experience of my life, trying to learn your lines,' Meghan told an apologetic McCoy afterwards. Ironically, no one gave a thought to asking a little girl with an unkempt mane of blonde hair, thick glasses and an awkward, clumsy manner, who was lurking in the chorus, to take the part. Her name was Scarlett Johansson, now one of the world's highest-paid actresses and who was briefly a pupil at the school.

McCoy, who these days is a renowned chef and scriptwriter, had another reason to thank Meghan. Two years Meghan's junior, Elizabeth was the self-confessed 'weird kid'. Intense, fiercely intelligent and overweight, she was interested in off-beat subjects like UFOs, the occult and ghosts. Other children thought her odd. Nor did it help that she suffered from petit mal seizures, a form of epilepsy that saw her going into a trance-like state from time to time that made her unreachable. As the seizures last for only a short time, children are often thought to be daydreaming or not listening.

Meghan, Elizabeth was to discover, was not like many of the other kids, who either walked on by or mocked her. The first time Meghan saw Elizabeth suffering from a seizure she came to her aid, sitting holding her hand and comforting her. Elizabeth also remembers how she provided friendship when she was being taunted by 'the mean girls', as she describes them. She recalls: 'I was bullied and miserable and my only salvation were the kids who liked me. I really liked Meghan a lot. She didn't turn me away if I started talking about off-beat subjects. She listened. She was cool and had cool things to say. I liked being around her.'

It was clear that Meghan had inherited her mother's strong sense of right and wrong, and was prepared to stand up for herself and for others. On one occasion the so-called 'mean girls' announced that they were starting a 'White Girls Only' club and wanted Meghan to join. 'Are you kidding me?' said Meghan to the gaggle of fellow pupils, dismissing them in a sentence. They went very quiet after that.

But that playground confrontation highlighted something that Meghan was struggling with herself. Around this time, Christmas 1988, she tells the story of how her father bought two sets of Heart dolls containing the traditional nuclear family unit of mother, father and two children. He bought one with black dolls, one with white, and mixed them together to represent Meghan's own family. Then he wrapped them in sparkly Christmas paper and placed the box under the tree.

Meghan's struggle to understand herself instinctively made her more aware of those who had difficulties fitting in. As Elizabeth McCoy recalls: 'You never forget the people who were mean to you and who was nice. That's why I have never forgotten Meghan. She was one of the most righteous people I have ever met. If someone was being treated unfairly she stuck up for them. On one occasion I made the girl who bullied me cry. I tried to apologize and Meghan sided with the other girl because she was the one in tears.

'Meghan called it like it was. She was going to defend those who needed it. Her attitude was: "I can see you are hurt and I'm going to protect you." She was a genuinely decent human being who looked out for people who needed help. She gave a damn about people other than herself.'

Even Elizabeth's father, Dennys McCoy, an internationally known animation scriptwriter, singles out Meghan. He recalls: 'She stood out because she was a level-headed kid who was smart and mature for her age. We were surprised that she became an actress. We thought she would be a lawyer.'

By the time she was ten, Meghan was fiercely switched on and loved to debate an issue, taking part in discussions about racism in America, most notably after the notorious beating of Rodney King by LA cops in 1991, the Gulf War that same year and the build-up to the 1992 Presidential contest between Bill Clinton and George H. W. Bush. During one classroom discussion about the looming war in the Gulf, a fellow pupil was in tears because he didn't think his older brother, who was serving in the US military, would make it home. The issue became such a hot topic that the children, led by Meghan, staged a protest on the school grounds. They made banners and signs daubed with anti-war slogans. Such was the interest that the local TV station, KTLA, sent along a camera crew to film the protest.

Even nearer to home were the LA riots in late April and early May of 1992, which were ignited after four Los Angeles Police

Department officers, who were filmed savagely beating Rodney King, an unarmed black man, were acquitted of assault and using excessive force. As the burning and looting spread like fingers along LA's thoroughfares, Meghan and her classmates were sent home. Meghan watched with wonder as ash from burning buildings floated onto her lawn. She thought it was snowing, but her mother knew better and told her to get into the house. Even when they returned to school there was a brooding sense of anxiety, the children, including Meghan, crowding around a second-floor school window as they watched police arresting a man. In total, the six days of rioting left 63 dead and more than 2,300 injured, and led to more than 12,000 arrests.

The experience awakened the nascent activist in her, Meghan becoming determined to use her influence when she could. She had already gained something of a reputation for writing to companies, especially food giants, about damaged or faulty packages and foods. Invariably, she was sent bags of crisps, biscuits or whatever by the food companies as compensation, and she regularly brought the fruits of her letter-writing to share among her schoolfriends.

Her most memorable coup was when she wrote to the household products company Procter & Gamble for making a sexist commercial that used the tag line 'Women all over America are fighting greasy pots and pans' to sell its dish-washing liquid. She and the rest of her classmates had been watching commercials as part of a social studies assignment. It was, however, the reaction of two boys in her class to the dish-washing liquid ad that particularly incensed her. She recalls them saying, 'Yeah, that's where women belong – in the kitchen.' Meghan felt confused. She was angry and annoyed, knowing that they were wrong, but she also felt, as she later recalled, 'small, too small to say anything in that moment'.

She went home and told her father, who suggested that she channel her feelings into handwritten letters of complaint. She wrote not only to the soap company chairman, saying that the phrase should be changed to 'People all over America', but also to Hillary Clinton, then the First Lady, Nickelodeon's *Nick News* anchor Linda Ellerbee, and prominent women's rights lawyer Gloria Allred, who was based in Los Angeles.

While First Lady Clinton and Linda Ellerbee wrote letters of encouragement, and Gloria Allred also offered her support, according to Meghan, she never heard from Procter & Gamble. However, when the ad aired again just a month later, she saw the impact of her handiwork. It had been changed to say, 'People all over America are fighting greasy pots and pans.' Her success once again had the TV cameras arriving at the school, this time with Ellerbee interviewing Meghan and her fellow pupils about her one-schoolgirl campaign.

'I don't think it's right for kids to grow up thinking these things, that just mom does everything,' Meghan told Ellerbee. 'It's always, "mom does this" and "mom does that".' Sometime afterwards, this and other incidents inspired her to join the Washington-based pressure group, the National Organization for Women, Meghan, as she proudly recalled, becoming one of the youngest if not the youngest member of the group, founded in 1966, which campaigns for women's rights.

More than twenty years later, in 2015, Meghan reflected on this chapter of her life while giving a speech as the newly minted UN Women's Advocate for Political Participation and Leadership. 'It was at that moment that I realized the magnitude of my actions. At the age of eleven, I had created my small level of impact by standing up for equality,' she said.

While her childhood experiences were the crucible that set her on the path to activism, her mother believes that she was hardwired from birth to try and make the world a better and more equal place. In short, she had a moral compass. Doria played her own part, strict at home but also ready to show her daughter that there was more to the world than Woodland Hills. She raised her to be what she called, 'a global citizen', taking her to places like Oaxaca, Mexico, where Meghan recalls seeing children playing in the dirt roads and peddling chewing gum so that they could bring home a few extra pesos. When Meghan, then aged ten, and her mother visited the slums of Jamaica, the schoolgirl was horrified to see such grinding poverty. 'Don't look scared, Flower,' her mother told her. 'Be aware, but don't be afraid.'

Her experience is reminiscent of the times the late Diana, Princess of Wales, privately took her boys, William and Harry, to visit the homeless and the sick in central London so that they would hopefully appreciate that life did not begin and end at the palace gates.

Meghan's letter-writing campaigns, her interest in current affairs, her purposeful travelling and gender awareness, were all of a piece with a young girl embarking on a journey where feminism could coexist with femininity, as well as an ethos of hard work that was matched by a willingness to try the new and the interesting.

Curiously, just as her letter-writing campaign got under way, another letter-writing campaign was kicking off, this one regarding the raunchy comedy show *Married . . . with Children*, for which her father was now the lighting director. Meghan often sat on the floor of the studio after school waiting for her father to finish work so that he could take her home. Indeed, she thrilled her fellow classmates when she was given permission to bring several friends on set to meet the cast.

As she sat quietly reading or studying, all kinds of ribald scenes were played out on set, some involving various stages of undress and semi-nudity, as well as off-colour jokes about sex. Hardly the normal after-school fare for a young schoolgirl. In January 1989, a Mormon from Michigan, Terry Rakolta, led a boycott of the show after the screening of an episode entitled 'Her Cups Runneth Over', which involved the purchase of a bra. That episode showed the character of Al Bundy ogling a naked model in a department store.

The resulting media storm led to some sponsors withdrawing advertising and the conservative Parents Television Council describing the show as 'the crudest comedy on prime time television … peppered with lewd punch lines about sex, masturbation, the gay lifestyle and the lead character's fondness for pornographic magazines and strip clubs'.

Meghan later described her own misgivings about spending time around the long-running comedy when she appeared on Craig Ferguson's late-night show. She told her host, 'It's a very perverse place for a girl to grow up. I went to Catholic school. I'm there in my school uniform and the guests would be [former porn star] Traci Lords.' While she wasn't allowed to watch the show when it aired, her mother would let her kiss the screen as her dad's name went by in the credits at the end of the programme.

Perverse it may have been, but it paid the bills – and Meghan's private school fees. At this time, unbeknownst to her, her father enjoyed a slice of luck that meant he no longer had to work such a brutal schedule. In 1990 he won the California State Lottery, scooping $750,000 with five numbers, which included Meghan's birth date. The win was ample payback for the thousands of dollars he had spent over the years buying lottery tickets.

As he still had outstanding financial matters concerning his divorce from Doria, he kept the win secret. But he was too greedy, and his duplicity proved to be his undoing. In order to avoid registering his name with the lottery authorities, he sent an old Chicago friend, who is now dead, to pick up his winnings. The plan, according to his son, backfired when his pal ended up swindling him out of the lion's share of his fortune in a failed jewellery business.

Before he lost his loot, Tom gave his son a substantial handout to start a flower shop and bought daughter Yvonne a second car after she wrecked the first one he had given her.

Within three years of his big win, Tom had declared bankruptcy, the lottery win proving more of a curse than a blessing. At least he had kept some money aside to pay for the next stage of Meghan's education, at Immaculate Heart, a private all-girls Catholic school just yards from his home in Los Feliz. From now on it made sense for her to live with her father during the week, as his home was walking distance from the school. It was a decision that would have far-reaching implications for the way she was seen by her new teachers and classmates.

3

A Street Called Gladys

Sixth Street in downtown Los Angeles is not a place for the unwary. And after dark, even the wary give it a wide berth. Danger lurks in the shadows, desperation loiters on the sidewalk. This is the heart of Skid Row, the mushrooming and endlessly shifting encampment of the homeless and the helpless that is a makeshift home to more than two thousand people. Los Angeles is the homeless capital of America. At the last count there were more than 57,000 men, women and children sleeping rough in the City of Angels, tent towns frequently springing up around the city underpasses, in empty buildings and other open spaces.

This particular stretch is more organized than most of the impromptu enclaves of Skid Row, with volunteers handing out water, food and clean socks. And there is one place in particular, at the corner of Sixth and Gladys, which offers a welcome oasis of calm and tranquillity amid the shouts, moans and shrieks of those who live in the tents and cardboard sheds that line both sides of the road.

This is the Hospitality Kitchen, more popularly known as the 'Hippie Kitchen', which is part of the Catholic Worker community founded more than eighty years ago by Dorothy Day and Peter Maurin. Their stated goal is to 'feed the hungry, shelter the homeless, care for the sick, clothe the naked, visit the prisoner'. In an average day, volunteers will hand out a nourishing but simple meal to around a thousand folk who line up around the block; for many it is their only food for the day. There is no prayer or proselytizing, just beans, salad, a hunk of bread and a thick slice of goodwill.

The charity's uncompromising ideals have, at times, placed them in head-on conflict with the Catholic hierarchy, local police and even other homeless charities. Catholic Worker activists are known to protest against unfair treatment of the homeless, American militarism and nuclear policy as well as the death penalty. Acts of civil disobedience, including lie-ins and noisy marches, have led some to suffer arrest and even jail. Former nun Catherine Morris, now eighty-three, and a stalwart of the Hippie Kitchen for more than forty years, has lost count of the number of times she and her husband Jeff Dietrich have been arrested for peaceful acts of civil disobedience. They like to think of themselves as the 'Merry Pranksters', the name derived from the early hippie followers of counter-culture author and poet Ken Kesey.

Though protest is an integral part of the Catholic Worker credo, feeding the homeless and the destitute takes priority. And it was in the garden of the Hippie Kitchen – a small outdoor haven that's filled with colourful murals, the chirping of Brazilian finches in an aviary and water bubbling over a fountain – that Meghan Markle had what could only be described as an epiphany.

With her mother's encouragement, she first visited the Hippie Kitchen when she was just thirteen and found the experience 'very scary'. By the time Meghan enlisted as a volunteer in the early 1990s, the composition of the homeless neighbourhood had drastically changed, from mainly old, white male drunks to a new younger and more volatile community of those high on crack cocaine and other deadly drugs. 'I was young, and it was rough and raw down there, and though I was with a great volunteer group, I just felt overwhelmed,' she later recalled.

She might well have chalked the visit up to experience and never ventured there again but for a classroom conversation with her Immaculate Heart High School theology teacher Maria Pollia some three years later. During class, Maria, who had already been a volunteer at the Hippie Kitchen for years, described her own early experience and how she faced up to her fears and doubts.

'It's one of the worst corners of Skid Row,' she says. 'One of the most distressed and distressing. It is heartbreaking. Driving through at night it looked like something Charles Dickens would be writing about. People huddled around blazing oil drums. It was very, very frightening. An awakening for me.' Her message to the class, though, was to put their fears aside and make contact with the homeless on a human level. They are people too, people with names, people with a past and hopefully a future.

'Life is about putting the needs of others above your own fears,' she counselled. It was a message that resonated with sixteen-year-old Meghan. 'That has always stayed with me,' she later recalled.

After class, Meghan spoke with her teacher, who advised on the practicalities of volunteering at the Hippie Kitchen. Heartened, Meghan began to go regularly, working as a server and clearing tables, which put her directly in contact with the Hippie Kitchen's guests. Maria Pollia recalls: 'What she learned was what I learned – that it is the human contact people crave. It's someone saying hello and knowing your name.' Meghan earnestly absorbed all the advice and began to come back with her own stories.

'It was remarkable that once in the situation she got right in it. She wasn't just handing out stew and letting everyone go by, but she was connecting with people, she was learning their names and listening to their stories.' And, as Catherine Morris observes, everyone on Skid Row has a story. It might be a hard-luck story, a never-catching-a-break story or a wrong-turn story; they would all be eye-opening for Meghan, offering a new perspective on what kind of life you could be dealt.

Meghan's experience was echoed by others, such as schoolgirl volunteer Sophie Goldstein, who described how she too confronted her fears and concerns. 'When I first came here, I have to admit, I was kind of nervous,' she wrote on the Catholic Worker blog. 'I saw the area and I was scared. Then I met the people. What the Workers told me was that a lot of the time these were people who couldn't meet up with their bills, and now they're stuck, or that they have drug problems. I got to put a face on my own prejudice.

'I realized that these are real people. They are not just the crazy homeless that you hear about all the time, or that my friends talk about, or the flippant remarks that people make about the homeless.' For Meghan it was a life-affirming and life-changing experience.

Up to that point, Meghan's only other experience of work was at Humphrey Yogart, a frozen yogurt shop where she worked when she was thirteen, serving customers and taking out the rubbish for four dollars an hour, employed under the California law that permitted youngsters enrolled in school to work ten to twelve hours a week. Owner Paula Sheftel told the *Daily Mirror* that Meghan was a hard worker and popular with the customers, 'She had to prove she had an outgoing personality and would work well with staff.

'A lot of the kids can't handle the pressure. It takes a special personality for somebody that young to deal with it. Meghan had that early on.' Meghan had ample opportunity to practise her people skills at the often fast-paced fro-yo shop, but she also gained another valuable lesson that would later serve her well. One afternoon, Meghan saw Yasmine Bleeth, one of the stars of *Baywatch*, and a particular idol of hers. Finishing up with the rubbish bin, Meghan approached the star and blurted out, 'I loved you in that Soft & Dri commercial.' Bleeth smiled, asked Meghan her name, and shook her hand. Later Meghan would say, 'That moment with Yasmine is exactly what I base every interaction with fans on.'

A yogurt shop in Beverly Hills was a far cry from the Hippie Kitchen at Sixth Street and Gladys, which like her travels with her mother to Mexico and Jamaica, honed her awareness. As she later observed for a book called *The Game Changers*: 'Yes, make sure you are safe and never ever put yourself in a compromising situation, but once that is checked off the list, I think it's really important for us to remember that someone needs us, and that your act of giving/helping/doing can truly become an act of grace once you get out of your head.'

If this was a practical application of her spiritual journey, her encounter with the work of Catholic theologian Tom Merton emphasized her intellectual curiosity and emotional maturity. In a world of black and white, Merton's mercurial thinking, with its endless shape-shifting vista of grey, of muted maybes and possibilities, is hard to pin down. 'As well as grappling with her personal issues, Meghan was taking on Merton whose thinking was at the core of her theology class,' says her former teacher Maria Pollia.

Merton is arguably the most influential American Catholic author of the twentieth century, his autobiography, *The Seven Storey Mountain*, selling more than a million copies. He lived a raucous and challenging life, fathering a child while studying at Clare College, Cambridge, in the UK, and briefly joining the Young Communist League before finally confirming to the Catholic Church in 1939 when he was in his mid-twenties. In 1941, he joined the Abbey of Gethsemani in Kentucky, where he gained a reputation as a monk who was a spiritual seeker, not a settler, a man who did not recognize absolute truth but saw the grand ambivalence, the contradictions and duality of existence.

For the average American sixteen-year-old, weaned on an academic diet of short sentences and multiple-choice questions, Merton is a complex and demanding character. Yet perhaps because of the racial duality of her own background, Meghan was attracted and inspired by the work of the American theologian. 'She was someone questing for knowledge; she had a profound desire to connect with people,' recalls Ms Pollia. There was a practical side to her perplexity. When she was in seventh grade at Immaculate Heart she was asked to fill in a form during an English class, on which one of the questions related to her racial background. There was no box for bi-racial. It was a quandary that would have welcomed the Merton touch.

Instead, she put her pen down and left the box empty, not wanting to offend one of her parents. 'So, I didn't tick a box,' she later recalled. 'I left my identity blank – a question mark, an absolute incomplete – much like how I felt.' When she discussed her experience with her father that night she could feel his impotent fury wanting to protect his daughter. He told her, 'If that happens again, you draw your own box.'

In her 1997 theology class entitled Experiencing God, Meghan was encouraged to think outside the box, proving herself undaunted by the intellectual challenges posed by Father Thomas Merton and other mystics. She embraced concepts that demand considerable maturity and considered reflection. For the first time in their school career, students were thrown into a subject without obvious answers, the course requiring more than an ability to memorize pages of a set text. Pollia observed to me, 'As we become more mature in the adult life we understand that there are many inconsistencies, many dichotomies, and that life is a continuing encounter with mystery.

'For a young person to feel comfortable with that conversation is very unusual. They get there in the end but rather than fearing these concepts and backing away, Meghan was already interested in pushing deeper and deeper into these questions. She was remarkable. Someone said, "Would you have remembered her,

Prince Harry notwithstanding?" Absolutely. She is one of the top-five outstanding students in my career and I promise you I am not just saying that.'

During this philosophy course, Meghan and her classmates were faced with a real-life paradox; namely, how could a young mother, a glamorous humanitarian in the prime of life, die in the cruel banality of a car accident. She and her friends watched the funeral of Diana, Princess of Wales, in early September 1997, tears coursing down their cheeks at the poignant moment when the cameras zoomed in on the royal coffin. Perched among the white flowers was an envelope with the one word, 'Mummy', containing Prince Harry's last note to his beloved mother. Meghan was not the only one to ask how this tragedy could befall a living icon; dozens of conspiracy theories sprang up on the internet and elsewhere as millions tried to make sense of the senseless.

Nor was she the only one to feel Diana's loss in a keenly personal way. After she heard about the tragedy, she and her friend Suzy Ardakani had sat and watched old videos of the 1981 wedding between Prince Charles and Lady Diana Spencer. According to family friends, she was intrigued by Diana not just for her style but for her independent humanitarian mission, seeing her as a role model. Inspired by the princess, she and her friend Suzy collected clothes and toys for less privileged children. In fact, such was her interest in the princess that Suzy's mother Sonia even gave her a copy of my biography, *Diana: Her True Story*, which remained on her bookshelves for the next few years. As her childhood friend Ninaki Priddy observed: 'She was always fascinated by the Royal Family. She wants to be Princess Diana 2.0.'

Diana's death was a painful reminder for the Ardakani family, who had just two years previously also experienced the life-changing force of a random act of fate. One afternoon in 1995, Matt Ardakani, Suzy's father, was working at his downtown car-body shop when a deranged Vietnam veteran who had murdered his family came into the garage and started shooting at random. Mr Ardakani was hit in the spine and lung and rushed to hospital. When Suzy was told about the shooting, it was Meghan who was the first to console the sobbing teenager and the one who accompanied her to the hospital, where they kept vigil for hours.

Suzy's mother Sonia Ardakani recalls: 'She and Suzy sat beside Matt's bedside for many hours, praying he would pull through. We feel sure those prayers helped him survive.' Though permanently paralysed, Matt did survive and is still working.

Meghan's instinctive empathy with others and her interest in giving back – a central tenet of Immaculate Heart's mission – as well as her evident maturity, thoughtfulness and positive attitude made her the clear first choice to be a group leader at a Kairos retreat in the autumn of 1998. Like hundreds of Catholic schools across America, Immaculate Heart regularly organized Kairos (Greek for critical moment) retreats for students, which were designed to help teenagers contemplate the place of God in their lives.

During the four-day retreat, which was held at the Holy Spirit Retreat Center at Encino, six girls were chosen to lead groups of eight in various discussions, their role being to encourage participation and debate. As a leader, the most daunting assignment was to make a thirty-minute presentation dealing with a challenging list of issues ranging from self-image and trust to core values and finding yourself.

Christine Knudsen, who has been organizing the Kairos retreat at Immaculate Heart for twenty-three years, described to me the qualities she watches for in the girls chosen as leaders. 'You are looking for a girl who has been through something and who has a certain amount of depth to her. The kinds of insights and comments Meghan made gave her a depth because she had had to struggle with her own issues.'

It was clear that her dysfunctional family background, the separation and subsequent divorce of her parents when she was still a youngster, were the concerns she grappled with. 'I know that was difficult for her, one parent over here and one over there and neither particularly fond of each other', recalls Mrs Knudsen. While Meghan was not the only girl on campus with divorced parents, what marked her out was the way she had managed them. Like many children of divorced parents, she had learned to become a skilled diplomat, mediating between the warring parties. This nihilistic parental interaction taught Meghan a valuable lesson: how to control her emotions. 'She is very poised,' observes a schoolfriend. 'It could be hard for her. Sometimes she felt she had to pick sides.'

The older she became the more she felt she was the one who was mothering her father. It was a source of friction, especially when she started dating. As a friend notes, 'Typical teenage stuff.'

There were other issues, too, which clearly troubled her, though she did not discuss them publicly at the time. Fitting in was a constant concern. As she later recalled: 'My high school had cliques: the black girls and white girls, the Filipino [sic] and the Latina girls. Being bi-racial, I fell somewhere in between. So every day during lunch, I busied myself with meetings – French club, student body, whatever one could possibly do between noon and 1pm – I was there. Not so that I was more involved, but so that I wouldn't have to eat alone.'

Photographer John Dlugolecki, who photographed Meghan and other students throughout high school, noticed that Meghan never appeared to be part of the African-American, Asian or any other ethnic group of girls. Dlugolecki also remarked that Meghan 'was not considered mixed race by her peers', adding, 'We only ever saw her with Tom, never with the mom.' And so it came as a mild shock to members of faculty when they finally got to meet Doria. 'Everyone thought [Meghan] was Italian because she was so light-skinned,' recalls one former teacher. 'Then we met her mother and realized she was bi-racial.'

As poised and confident as she seemed at Kairos when she discussed her own demons, at least those related to her family discord, having had those experiences clearly enabled her to encourage her classmates to confront their own. As Meghan recalled in a 2016 issue of *Sharp* magazine: 'In middle school and high school, there was this huge span of my life where I was just the girl with the crazy curly hair, a big gap between my teeth, with skinny legs. I was always the smart one. My self-identification was wrapped up in being the smart one.'

Mrs Knudsen recalls: 'You have to be very honest about who you are and be willing to share all the things that you struggle with, your successes and failures. She was articulate, confident, feisty and spunky.

'I remember her saying, "Why can't we do it this way, has

anybody thought about that?" She was always thinking about a better way to do something, not just complaining.'

For many students the retreat is a turning point in their young lives, a time when they face up to their own emotional issues honestly. Realizing that their classmates have their own problems is seen as a critical catalyst. 'It's a time of truth telling and the leaders are the ones who set the tone,' observes Mrs Knudsen. 'The atmosphere is: "I am willing to share my truth with you, and that makes you willing to share your truth." So there is a lot of crying but it is healing crying. Everything out in the open, you realize everybody has to struggle and that nobody is perfect no matter how they look.'

❖

While her fractured family background and her sense of isolation caused Meghan a great deal of heartache as she grew up, it also helped provide some of the psychological drive that would propel her towards her overarching ambition. From a young age, Meghan dreamed of becoming a famous Hollywood actress. She fantasized about winning an Oscar one day, practising her acceptance speech in front of her bedroom mirror. As James Lipton, the venerable inquisitor for the long-running *Inside the Actors Studio*, never tires of reminding his audience, most actors come from broken homes. This often bitter experience gives them the emotional rocket fuel to power a star-making screen performance.

From day one at Immaculate Heart, Meghan threw herself wholeheartedly into the drama department. Besides being a stepping stone towards following her dream, at school the drama department has a rather different function. It acts as a welcoming club, an unofficial sorority and a close-knit family. As a six-times Daytime Emmy award winner told me: 'You might be a misfit everywhere else but here you have a sense of belonging.'

As well as taking to the boards, Meghan held numerous offices, including president of the school's Genesian Society, a group devoted to the preservation of the performing arts that actively hosted or attended plays, dramatic festivals and apprentice stage productions. However, as she didn't hold a formal office, she was always at the edge of the student council, never quite a part of it.

Immaculate Heart was able to call on a rich roster of Hollywood luminaries to direct and produce plays and musicals. There was leading voice coach Rachael Lawrence, choreographer and *Jersey Boys* star Joseph Leo Bwarie, and, most prominently, Gigi Perreau, a former child actor whose work is honoured with a star on the Hollywood Walk of Fame. Ms Perreau started her career in movies at the tender age of two when she played Greer Garson's daughter in the 1943 film *Madame Curie*. By the age of ten she had appeared in twenty-five films, including working on set with Nancy Reagan in the 1950 thriller *Shadow on the Wall*. When she retired from acting work, Ms Perreau, now seventy-seven, brought her experience to staging plays and musicals at her alma mater, as well as to teaching drama classes.

Gigi remembers Meghan as a skinny kid who developed and blossomed into a beautiful and confident young woman during her time at Immaculate Heart. She told me, 'We never had a moment's problem with her, she was spot on, learned her lines when she had to, very dedicated, very focused. She was a wonderful student, a lovely girl even then, and very hard-working. She was very dedicated. I knew she would be something special.'

In drama class they often discussed topics of the day and Gigi remembers Meghan as an inquisitive youngster who loved hearing tales of Gigi's time in France and other European countries. She was keen to explore the world beyond the nearby 'Hollywood' sign.

When she was rehearsing for a play, her father was always around. As an Emmy winner who had been nominated almost every year while working on *General Hospital*, he was soon roped in to becoming the technical director for every school production Meghan was involved in. The majority of students were not aware that he was Meghan's dad. He was known simply as 'that guy in the overalls'. Those in the drama group were rather more respectful, calling him 'Mr Markle'. 'He liked to be thought of as gruff,' recalls Ms Perreau, 'but he was always very generous with the girls. If we had a late rehearsal he would go out and buy a boxful of McDonald's to feed them. Modest too. He never asked to be credited for any work he did.' He was single and shy and Gigi admits to having a 'bit of a crush' on the burly guy in overalls who was clearly trying to bring up his teenage daughter on his own. She asked him out, and they went to see a play together at the Doolittle Theatre, just south of Hollywood and Vine. Though they had a good time, nothing ever developed.

Tom's focus was on Meghan. A keen photographer, he took endless photographs of Meghan on stage, teaching her how to pose and coaching her on angles. He was proudly watching from the wings when, on 28 March 1996, she made her first solo singing performance, playing the secretary in the school's production of the musical *Annie*. Director Perreau remembers that the fourteen-year-old budding actress was 'very excited and nervous about her song', and describes her performance as 'delightful'. Meghan went on to play an aspiring actress in the 1937 comedy *Stage Door* and was featured in *Back Country Crimes*, a black comedy by American playwright Dr Lanie Robertson. In the March 1997 programme notes for Immaculate Heart's production of Stephen Sondheim's musical *Into the Woods*, in which she played Little Red Riding Hood, Meghan announced her ambition to the world. In between thanking her friends and her 'adorable' boyfriend, she revealed that she wished to attend Northwestern, a prestigious university near Chicago. This, she predicted, would be her next stop on her way to Broadway. Meghan was clearly not a girl wanting in confidence.

For her junior year she appeared yet again in a school production, *Steppin' Out*, but for her senior year she decided to test her ability beyond the confines of Immaculate Heart. It was a new challenge and offered the chance of branching out on her own without her father looking down on her from the lighting gantry. There was also the small matter of spending time alone with her then-boyfriend. Thus she found herself in a room with forty other girls waiting to be auditioned for Sophocles' Greek tragedy *Oedipus Rex* staged in the autumn of 1998 by the all-boys St Francis High School in La Cañada Flintridge.

As it was drama director Emmanuel (Manny) Eulalia's first big production at St Francis, he wanted to make an impact, so he carefully chose the girl who would play the lead role of Jocasta. It was no contest. 'Meghan was a standout,' he recalls. 'She had that something of the "it" about her. As a director it is what you are always looking for. She had charisma, no doubt.'

After signing a formal document pledging to arrive on time, dress appropriately and refrain from sexual and racial innuendoes – a code of behaviour somewhat ahead of its time – Meghan and the rest of the cast got down to a gruelling two-month schedule of rehearsals. Early on she impressed the show's director with her timekeeping, preparation and command of the stage. In the show's musical numbers her voice packed a punch, even if she quavered somewhat on the higher notes.

While she was the only girl from Immaculate Heart to audition, she had star status at the all-boys school. She had already dated several pupils from St Francis, including her first long-term boyfriend, Luis Segura. In time-honoured fashion it was his sister Maria who set them up on their first date, the couple seeing one another regularly for nearly two years. She got to know the Segura family well, including Luis's younger brother Danny, who played Creon in *Oedipus Rex*, and always credits Meghan, who was then sixteen, with encouraging him to take to the stage. In turn she accompanied Danny to the St Francis Junior-Senior prom in April 1998 held at the InterContinental Hotel in downtown Los Angeles. Through them she also became friendly with other boys from St Francis, everyone hanging out at each other's homes.

Describing her as 'sweet and fun', Luis – now a successful realtor in downtown Pasadena – was no doubt one of a number of voices encouraging her to enter for the contest for St Francis Homecoming Queen that autumn.

This pinnacle of high-school social standing came with

serious competition from dozens of other girls. Hopefuls had to write an essay listing their accomplishments – Meghan's regular work in the Hippie Kitchen made her an instant standout – before facing a grilling from members of the student body and faculty. The names of the finalists were read out at the fifty-yard line on a hastily erected stage during the half-time interval at a St Francis football game. Amid whistling and cheering, Meghan was proclaimed that year's queen and was duly crowned by the previous incumbent. The entire 'court' then left the field in a procession of classic convertibles so that the game could continue. It was an indication of her popularity and appeal that a girl who was neither a cheerleader nor hailed from one of the local all-girls Catholic schools was chosen.

Even though she was now 'Queen Meghan', her drama director Manny Eulalia recalls that she didn't let the adulation go to her head. She remained grounded, joking around as she accepted the congratulations of her fellow cast members. Once word got out that 'Queen Meghan' was the female lead in the show, tickets sold briskly for the sombre tragedy. For three nights in early January 1999 the teenage cast played to a full house in the 250-seater theatre at nearby Flintridge Preparatory School. In previous years, interest in school productions had been disappointing. Not this time. When Meghan first appeared, there was a rustle of applause, despite the audience having been warned to curb their enthusiasm.

'A lot of pupils went to the show just to see Meghan,' recalls Manny with a smile. 'She certainly had a fan club. Quite a few of the boys had crushes on her.' At the end of the eighty-minute production, the audience gave Meghan and the rest of the cast a standing ovation.

In the programme notes she wrote, 'I would like to give thanks to Mommy, Daddy, Sushi, Aubergine, Danny boy, Brad, Gabe, all the beautiful, amazing, gorgeous sweeties at Immaculate Heart, the great guys at St Francis, and the phenomenal cast and crew.'

Though she was deemed a standout in *Oedipus Rex*, Meghan Markle's high-school acting career is best remembered for her performance as the sexy South American vamp Lola Banana in the 1955 musical comedy *Damn Yankees*. As the production was being staged by another all-boys Catholic school, this time Loyola High School in downtown Los Angeles, once again she had to compete against girls from other Catholic schools. Fresh from her triumph in *Oedipus Rex*, she snagged the star role of Lola Banana. The story, based on a modern retelling of the Faustian pact, involved the vampish Lola, her deal with the devil, and her attempts to seduce a baseball fan turned star player, Joe Hardy. When Meghan, dressed in long satin gloves and a sequinned leotard, shimmied across the stage in the sassy burlesque number 'Whatever Lola Wants', she brought the house down.

'It was like WOO,' a member of the audience told me. 'She was extraordinary. I remember sitting there thinking: "Oh my goodness, this is an Immaculate Heart girl." She was wearing the little spangly number, doing the shimmies, the whole bit. It wasn't lewd, she was playing a character. It was sweet in a way but it was also like WOW. This was a girl with star quality.'

At another time, in another country, something very similar happened when the normally demure student Kate Middleton sashayed down the catwalk in a sheer shift dress over a bikini at a college fashion show. Prince William, watching the parade from the front row, whispered to his companion, 'She's hot.' The rest is royal history. On this occasion, it was an eye-opener for those teachers and classmates who were seeing a very different side to Meghan. Normally seen as fun but thoughtful, mature and controlled, Meghan's amorous song-and-dance routine was a revelation. After the show, her theology teacher Maria Pollia and her boyfriend went backstage and presented her with a bouquet of red roses. It was a touching moment. Meghan, who had been beyond excited to win the role, burst into tears. 'Oh, you didn't have to do this,' she sobbed, suddenly overwhelmed by the moment. As Ms Pollia recalls: 'She had appeared in many productions and she was always good. This time, though, she was a star. And that night a star was born.'

It was perhaps appropriate then that it was a Loyola High School boy who accompanied Meghan to the Junior-Senior Immaculate Heart school prom in April 1999, again at the InterContinental, now Omni, Hotel. Meghan and her beau, Giancarlo Boccato, now a New York property manager, looked a very glamorous couple as they danced cheek to cheek. They were, as photographer John Dlugolecki observed, 'a star couple'.

An academic star too. Her graduation ceremony in June 1999, which was held at the Hollywood Bowl, was another chance to shine. She walked away with a clutch of glittering prizes that touched on her intellectual, artistic and charitable work. She was presented with the Bank of America Fine Arts award and the Notre Dame Club of Los Angeles Achievement Award, earned a commendation in the National Achievement Scholarship Program for outstanding black students, and won a service award for mentoring younger students.

The future was looking very bright. As she had predicted three years earlier, she had been accepted at Northwestern University, where she intended to study English as she wanted to explore her writing ability. She resisted the idea of studying drama, considering it a cliché of the California girl going to college and then returning to her roots in Hollywood without attempting another discipline. She was accomplished in so many fields that some expected her eventually to enter politics or the law. All felt that she would do something worthwhile with her life and at the same time give back to the community. The word 'classy', which she used to describe herself in her final yearbook, and her choice of a quote attributed to former First Lady Eleanor Roosevelt to illustrate her senior-year photograph, reflected her rounded personality. It read: 'Women are like teabags; they don't realize how strong they are until they're in hot water.'

As her drama teacher Gigi Perreau recalled: 'I wasn't sure which direction Meghan would ultimately be going in because she also had interests in humanitarian activities. She had a good heart, had absorbed the school's philosophy that there is nothing we cannot do, and she seemed to be focused on her future.'

❖

A couple of years after she graduated from college, Meghan returned to her alma mater. She chatted to a few of her old teachers and caught up on the news. 'Keep in touch, sweetheart,' Gigi told her as Meghan was preparing to leave. The budding actress was still struggling to get a foothold on the greasy pole that is Hollywood and was working as a hostess in a Beverly Hills hotel restaurant to pay for acting lessons. Somewhat ruefully she told her former acting mentor, 'I don't want to come back until I have really made it.'

The staff and pupils of Immaculate Heart figure it might be time.

4

'Can You Say, "Hi"?'

ummertime, and the living was easy for Meghan. Freshly graduated from Immaculate Heart and with her Northwestern University future beckoning, Meghan packed her last Los Angeles summer with memories and then packed her suitcases for her first semester away from home. She would effectively be starting a new life. Not one of her classmates from Immaculate Heart or anyone she knew from LA was going to Northwestern and she was determined to make a good impression. The orthodontics she'd had during her high school years had gradually adjusted her bucked, gap-toothed grin, and now she was smiling widely without feeling self-conscious.

Once her dental work was complete she had some head shots taken to send out for auditions. As she was leaving for Chicago in the autumn, the best she could hope for was a day or two's work on one of the many music or short videos that were being shot around town. She had already earned around $600 for a couple of days' work in a Tori Amos video, '1000 Oceans', which was shot in a car park in the downtown LA streets. Meghan, dressed in a low-cut blue spaghetti-strap top, appeared as one of a crowd curiously examining a glass box containing

Amos, writhing around as she sang. It comes across as a kind of performance art – but to a melody. The four-and-a-half-minute video, directed by Erick Ifergan, climaxes with scenes of rioting kids facing police horses and hoses, a musical reprise of the LA riots. Amos's video is, for dedicated Markle watchers, the first public appearance of one of Meghan's most distinctive mannerisms: continuously brushing back her long hair from her face with her hand.

That weekend, she had another audition lined up, this time for a Shakira video. It was to be a high-energy dance fest, a world away from Amos's vision of urban alienation. Meghan's best friend Ninaki 'Nikki' Priddy was going to drive with her to the audition, then they were going to go shopping so that she could find something new to wear for the Northwestern students' reception at the Beverly Hilton Hotel. The meet-and-greet was her first chance to scope out her fellow undergraduates and to make some first impressions herself. During the day, Nicki and Meghan also planned to goof around, filming LA street scenes – and themselves – with Nikki's new video camera.

The audition for the Shakira video didn't go quite as well as Meghan had hoped. It was fun to dance crazily, but afterwards she told Nikki, 'I am burning up; I was really nervous I was going to fall out of my top I was just shaking around so much.'

She knew her performance hadn't won her a gig as a $600-a-day featured dancer, but she was hoping for a spot as an extra. It was less money and no real camera time, but still, it would be fun. As she waited in the audition room, she ran into a girl she had met at the Tori Amos video shoot. It was the last time they saw one another – Meghan did not get a call back.

After hitting the mall, Meghan and Nikki drove through Los Angeles in Doria's Volvo station wagon with the personalized number plate MEGNMEE, Meghan keeping up a running commentary – Nikki was in charge of the camera. The duo dismissed the gay majority of West Hollywood with the jejune, 'We could walk down the street naked and no one would care.' They zoomed in on a woman who seemed to have just had collagen injections in her lips and they marvelled at the houses along Beverly Glen and other wealthy enclaves in Beverly Hills and the surrounding area.

Back home at her mother's house, Meghan tried on her new outfits for the student gathering at the Beverly Hilton. She had a vision of how she wanted to project herself at Northwestern and had decided that she would focus on a monochromatic look, black and grey, a colour scheme that would make her look stylish, sophisticated and pulled-together. With that in mind, she'd chosen a pencil skirt, tube top and white structured, open-front blouse that doubled as a jacket. It was a prescient foreshadowing of the office-wear she would don to play Rachel Zane over a decade later.

Meghan made that last summer at home count, but she was also troubled. She and her father weren't getting along, and she was deliberately avoiding him. The emotional shutters had come down – Meghan went to stay with her mother and did not even visit her father's house to pick up her mail. It was a situation that perplexed her friends, as they knew that Meghan was the apple of her father's eye and could get away with blue murder. Not that any of his children, Tom Junior and Yvonne included, took advantage of his *laissez-faire* attitude; they always did their homework on time whatever the distractions. It was Meghan's mother who was more of a stickler for boundaries. Though she would join Meghan and her friends dancing to music on the radio or talking about make-up, she was stricter than her ex-husband. Meghan could twist him around her little finger. Yvonne often told the story of the time before Christmas when Meghan was looking at a jewellery catalogue and picking out a ring, which Tom Senior had promised as a gift. She teased her much older sister by saying that whatever her father bought Yvonne, Meghan would receive the most expensive gift as she was the most favoured child. So while the split between father and daughter was unusual, her friends dismissed it as simply a summer storm. It was not the best send-off for her college career, though.

As well as leaving behind her childhood home, she was also leaving the girl she considered her 'sister', Ninaki Priddy, who had been her best friend since they could barely walk. Meghan and Nikki became best friends at the Little Red School House, spending countless sleepovers together, playing in the pool at Nikki's parents' modest three-bedroom home in North Hollywood. They remained close when they transitioned to Immaculate Heart, the duo travelling around Europe together with Nikki's parents, Dalton and Maria, and her little sister Michelle. Nikki loved Paris so much that she studied at the Sorbonne the following summer. When they landed in London and posed in front of Buckingham Palace, they never for a moment thought that one day Meghan would be welcomed inside the black wrought-iron gates. Now college and separation loomed and they were trying to crowd every moment with laughter and fond memories.

❖

Meghan looked around her dorm room and began unpacking. She was bunked in the freshman dorm known as North Mid-Quads, next door to the Kappa Kappa Gamma sorority house. She hadn't decided yet if she would rush – the peculiarly American college system where students visit all the sorority or fraternity houses and find one that suits them, then hope they will be selected to join it – or just stick to friendship groups in her dorm and classes. The first few weeks at a new college are difficult enough; there is a lot of judging and sizing up as hundreds of anxious teenagers, bubbling over with hormones and excitement, try to orientate themselves both physically and psychologically. Rush merely exacerbates that feeling of vulnerability, of wanting to belong. Without a friend, or even an acquaintance, from back home, Meghan, a naturally gregarious character, worked hard at making new friends.

But her self-esteem was about to take a most unexpected blow. She had grown up in the melting pot that is Los Angeles. Her school, Immaculate Heart, was a kaleidoscope of girls of different colours and nationalities. Now, she discovered that even though the town of Evanston, where Northwestern University is based, is just a few miles from Chicago, the college itself is overwhelmingly white. African-Americans make up a third of the town, but only 5 per cent of the student body. There were even fewer bi-racial students. Here at Northwestern she stood out.

Just one week into her first semester, as Meghan sat reviewing her class schedules for her chosen major, English, a dorm mate came up and asked, 'You said your mom is black and your dad is white, right?'

Meghan smiled weakly and nodded, suddenly uncomfortable. 'And they're divorced?' her dorm mate continued. Meghan nodded again. The girl gave her a knowing look. 'Oh. Well that makes sense.' Meghan felt a stab. The snide remark cut her deeply. 'Makes sense how?' she wondered. Of course, she understood the implication: that the failure of an inter-racial marriage was inevitable. The interaction stayed with her and was one of the memories she referred to years later in an article she wrote for *Elle* magazine in 2015.

Los Angeles had been a huge multicultural bubble, and now Meghan was being exposed to narrow minds and outdated, provincial thinking. This wasn't the first, nor would it be the last time she would hear or be subject to a crass racial slur. As she was light-skinned, many fellow students didn't realize she was bi-racial, which left her as a fly on the wall as they made racist jokes or expressed bigoted opinions. The above incident, in particular, stayed with her, shaping her reflections about how others viewed her, her family and her heritage. 'My lasting memory of Meghan is her profound sense of self,' remembers Professor Harvey Young. 'She was thoughtful and understood what it means to face prejudice and discrimination.'

But Meghan was tough enough not to let it bring her down – she was too busy cutting loose. Now that she wasn't under the watchful gaze of her mother, she started wearing heavier make-up and experimented with highlighting her hair. Having made up her mind, she rushed Kappa Kappa Gamma and was initiated into the sorority, which was full of girls who were considered 'intelligent hot messes'. As KKG member Melania Hidalgo observed: 'The thing we all have in common is that we're all very driven, ambitious and passionate.' The sorority embraced her warmly, Meghan eventually being elected as the sorority's recruitment chair, responsible for bringing new girls into the KKG clan. As an outgoing, confident and articulate young woman, she was well suited for the role of selling the sorority. Sometimes she was a tad too persuasive, some students, according to classmate Ann Meade, thinking her overly assertive. For the most part, fellow students remember her thirst for life and her 'explosive personality' – a dynamic, self-possessed young woman.

As a sorority member, she also participated in the Northwestern University Dance Marathon, one of the biggest student-run charities in America. The year Meghan danced was the first time since the event's inception in 1975 that a woman, Ginger Harreld, was the emcee, though she shared the duties with a male student. While the dance marathon was no longer the gruelling win-or-die dance fest of the Depression era, the thirty hours Meghan spent on her feet, day and night, certainly helped her work off her 'freshman fifteen' – the weight she had packed on from drinking, munching starchy dorm food and making late-night trips to the twenty-four-hour Burger King.

Of course, all this socializing did have a focus for many students: the search for a boyfriend. More sophisticated and put-together than most of her contemporaries, Meghan was seen as a cool catch. Normally she went for well-dressed Latin boyfriends like Luis Segura, but she changed gears during her time at Northwestern. Her first boyfriend was Steve Lepore, a chiselled, white, six-foot-five-inch sophomore basketball player from Ohio. He made Meghan, at five foot six inches, feel petite. Her association with Lepore raised her stock with her KKG sorority sisters, who were 'impressed that she had snared such a hottie'. 'They made quite the pair,' recalled a former classmate. But their relationship was short-lived. For his junior and senior year, the high-scoring basketball star accepted a transfer offer to Wake Forest University in Winston-Salem, North Carolina. Goodbye Meghan, hello basketball pro prospects.

While they made a perfect-looking college couple, they had their differences. Steve's sporting ambitions meant that he had to forgo partying, turn in early, and the night before any game Meghan was not welcome to stay over. Meghan, on the other hand, was a party animal, who enjoyed the freedom college offered away from her parents, drinking and staying out late.

While she might have lost her freshman-year boyfriend, Meghan did make two very close friends at Northwestern who would stay with her for life.

It was during a literature class, discussing the work of African-American writer Toni Morrison, that she first met Lindsay Jill Roth, a petite blond from Lattingtown, New York, a wealthy Long Island suburb with million-dollar homes overlooking Oyster Bay. Her parents were attorneys, though her mother had retired. Unlike Meghan's friends from Immaculate Heart, Lindsay was Jewish. Smart, funny and articulate, the two girls would study together, go out drinking and dancing, and chat long into the night, talking up a storm.

Her other best friend could not have been more different. The son of two pastors, Larnelle Quentin Foster was a flamboyant, larger-than-life African-American who hid the fact that he was gay from his family and friends – although he eventually confided in Meghan. Meghan and Larnelle took classes together in the School of Communications after she changed her major from English to a dual major of theatre arts and international relations. The twin major reflected her indecision – she was unsure whether to pursue a career in politics and the diplomatic world or to strive for screen stardom. Though the latter was, as she recognized, something of an LA cliché, she was in good company – Warren Beatty, Stephen Colbert, Zach Braff and David Schwimmer all learned their trade at the university. Larnelle, however, couldn't help but notice that her enthusiasm was more for Hollywood than the State Department. The couple, who attended everything from student productions to avant-garde offerings, enjoyed discussing the theatrical structure and language of a play as much as performing, Meghan taking parts in short films made by fellow students. She also slipped away from campus to attend auditions for TV commercials.

On weekends Meghan would often go to Larnelle's family home for meals, the two friends trying out different recipes, including Meghan's current speciality, Indian food.

The Foster family adored Meghan, attracted by her quirky sense of humour and her effervescent smile. She even accepted their invitation to join them at church. 'If my mother had had her way, of course I'd be with Meghan,' he says. 'She would say: "Oh, I love Meghan so much." I was like, "Yes, Mom, I do, too."' He also knew that he would break his mother's heart if she discovered that he was gay. For the time being, Meghan was his cover, and he in turn provided her with companionship and an escort, a role which made him the envy of many of the straight guys on campus. 'How do you go out with her?' they asked him. 'Because I'm not trying anything!' Larnelle told the *Daily Mail*.

Meghan's two closest friends represented the duality of her heritage: the iconoclastic, eccentric and independent African-American and the white professional. Their presence helped her to explore and integrate these sides of her personality, absorbing and synthesizing as she grew into her own identity.

Between semesters, it was a relief to return to Los Angeles, not only for the weather but also to be back in such a diverse city, where the blonde and blue-eyed are in a minority. As she learned, though, the image of tolerance and acceptance was a veneer that easily scratched.

She tells a story about the night she and her mum went to a concert. As Doria was slowly backing her Volvo out of the parking space, another driver impatiently yelled at her, using the 'N' word. Meghan flushed, her skin prickling with frustration, sharing Doria's pain and rage. She looked at her mother, and saw her eyes welling with tears. Meghan whispered the only words she could manage: 'It's OK, Mommy.' But it wasn't OK. They drove home in silence, blood pounding in Meghan's ears, Doria's fingers gripping the steering wheel tightly.

❖

The experience of growing up bi-racial was used as a jumping-off point for discussions that Meghan and seven other classmates had with their history and theatre professor Harvey Young, whose seminars focused on African-American plays, their meaning, their impact and their history. Meghan, who had moved between two communities throughout her life, was very aware of how people responded to race, racial differences and the idea of otherness. Young said, 'She had a very sophisticated understanding of what it means to live in a racial body that gets perceived and is treated differently based upon communities in which you find yourself.'

Young's class brought into focus Meghan's ambiguous place in society. She later recalled: 'It was the first time I could put a name to feeling too light in the black community, too mixed in the white community.'

Her experiences at Northwestern, both in and out of the classroom, and the self-knowledge she gained would serve her well, arming her with insight and inner strength when she tried to penetrate the smooth, evasive structure that is Hollywood.

❖

By the start of her junior year, it was clear that if Meghan continued at her current pace she would earn most of her credits for her degree way ahead of schedule. Just for fun she took a course in industrial engineering, her professor setting the French classic *The Little Prince* by Antoine de Saint-Exupéry as set text. As she later wrote in her blog, The Tig: 'It was a seemingly odd choice, but at the end of the day, the takeaway was a self-empowerment and motivational bent that I apply to decision-making in my life to this very day.' As she had time on her side, and was still unsure about her path after university, she decided to go into the field to gain some practical experience in international relations. She knew that her uncle Mick Markle was employed as a specialist in communication systems for the US government – the talk in the family was that he worked for the CIA, the government's overseas spying arm. So she approached him to ask for his help in getting her an internship abroad with the State Department. 'Meghan, I will help you if I can,' he replied. Help he did. Uncle Mick pulled a few strings, and even though Meghan was quite late in getting in the application paperwork, that was overlooked because of her excellent academic record and her uncle's influence. Soon afterwards, she was informed that she had secured a six-week internship as a junior press officer at the American Embassy in Buenos Aires in Argentina. It was quite the adventure for the twenty-year-old, flying from Los Angeles to Buenos Aires on her own. She joined a team of around 28 State Department officials and guards in the mid-sized American enclave. Before starting work she was given an orientation of the building complex and the city, safety being the primary focus. The young student was warned about where to avoid, what to do in an emergency and which telephone numbers to call. Basic but vital information. With the anniversary of 9/11 approaching, all American embassies around the world, including that in Buenos Aires, had been placed on Code Orange security, the second-highest level.

For the most part, her day-to-day life was the routine and mundane world of the office grunt, filing, answering phones and drafting letters. As a consummate team player, she impressed her superiors with her enthusiasm and demeanour.

She was a willing worker, undertaking the tedious, run-of-the-mill jobs quickly and efficiently. Her superior, Mark Krischik, now retired, recalled her as a young woman who was good to work with and who carried out her assignments with 'efficiency and ingenuity'. Though memories are hazy, there was talk of a dalliance with a US Marine tasked to guard the embassy compound. But what was more certain was her love of Spanish cuisine, and the city's buzzing nightlife.

As it was her twenty-first birthday on 4 August 2002, she was given permission to travel in the convoy that was picking up the US Finance Secretary Paul O'Neill, who was making a whistle-stop visit to South America. It was a treat. However, her opportunity to be treated like a VIP for an hour or two rapidly turned into a terrifying ordeal.

She was waiting in the motorcade when Secretary O'Neill landed at Ezeiza airport, fifteen miles outside the centre of Buenos Aires. Argentina had recently defaulted on a $141 billion debt and neither the International Monetary Fund nor the American government were in any mood to bail them out. Before he left Washington, O'Neill had announced that South American nations should have policies in place to 'ensure that aid is not diverted to Swiss bank accounts'. Though his target was the corrupt political elites siphoning off billions of dollars into their own personal bank accounts, the suffering man and woman in the street blamed the United States for the economic calamity that had befallen them. After he landed at precisely five o'clock, O'Neill's motorcade drove to a meeting with President Eduardo Duhalde, head of the interim government. Though O'Neill was expecting a bumpy ride, even he was perturbed when banner-waving demonstrators surrounded the convoy. 'I remember the arrival because protesters banged on my limo with their placards. It was a memorable event,' he later deadpanned.

The junior press officer was terrified, recalling that it was the scariest moment of her life. It was all the more concerning, not only because of the impending anniversary of 9/11 but because of intelligence reports suggesting that Islamic militants could be setting up a network in South America. Meghan would have already been wary, and it's easy to imagine how frightening she would have found an angry mob of protesters attacking her car.

However, the experience didn't seem to put her off considering her future working for the government agency. 'If she had stayed with the State Department she would have been an excellent addition to the US diplomatic Corps. She had all that it takes to be a successful diplomat,' Mark Krischik later recalled.

Certainly she was sufficiently committed to a career with the State Department to take the Foreign Service Officer Test while she was still in Argentina. The three-hour exam is a mix of politics, history, general knowledge and maths, requiring an awareness of everything from the origin of be-bop to East Asian labour laws. It proved a stretch too far; Meghan failed the exam. She did, though, fly to Madrid to take a six-week course in Spanish at the International Education for Students programme. It was an added string to her bow just in case she wanted to give the world of diplomacy another try.

When she returned to Northwestern she was able to regale her friends with tales of tapas and tango, and tried to brush off her disappointment at missing the mark on her Foreign Service Officer Test. In any case, fate, it would seem, was pushing her into the world of entertainment. Her lighting-director father pulled favours to put her forward for a casual role in *General Hospital*, just as he had done with his eldest daughter almost a decade earlier. In November 2002, Meghan auditioned for a 'day player' role in which she said around five lines. Thanks to her father's influence, she got the part. The episode aired just before Thanksgiving.

A few weeks later she was at a holiday party with friends when she was approached by a man who introduced himself as Drew. Instead of wanting to date her, he wanted to manage her. A friend had slipped him a copy of a student film in which Meghan had appeared, and he was impressed, calling Meghan to tell her: 'You know what, you're going to make money, and I'll take 10 per cent. I think you should stick around.'

But at that time in her life, Meghan couldn't stick around. She had courses to finish back at Northwestern and a graduation to attend. She promised, though, she'd be back. As she saw it, as one door had closed, another one opened. If the State Department didn't want her, maybe Hollywood did.

❖

Once home from Northwestern, diploma in hand, Meghan went out and auditioned for commercials, none of which she booked, but which were good experience. By now this was a well-trodden route, Meghan having attended numerous auditions when she was still at Northwestern. Then she got a call. Her best friend from college, Lindsay Jill Roth, was working in casting for a film called *A Lot Like Love*, starring comic heartthrob Ashton Kutcher. She had snagged Meghan an audition for a one-word role.

'Can you say, "hi"?' asked the director.

'Yes, I can,' replied Meghan. 'But I read the script and I really respond to this other character and I would love to read for that.' Naturally, the other character had a bigger role.

The director and the casting staff exchanged glances. 'This girl certainly has some balls,' their looks said. Meghan didn't get the role she pitched herself for but she did get the part for which Roth had recommended her. Once on set, the director allowed her to improvise, expanding her lines from one to five. In movie terms that was a triumph.

Next up she landed another small part in the futuristic law office drama *Century City*, starring Viola Davis and Nestor Carbonell, among other old hands. She played a staff member and delivered one line: 'Here's to Tom Montero, who had the vision to install this amazing virtual assistant.' Her scene was over in one day, and she was back to casting calls, at the mercy of the Abominable No Men. It was a scratchy hand-to-mouth existence, one experienced by thousands of Hollywood hopefuls.

On the way to an audition one day, the electric button that unlocked the doors to her Ford Explorer failed to open. She tried the key but to no avail. Trying not to panic, she went around to the hatchback trunk, which used a different key. By some miracle, it opened. Running short on time, she had no choice but to crawl in through the back and clamber over the seat. Thank goodness she was in shape from yoga and running, and thank goodness the car started and had a full tank of petrol. When she got to the casting studio, she pulled into a deserted part of the parking lot and exited the same way.

Too broke to get her SUV repaired, Meghan repeated this

routine for months, parking far from other cars and waiting for the coast to clear before emerging from the hatch, feigning that she was searching in the back of the car for a script or photos before climbing back inside.

Of course she knew there would be setbacks; Meghan had been around the entertainment industry for too long to believe in rags-to-riches stories. So she stayed optimistic. Her motto was, 'I choose happiness', and she made it a point to stay happy, getting together with friends over pizza and wine, taking yoga classes, and going out as often as her budget permitted. One night her budget took her to a dive bar in West Hollywood that had been popularized by the 'Young Turks' in the entertainment industry (young hotshots keen on challenging the older Hollywood establishment) who liked to feel that they were slumming it in an authentic beatnik environment. A loud drawl, tinged with a New York accent, caught her attention. The owner of the voice was chatting with a couple of friends.

Over six feet tall with reddish blond hair and blue eyes, Trevor Engelson looked like a surfer or volleyball player, an archetypal California golden boy. He had the tone and the air of a Matthew McConaughey Lite, although he was born and raised in Great Neck, New York, the son of a successful orthodontist and great-grandson of Jewish immigrants.

Like Francis Ford Coppola, Trevor had attended Great Neck North High School, and like Coppola, he originally wanted to direct movies. 'I realized you needed talent to do that, so that was out the window,' he says self-deprecatingly. While still in high school, he managed to get himself hired as a production assistant on shoots in New York City, working tirelessly on weekends and during school breaks. The experience paid off and he was admitted to the Annenberg School of Cinematic Arts at the University of Southern California. He was on his way.

After he graduated in 1998, Trevor worked on the low-budget movie *Safe Men*, notable only for the appearance of Paul Giamatti as the strangely monickered Veal Chop. Then Engelson, who liked to think of himself as a hustler, was hired on *Deep Blue Sea* – a film which needlessly demonstrated the inevitably bloody consequences of genetically engineering super-intelligent Great White Sharks – as a staff assistant. During his time in the office he studied how his bosses, the movie's producers, worked. He liked what he saw. It didn't seem that they were working very hard and yet they made a lot of money and got the prettiest girls. He approached one of the producers, Alan Riche, and told him earnestly: 'Alan, I want to do what you do, I want to produce.' Riche advised him that, first, he had to work as an agent. Once *Deep Blue Sea* wrapped, Riche got the ambitious assistant a referral to the Endeavor Talent Agency. He started at the bottom of the ladder in the mail room working as a driver, delivering scripts and other agency-related packages, around town.

Trevor was personable and eager, and in due time he worked his way up to become assistant to the motion-picture literary agent Chris Donnelly. He was on the fast track to higher things. Then his ruthless ambition got in the way. While Donnelly was on vacation, Trevor sent out uncommissioned scripts, known as spec scripts, to actors and directors under the Endeavor letterhead. 'I thought I was being a self-starter,' Trevor admitted later. While there were no lasting hard feelings, he was fired for

Above: After graduating from Fairfax High School in Los Angeles, Doria Ragland (far right, second row) worked for her father, Alvin Ragland, at his antiques business. Later she took on a job in the makeup department at ABC Studios. It was here that she met her future husband, Thomas Markle, then lighting director for the long-running drama *General Hospital*.

Left: Thomas Markle, pictured in this 1962 high school portrait when he was eighteen. Shortly after graduating he headed to the Poconos, where he worked in local theatres. Later he moved to Chicago to pursue his ambition of working in stage lighting.

Above: On 23 December, 1979, African American Democrat Doria Ragland married Pennsylvania-born Republican Thomas Markle Sr. at the Self-Realization Fellowship Temple in Hollywood.

Left: Meghan, then a two-year-old toddler, was photographed endlessly by her doting father. But soon after this picture was taken, Doria and Thomas went their separate ways.

Above: Meghan, seen here at age five, and her mother, Doria, who worked as a travel agent, would often take trips together, visiting Mexico and Jamaica.

Below: Meghan's grandfather Alvin Ragland, standing next to her Aunt Saundra, holds a smiling Meghan at a family gathering while her half-brother Tom Markle Jr. holds her ponytail. Seated are her mother, Doria (left), and grandmother Jeanette (right).

Left: Meghan, age five, sings 'The Wheels on the Bus' at her private school, the Little Red School House, in Hollywood. The budding actress appeared in numerous productions, including *West Side Story* and *How the Grinch Stole Christmas*.

Below: Meghan at Ninaki Priddy's ninth birthday party in 1990. They were such good friends that both families considered them sisters.

Following page, top: Meghan, around age ten, with her Uncle Fred Markle (left), now presiding bishop of the Eastern Orthodox Catholic Church, with her father, Tom Markle Sr., and grandmother Doris. Meghan was devoted to her grandmother and regularly visited her at her Glendale nursing home.

Below: Tom Markle Sr. worked as the lighting director for the sitcom *Married … with Children*. Meghan would often bring friends, seen here with series star David Faustino, to visit the set.

Top, left: Meghan in seventh grade, 1993, at the start of her first year at Immaculate Heart, an all-girls Catholic high school in the Los Feliz area of Los Angeles.

Top, right: Meghan in eighth grade, August 1994. That year she first volunteered at the Hippie Kitchen but found the experience 'very scary'. She would return four years later.

Below: Meghan's Immaculate Heart High School was just a few minutes walk from her home in Los Feliz. Here she is fooling around with her school friends.

Top, left: Meghan posing by the Christmas tree with her boyfriend Luis Segura. They were introduced by his sister Maria.

Top, right: Meghan and her classmate Cecilia Donnellan strike a pose at the senior year Christmas dance held in December 1998.

Left: During her time at Immaculate Heart, Meghan featured regularly in stage shows and was photographed frequently for programme notes and yearbooks. Note that here she is wearing the distinctive art-deco-style Immaculate Heart class ring.

Above: A prescient photograph of Meghan and her best friend Ninaki Priddy outside Buckingham Palace during their summer trip to Europe in 1996.

Below: Meghan and her lighting-director father, Tom Markle Sr., enjoying the sunshine at a school picnic. He was devoted to his daughter, spending hours setting the stage lights for her many theatre performances.

Above: Meghan and her fellow thespians are given a standing ovation by the appreciative audience at St. Francis High School.

Bottom, left: Meghan, starring as Jocasta in the Greek tragedy *Oedipus Rex*, kisses Oedipus, played by Alejandro Santiago Fresquez, in the dramatic last act. The play, which was staged at Flintridge Preparatory School in La Cañada Flintridge, was a sellout, largely because Meghan, that year's homecoming queen, was the star.

Bottom, right: Meghan, as Jocasta, expresses her tearful despair when she realizes that she had committed incest with her son.

Above: The young actors take a break between rehearsals. Meghan hitches a ride on the back of a grinning Danny Segura, kid brother of her boyfriend Luis, while Brent Giannotta, who played a shepherd, makes a mock attack with his staff.

Below: Homecoming queen Meghan is all smiles at the St. Francis High School homecoming dance. Here she is dancing cheek to cheek with Giancarlo Boccato.

Right: On the day of her graduation, which was held at the Hollywood Bowl in the summer of 1999, Meghan collected a raft of awards for academic ability and community service.

Below: Meghan customized her room on campus at Northwestern by painting the walls in vivid colours. Before she handed back the keys she had to repaint the walls standard white.

Above: After Meghan graduated from college, she and her friend Ninaki Priddy took a road trip back to Los Angeles, stopping off at the Hotel Bellagio in Las Vegas, the setting for her favourite film, *Ocean's Eleven*.

Left: Meghan backstage on *Deal or No Deal* in one of the show's less revealing and more comfortable costumes.

Above: Meghan and her husband, film producer Trevor Engelson, seen here enjoying a break on a Greek island, worked hard and played hard. Engelson boasted that even on the plane he was working. 'But I'm always having a lot more fun than most other people I know.'

Below: Meghan and her husband Trevor Engelson enjoy a candlelit dinner for two during a romantic vacation on the island of Santorini in the Mediterranean.

Left: In 2008, when Meghan appeared as junior FBI agent Amy Jessup in director J. J. Abrams's sci-fi drama *Fringe*, she hoped that she would last the series. That she appeared in only two episodes came as a disappointment, one of many she faced as an aspiring actor.

Below: Suits producers cast Gina Torres (left) as a founding partner of the fictional law firm; Rick Hoffman as her devious colleague, Louis Litt; Meghan Markle as the sophisticated paralegal Rachel Zane; Gabriel Macht as hot-shot lawyer Harvey Specter; and Patrick J. Adams as brilliant lawyer Mike Ross, Rachel's love interest.

Following page: In 2011 Meghan got her big break in the legal drama *Suits*, a TV series in which the designer clothes were as important as the script. Meghan's sleek, sophisticated look attracted a huge fan following. Her hair was so important to her character, Rachel Zane, that she was contractually obligated to wear it down on camera.

Left: At the Elle Women in Television dinner in January 2013, Meghan joined Nicole Richie, Ellie Kemper and Erika Christensen to celebrate the work of women in TV.

Right: Meghan's fashion style is effortless, confident and polished, here posing for photographers in Toronto in January 2012.

overstepping his remit. Never down for long, he quickly found work as an assistant to fellow USC alumni Nick Osborne and his partner Jeffrey Zarnow at O/Z Films. As Trevor put it: 'They needed a hustler who could bring food to the table.' After he sold his first script, *The Road to Freaknik,* to Fox Searchlight for $25,000 he celebrated by partying hard.

When Osborne began his own movie company, Underground Films, Trevor became his assistant, several years later taking over the company. Beneath the banter and the wisecracks, Trevor was a driven soul, a young man out to make his mark in an uncompromising industry. When Meghan first met him on that night out in West Hollywood, she liked what she saw, attracted to his passion, his drive and ambition. Trevor was a typical New Yorker: brash, blunt, no bull and ballsy. At times, though, he was maybe a little too gauche for a sophisticated girl who liked classy rather than crass. He was a guy too with an aphorism for every occasion. 'Hope is the greatest currency we have in this business,' he told the wide-eyed wannabee. True or not, it's a great pick-up line.

His favourite saying belonged to the legendary Hollywood producer Neal Moritz, the man behind *The Fast and the Furious* franchise: 'Don't give it five minutes if you're not gonna give it five years.' Trevor said it so often that, in time, Meghan began to use it herself, presenting the phrase as though it had sprung fully formed from her head. Her version is more refined: 'Don't give it five minutes unless you can give it five years.' But Trevor had aphorisms – and chutzpah – to spare. As he once told a former USC buddy in a podcast interview for *Scripts and Scribes*: 'I'm a gigantic believer that all this shit can come to an end any minute now, and you've gotta take advantage of [it]. I'm Jewish and all that, but I think you got one shot at this life, so if you have a chance to have some fun and you're not hurting anybody else and you can still take care of everything else to be taken care of and – I always find a way to have a lot of fun. That's never an issue.'

He was the quintessential example of the young man who burned the candle at both ends, playing and working hard. Cuba, Palm Springs, New York: the world was his oyster – at least until he reached his credit card limit. As he said: 'If I'm on a plane going somewhere, when I land I'm working, on the plane I'm working, when I'm drinking I'm working. But I'm always having a lot more fun than most other people I know.' A thirsting producer and an ambitious actor. It was a classic Hollywood combination.

When Trevor's movie *Zoom* began production in early 2005, Meghan had recently bagged a brief appearance on the sitcom *Cuts*. It was one line, one measly line, but for Meghan she felt that she was on her way to the stars. Later in an anonymous blog, *Working Actress*, which she has been credited as writing, she described that feeling: 'At the start of my career, I remember freaking out, and celebrating over getting one line on a shitty UPN show. At the time, that was a big success. It was phone calls of congrats, and flowers, and celebratory dinners with wine glasses clinking. It was a landmark of more work to come, and a glimmer of hope that said "holy shit, you're really doing this."'

While she waited for her close up, to pay the bills she was making ends meet as a hostess in a Beverly Hills restaurant, working at a local store where she taught classes on the art of gift wrapping and used her other skill, her impeccable handwriting, to earn decent money as a calligraphist. She had learned the skill back at Immaculate Heart, and as she later commented: 'I've always had a propensity for getting the cursive down pretty well.' At that time, her claim to fame was writing the envelopes for the June 2005 wedding of singer Robin Thicke and actor Paula Patton.

The roles were coming, but not as quickly as she would have liked. In the summer of 2005 she was booked for a role on the show *Love, Inc.*, and later in the year, around Thanksgiving, for a TV movie called *Deceit*, followed by an appearance as an insurance salesperson on a short-lived sitcom *The War at Home*.

While Meghan was steadily but slowly chugging along, Trevor went from boom to bust, *Zoom*, which was released in the summer of 2006, proving an unmitigated disaster. The family action film, described as a 'dull and laugh-free affair', received a 3 per cent rating on Rotten Tomatoes. The movie's star, Tim Allen, even received a Razzie nomination for Worst Actor.

It was not much better for Meghan. So far, 2006 had been a bust both for film and TV roles. The couple's social life, though, got a bit of boost when, in August, they were invited to the Hamptons for the Coach Legacy Photo Exhibit. The event celebrating the American handbag manufacturer saw the couple sipping champagne and rubbing shoulders with wealthy socialites and the celebrity fringe – but it didn't help them up the Hollywood ladder.

The daily rejections would have broken someone with less grit, but Meghan knew it was a numbers game. As girls dropped out and headed home, defeated, the greater her chance of booking something became. As Trevor said, don't give it five minutes unless you can give it five years. And her five years were not even close to being up.

Like other girls doing the rounds, she had a gym bag containing the essential wardrobe for every possible part she might be called for: red for feisty Latina, pastels for the girl next door, mustard yellow for African-American. Short skirts, long skirts, blazer, bikini and tops; everything she needed was in her trusty tote. As she acknowledged, being ethnically 'ambiguous' allowed her to go for virtually any role. 'Sadly, it didn't matter,' she later wrote for *Elle* magazine. 'I wasn't black enough for the black roles and I wasn't white enough for the white ones, leaving me somewhere in the middle as the ethnic chameleon who couldn't book a job.'

She was sitting in her sweats, fabric tubes covering her forearms to keep skin oil off the envelopes she was hand-addressing for a calligraphy client, when her agent Nick Collins called. Collins, Boston-bred and a graduate of Brown University, knew all about the struggle to get on the Hollywood ladder – he had made ends meet waiting tables at a Brentwood restaurant before Bob Gersh made him his assistant at his eponymous talent agency. So he sympathized with her struggle to stay afloat.

He had secured an audition for her. There was one hitch. She had to appear in what the producers coyly described as a 'body conscious outfit', that is to say, a bikini, swimsuit, short skirt or shorts so that they could get an idea of what her body looked like. Yes, it was a cattle call for the position of briefcase girl in the popular TV game show, *Deal or No Deal*, but with nothing else lined up she agreed to go. After all, it was only a short drive from the West Hollywood home she now shared with Trevor to Culver City where the auditions were taking place. As she picked out her shortest skirt, she could have been excused for wondering: 'Is this why I earned a Bachelor's degree in international relations?'

5

Short Skirts, High Heels

Like so many teenagers, Tameka Jacobs arrived in Hollywood wide-eyed and eager to make her mark as a model or an actor. At five foot ten inches she was a head above the competition. Striking too, having Creole, Norwegian, African-American, French and Spanish in her genes. And that's just what she knows about.

First, she did some modelling before auditioning for a new entertainment show, *Deal or No Deal*, hosted by Howie Mandel. The show, based on the Dutch original and replicated across the world, was predicated on the tension between greed and prudence, a sure-fire ratings winner. Contestants choose from twenty-six briefcases which contain a cash value ranging from a cent to one million dollars. During the game the contestant eliminates various briefcases in the hope of being left with the million-dollar case. Periodically, the contestant is offered a deal by an unseen banker. The offer to quit the game and take modest winnings is matched by the possibility of going on and winning the big prize. The audience is always eager to see them risk it all.

The briefcases themselves are held by twenty-six beautiful smiling girls arranged temptingly in front of the contestant. This is where Tameka came in. She was asked to be briefcase girl 21, a position she held from the day the show opened in December 2005 to the end of its run in 2010.

When she was first asked to join, Tameka was over the moon. It was almost everything she could have asked for. She was paid $800 per episode and they regularly recorded seven episodes a day. That was $5,600, more than $23,000 a week, when the going was good. Then there were endorsements and personal appearances thrown in. Fame and riches for standing for hours on end holding a briefcase full of pretend cash. The irony was not lost on her.

Plus it was fun being a briefcase girl. The other girls were rowdy, catty and goofy; it was just like being in a sorority house. They only had two enemies – the cold in the studio and the achingly high heels they were all asked to wear.

Meghan joined the gang in 2006 for season two after successfully passing the audition. Along with model Chrissy Teigen, she began as a back-up in case regular girls were ill or failed to show up. Eventually she got a full-time slot as briefcase girl number 24 – close to Tameka. When she first arrived, Tameka clocked her as another multi-racial girl. 'It was never discussed between us,' she recalls. 'We just looked at one another and knew.' It was an unspoken code, a shared understanding of a lifetime of misunderstandings, quizzical glances and snide comments condensed into one knowing look. They had connections in common, too – early on, Tameka had been taken under the wing of model, talk-show host and all-round superstar Tyra Banks, who was, as Meghan well knew, a legend back at her old high school, Immaculate Heart. Now it was Tameka's time to return the favour, giving Meghan the low-down on the personalities, on who and what to look out for. She briefed her on the daily routine and what to bring to set – a pair of cosy Ugg boots after a day in high heels in near-freezing temperatures was a must. As they chatted it was clear to Tameka that Meghan saw this as a stepping stone to earning some money before trying for more serious acting jobs.

The average *Deal or No Deal* day began at 5.30 in the morning as Meghan and the other briefcase girls gathered for hours of hair, make-up and the final fitting for their skimpy outfits. With outfit changes every episode, and multiple episodes filmed per day, they often had to endure three separate fittings. A rack of beautiful matching ball gowns would arrive, to be unceremoniously hacked to pieces so that the girls' legs and décolletage were on full display.

After rough fittings for length and shape, there would be a final wardrobe session in which the girls sucked in everything and the dresses were pinned down. Some dresses were so tight that the girls couldn't even bend down to put on their agonizingly high heels, so an assistant would be on hand to help.

The briefcase girls all wore Spanx shapewear, not only to make their stomachs flatter but to keep them warm in the Arctic studio temperatures. As a final touch, they inserted what briefcase girl number 13, Leyla Milani, liked to call 'chicken cutlets' – or sometimes wodges of tissues – into their bras to enhance their cleavage.

As Meghan stood there for hour after hour, trying not to shiver, her feet sore from the cheap high heels, a painted smile on her face, she thought of the pay cheque at the end of the week.

This was not what she had in mind when she went into acting but, at only twenty-five, she was earning more money than she had ever earned in her life, and the shooting schedule was perfect: long blocks of filming followed by weeks of down time which gave her the opportunity to attend more auditions and go travelling with the man she playfully called Trevity-Trev-Trev, a nickname he had originally been given by the rapper LL Cool J.

While the Hamptons had been sampled, there were other spots she wanted to visit, schedules permitting: Greece, Mexico, Thailand, anywhere in the Caribbean, were all on her list. The foodie in her fantasized about going to Bangkok and sampling the menu at Chote Chitr, the restaurant which had been featured on National Public Radio and in the *New York Times*. Their mutual ambition as well as their love of adventure, of hopping on a plane to somewhere unusual and faraway, was a central plank of their relationship. Over time, Meghan gained something of a reputation for knowing about the newest restaurants or the quirkiest hotels in odd parts of the world.

He would join her – if he had the time. They were both driven individuals, Trevor as busy, if not more so, than his girlfriend. It was noticeable that, unlike the boyfriends and husbands of her *Deal or No Deal* 'sisters', Trevor never visited Meghan on set. It was so unusual that his absence was commented upon by the other girls. However, there were plenty of other celebrities, mainly sports stars, who dropped by, some clearly trying to get up close and personal with the girls. One frequent guest caused quite the frisson: Donald Trump, then organizing the Miss Universe pageant, and once making a guest appearance as the banker on *Deal or No Deal* to cross-promote *The Apprentice*.

The frequently bankrupt real-estate mogul toured the set, giving girls his card and inviting them to play golf at one of his courses. Tameka Jacobs told me: 'He was a creep, super-creepy, but some girls were attracted to money and power and took his number.'

Meghan was one of the girls who gave the future president a wide berth. Not that she was known for joining in much with any of the 'after-work' events – occasions when a bevy of beautiful women, several minders in tow, trawled the bars of West Hollywood. As Meghan is now known as a thirsty socialite, it is surprising that she rarely, if ever, joined in these raucous nights of karaoke and chasers.

For a girl who would end up living her life on Instagram, it is remarkable, too, that she never posed for a silly picture, mugging for the cameras like the rest of her colleagues. Meghan knew her angles – after all, she had been taught by the best, her father – and always posed sweetly. If caught with a drink in her hand, it was only ever champagne, and she was never heard to swear.

Aside from promotional photos in costume on the *Deal or No Deal* set, Meghan's only promo work for the show was self-serving; at the 2006 Emmys she appeared at a gifting suite, where celebrities are given products in exchange for posing for a photograph by the company logo, and was duly photographed looking at yoga mats and resort wear. Meghan's lack of involvement in 'office' gossip – she was always studying lines for an audition, recalls Leyla Milani – and after-work play was just one of the reasons she stood out. Another was her eating habits. While the other girls 'sucked hard candy and ate raw vegetables' between scenes, Meghan would eat pizza or bags of crisps, seemingly unconcerned about bloat or weight gain. And while many of the other girls thanked their lucky stars for this opportunity, Meghan saw the gig as a temporary berth. As Tameka recalls: 'She was super-sweet, adorable, a little sheltered, wholesome, with a good head on her shoulders. Looking back, it was clear that she had a brand and wanted to protect that brand for a future career as a serious actor.' She knew where she wanted to go, and it certainly wasn't spending her days on *Deal or No Deal*.

During the shooting break in November, Meghan auditioned for and got the part of a Latina murder suspect on *CSI: NY* – the part once again had Meghan flashing the flesh when her character was introduced wearing a corset and suspenders. Then it was back to the cold NBC soundstage in Culver City.

During Meghan's time on *Deal or No Deal*, Trevor had a film in production, a marital comedy called *License to Wed*, starring funny man Robin Williams and Mandy Moore. Meghan secretly hoped there would be a role for her, but the bit parts that might have suited her went to more experienced actresses who had worked with the director, Ken Kwapis, on the TV series *The Office*. It was to become a source of conflict between the couple, Meghan becoming disappointed that Trevor didn't try harder to include her in some of his productions.

No matter. She had the feeling that this could be her year. During the February round of auditions for the 2007 pilot season, she came away from a meeting with top casting agent, Donna Rosenstein, with a positive spring in her step. Rosenstein had been senior vice-president at ABC for many years, overseeing the casting of such series as *NYPD Blue*, *Roseanne* and *Twin*

Peaks, and had since set up her own company. She was Meghan's best chance yet at the big time.

Meghan loved the part she had been asked to read for, a former stripper and street walker called Kelly Calhoun who had been rescued from her seedy life by a born-again Christian cop who had fallen in love with and married her.

The show, named *The Apostles*, was part police drama, part *Desperate Housewives* complete with similar voiceover narration, and was set in a suburban Southern California cul-de-sac where all the residents were police officers and their spouses. Shortly after her reading, Meghan got the news she had been longing to hear: 'Meghan, you got the part,' her agent excitedly told her. When she told her father, he wrote her a loving note of congratulations, the actor keeping his tender letter in a hand-carved box by the side of her bed.

Meghan's character wasn't the most feminist of women, but compared to her role as a briefcase babe, Kelly Calhoun was at least a step in the right direction. Her African-American husband, played by Keith Robinson, finds himself conflicted, berating her for her immoral past but drawn to her sassy, yet vulnerable, personality. In the tight-knit enclave, Kelly finds empowerment and friendship with the other wives. She startles them first by sharing sex tips on how to keep things hot in the bedroom and then by teaching them the tricks of the stripping trade, demonstrating how to disrobe seductively. Meghan had a good feeling about the show. It ticked all the boxes: a strong cast – Shawn Hatosy from *Alpha Dog*, who specialized in playing tightly wound, edgy characters, was one of the leads – a solid back story, feminist themes, and plenty of room for conflict and tension in the insular cop community.

The pilot, shot as a full-length feature, was delivered in June 2007. After several viewings and much back and forth, Fox Studios decided to pass on making a full-blown series, airing it the following year as a standalone movie. It was a real blow for Meghan, who had harboured high hopes for the show. At least she could now add 'stripper' to her acting résumé. Which she promptly did.

While Meghan worked on *The Apostles*, Trevor was in production on a Sandra Bullock/Bradley Cooper comedy, *All About Steve*, written by two of his clients. Bullock had taken control of the film as producer, leaving Trevor to manage his growing stable of writers and directors.

He was always hustling to get them work and to find new clients. When he went to coffee shops he handed out business cards to whoever was tapping away at their laptop. 'What's the worst thing that happens? I read a shitty script?' he laughed. He read scripts non-stop, going so far as to keep a stack of them in their bathroom at home as well as a supply of waterproof pens so he could make notes.

As for Meghan landing a role through her boyfriend – that had proved to be a bit of a washout. At least, so far. Not so with casting agent Donna Rosenstein, who called her in to read for the role of Sadie Valencia, the spoilt daughter of a Las Vegas casino owner in the story of a crime boss's family who were struggling to go straight. There were solid expectations that the comedy, *Good Behavior*, which also starred *Chicago Fire*'s Treat Williams as her father and *Schitt's Creek*'s Catherine O'Hara as the family matriarch, would be well mannered – and funny enough – to make a series for the ABC network.

When the show, which was filmed in Las Vegas and Los Angeles, and also starred the Canadian actor Patrick J. Adams, was tested to a wider audience, it got the thumbs down. In the end it was just another pilot to wind up being broadcast as a standalone TV movie.

Work did keep coming, though. Now twenty-seven, Meghan, once she was finished with *Good Behavior*, was cast as Wendy in *90210*, a reboot of the long-running series *Beverly Hills, 90210*, which she had watched as a teenager. The new version was trying to be equally iconic but updated and raunchier.

In the series premiere, Meghan's character once again had a bawdy introduction, first being shown outside West Beverly Hills High performing oral sex in another student's car while pupils go back and forth. Her character lasted for just two episodes before vanishing without any plot explanation. The series, however, would run for five seasons. With various guest spots in established series like *Knight Rider*, *Without a Trace* and the sitcom *The League*, Meghan was almost becoming a familiar face to TV audiences. Real fame, however, or even just a steady pay cheque – she was barely earning enough to pay for actors' health insurance – continued to elude her. She was always on the cusp of making a breakthrough.

When director J. J. Abrams – who even before his mega successes with *Star Wars* and *Star Trek* was lauded as the mastermind behind *Mission Impossible III* and *Lost* – had Meghan playing a junior FBI agent, Amy Jessup, in his sci-fi procedural, *Fringe*, she once again had high hopes that something would come of it. She appeared in the first and second episodes of the second season, and though director Akiva Goldsman, best known for his hit *A Beautiful Mind*, hinted that audiences might be seeing more of Agent Jessup, she never returned to the creepy tale of spooky shapeshifters and parallel universes. In fact she was next seen altering her personal universe in a more conventional way, snorting a couple of lines of cocaine in the knowing TV-movie comedy, *The Boys and Girls Guide to Getting Down*. Based on the award-winning 2006 independent film that featured her *Deal or No Deal* co-model Leyla Milani, the show charts the vagaries of the LA dating scene.

In the sex, drugs and anything goes movie, Meghan is shown as a single girl pouring herself into a super-tight black dress – shades of *Deal or No Deal* – before heading out for the night prowling the singles scene of downtown LA, where she knocks back some blow to keep the mobile debauchery moving.

With roles to her name in which she had snorted coke, performed oral sex and taught striptease, what better credentials could she have had to share an on-screen smooch with former junkie, funny man and now British movie star Russell Brand. Her 'exotic' looks won her the role of Tatiana in *Get Him to the Greek*, which filmed in the spring of 2009. With no lines, she remained uncredited in the official cast list. Still, she fared better than Brand's ex-wife Katy Perry and singer Alanis Morissette, whose scenes were deleted.

During this time, it was her partner who was getting the plaudits. Trevor was named by the *Hollywood Reporter* as one of the 'Top 35 Under 35' in the Next Gen Class of 2009 for his work as a manager and producer. All those years of meetings and schmoozing were paying off – and he already had the pretty girl he had always dreamed of. Along with that glowing write-up in the *Hollywood Reporter*, the honour came with a party at My House, a Hollywood club famous for its velvet ropes and bottle service, where Meghan did her best to shine as the beautiful and talented, as well as supportive, girlfriend of a bona fide mover and shaker.

Trevor could now afford to give Meghan a few crumbs from his groaning pile of scripts. At least it would stop her continuously nagging him to give her a part in one of his productions. Two clients, Marcus Dunstan and Patrick Melton, the writers behind the *Saw IV, V* and *VI* movies, had put together a nineteen-minute film, *The Candidate*, based on the short story by Henry Slesar. Meghan was cast as the secretary, in one scene showing off a beautifully written, hand-addressed envelope – an in-joke about her calligraphy skills.

Trevor then found a small role for her in *Remember Me*, a 9/11-themed melodrama starring the British heartthrob Robert Pattinson. The movie, which was shot in June, was written by his client Will Fetters and turned out to be the producer's biggest hit to date, a ratings and box-office success. Meghan might be proving to be his lucky charm.

Not that she thought so. Earlier that year, in January 2010, the young actor began an anonymous blog which she called *Working Actress*, where she described in often heartbreaking detail the life of a jobbing actor. In one post she wrote: 'I'm not gonna lie. I've spent many days curled up in bed with a loaf of bread and some wine. A one-woman pity party. It's awful and ridiculous.' She described what it was like to have her minor scenes cut from a movie, the endless rejection, bitchy fellow actresses at auditions, and test shoots gone wrong. 'All you are doing is setting yourself up for heartbreak,' she said of this most demanding of professions. Though her blog, which abruptly ended in 2012, was anonymous, the *Daily Mail* reported in February 2018 that fellow bloggers and actors had confirmed she was the author. 'Yes it was definitely Meghan Markle who wrote it,' said actor Lance Carter who communicated with her before reproducing one of her posts on his own site.

Shortly after beginning the blog in July 2010, Meghan was ready for her own close-up. She was cast opposite comedian Jason Sudeikis in the comedy *Horrible Bosses*. In her thirty-five-second scene she played a FedEx girl whom Sudeikis creepily hits on, saying that she is too 'cute' for the job. Meghan was cool and polite, a professional just doing her job. That was it. Blink and you would miss her. She did, though, get to meet her screen idol, Donald Sutherland, who played Jack Pellit in the movie. 'I was so excited to work with him,' she enthused in her blog, *Working Actress*. 'The woman in the hair department said he was a gem and that I would love him, so when I met him (and his oh-so-debonair self), I said: "Mr Sutherland, I hear I'm going to fall in love with you before lunch-break." He laughed, it broke the ice. And I resisted the very major urge to squeal.'

Despite enjoying her fan-girl moment, she had to recognize that this was yet another acting job that traded exclusively on her looks and sex appeal. Time to recalibrate. She was approaching thirty, an age in a notoriously cruel place like Hollywood when she would soon be considered over the hill. If she was not careful, her agent would be dropping hints about changing the date of birth on her CV.

Another casting season had passed her by and she had nothing apart from a series of auditions in her diary. It was hard not to feel discouraged, especially when she heard of the successes of her contemporaries. Those five years were up and she just hadn't quite made that extra leap.

Time to dip into Trevor's pick 'n' mix bag of aphorisms. Along with 'give it five years' he had another favourite: 'This is not a business for the weary. You're either gonna buy an island or be sent to one.'

Meghan straightened her skirts, focused her gaze, and walked into the next casting room. She wasn't ready to be marooned just yet.

6

A Star is Tailor-Made

Rachel Zane was a ball buster. A ball buster to cast, a ball buster to play, and a ball buster even to name. Sexy but unapproachable, Rachel Zane was a character created as the love interest on a new show; so new they hadn't even worked out the title. Opinion was split. Some executives at the USA Network, who were developing the show in 2010, went for *A Legal Mind*. Others thought the title *Suits* was tailor-made for a snappily dressed office full of sharp lawyers. *Suits* won out. That was just one of numerous daily battles to give the show a distinct identity. Casting and chemistry were critical to give *Suits* crackle and pop. Patrick J. Adams was perfect for the part of Mike Ross, the legal genius with an eidetic memory who couldn't afford law school because he was paying to keep his sick grandma in an upscale nursing home. The actor's eyes were the key to him winning the role: piercing blue, long-lashed. The rest of him was just average-looking boy-next-door. He combined a vibe of intelligence with just enough seediness to flesh out the part of the brilliant college dropout who made a living by taking law-school entry exams for other students.

After several weeks of casting, on 7 July they had signed up *The Others* star Gabriel Macht as top lawyer Harvey Reginald Specter, and cast Rick Hoffman as the duplicitous partner Louis Litt, as well as Gina Torres, who played the sharp-tongued founding partner Jessica Lourdes Pearson.

One part remained, the role of Rachel Zane. She was a paralegal who was smart, elegantly upper class, and so highly regarded at the fictional law firm that she had her own office, while several of the fictional lawyers still laboured on the main floor. She had to be sexy without being overtly so, secure in her own power as a woman, but with a certain vulnerability as shown by the fact that she was unable to pass the LSAT, the exam which determined eligibility for law school. The show's producers were looking for a woman who had toughness and attitude while still being engaging.

'The part was just a nightmare to cast,' recalls one studio executive. 'Then Meghan Markle came along.' Once told by famed casting director April Webster to use 'less make-up, more Meghan' when auditioning, Meghan had dressed sexy-professional-casual to screen test for the role. Somewhat belatedly she realized that the plum-coloured spaghetti strap top, black jeans, and high heels she was wearing were more single lady lawyer on the prowl than attractive paralegal with an encyclopaedic knowledge of the law.

Before her audition Meghan ran into an H&M store, picked out a simple black dress for thirty-five dollars and raced back to the studio. She hadn't even time to try it on for size. The producers of the then-titled *A Legal Mind* asked her to change into the new garment before taking the screen test. It was the best thirty-five dollars she had ever spent. As the show's creator

Aaron Korsh told writer Sam Kashner: 'We all looked at each other [after the Meghan Markle screen test] like, "Wow this is the one." I think it's because Meghan has the ability to be smart and sharp but without losing her sweetness.'

With the casting of Meghan Markle, the character of Rachel Zane was made flesh. Originally, the brainy and beautiful paralegal was named Rachel Lane, but the clearance department felt the name was too similar to that of a real person. Instead, they chose the surname of the show's casting director Bonnie Zane, an insiders' compliment to the storied Hollywood professional for her work on the show.

It was not as if Meghan was a shoe-in for the role. Now thirty, she was on paper too old to play a young paralegal, and the multi-racial Gina Torres, who played partner Jessica Pearson, had already put a tick in the box marked 'ethnic diversity'.

Meghan's main rival was a younger, more experienced Canadian actor, blonde, blue-eyed Kim Shaw. By now Meghan had learned to manage her expectations and not take rejection too personally. She was too light, too dark, too skinny, too something or other for so many roles.

Meghan didn't feel great about her audition, and called her agent Nick Collins at the Gersh Agency from her car. She told him that she could not get her head around the lines. It was a mouthful, the worst audition of her life. 'I don't think I did a good job in that room, and I need to get back in there,' she wailed. 'I really want this part.' Her agent, as she later recounted to *Marie Claire* in 2013, had heard this before from many of his clients, and his answer was always the same: 'There's nothing I can do. Just focus on your next audition.' Once again she felt that moment of: 'Why am I subjecting myself to this torture?' She had a top degree, a sparkling résumé, great connections; she didn't have to put herself through the ringer every day. But there was an inevitability to it that Meghan found hard to resist. As she once said in an interview with Al Norton: 'If you grow up in a coal-mining town, you will probably become a coal miner. I grew up in the industry, and was always on set because of my dad, so it seems natural for me to be an actress.'

In spite of her considerable misgivings, she tried to stay optimistic, going to yoga classes and meditating to stay grounded. All the while she headed out to other auditions, though none of them inspired her as much as *A Legal Mind*. In her heart, she felt the role would be perfect for her. And the fact that the character shared her first name, Rachel, added that extra something – it was kismet.

While Meghan felt she had blown the audition, unbeknownst to her, behind the scenes the executives were busy drawing up the contract for the pilot if the network approved. As she recalls: 'We had no idea that they ... loved my read. They loved my take on Rachel and they were putting together a deal for me. It was a really good lesson in perspective. I think we are always going to be our own worst critics.'

The head honchos at USA Network had chosen Markle over Shaw, formally casting her on 24 August 2010. As then-USA Network co-president Jeff Wachtel explained: '[Shaw] was a little bit more traditional blonde girl next door; [the decision] was a tough one because they were both really good. Meghan had a certain type of sparkle and was a little more urbane, a little more worldly.'

The deciding factor was how they wanted the relationship between Rachel and Mike to play out. As Wachtel told the *Hollywood Reporter* in 2017: 'One of the things that we needed at the beginning with *Suits* was Patrick's character comes in as the hottest thing in town: he's brilliant, has a photographic memory and fakes his way into being a lawyer and then he comes up against this girl who turns out to be the love of his life. We needed somebody who had a real authority to shut him down and still be the coolest thing around. And they had it right away. It was a lot of fun.'

Meghan was still taking other auditions when her mobile phone rang with a call from her agent, telling her she had been cast in the *Suits* series pilot and would begin filming in autumn in New York. She was overjoyed but also wary. After all, she had gone down this road before, especially with *The Apostles*, which, at the time, she felt confident was going to be her big break. After eight years going from audition to audition, had she finally caught a break? Meghan's casting garnered a short article in the *Hollywood Reporter*, noting her uncredited role in the 2010 comedy, *Get Him to the Greek*.

When she began with a standard table-read of the script, it was obvious that Meghan and Patrick generated chemistry, this elusive quality that is the showbiz equivalent of lightning in a bottle. It was vital that they had a spark, as the ups and downs of their love story would be a narrative arc throughout the series – if the show was picked up by the network, that is.

In the autumn of 2010 Meghan flew to New York to shoot the ninety-minute series pilot. Since the elation of winning the part, reality had set in. She had already shot five pilots, including one for ABC with her current co-star, Patrick J. Adams, and none of them had got any further. Maybe he was her unlucky charmer. As she later observed: '[A pilot is] like your baby, then you wait and wait to see if it gets picked up and it's a hard thing to let go of. The one I had the most attachment to was one called *The Apostles*, which was my very first pilot. It's probably revisionist history but I look back on it now and think: "That would have been amazing." But who knows?'

On her first day of the shoot, the normally nerveless Meghan was a little edgy. Though she had grown up on sets, and was no novice to TV productions, it was one thing sitting in the wings watching the action, or hovering on the edges as a bit part, quite another to be centre stage. Nonetheless, all those hours after school on professional soundstages, observing the interaction of actors and crews, overhearing the snatches of conversation and gossip between production assistants, and hanging around the craft service table, had taught her how to behave on set. She was charming to everyone, from grips to the lighting director. There was a degree of self-interest at work, Meghan having learned from her father that the placement of a light could enhance or slightly deform a pretty face, and that some of the placement depended on goodwill.

Meghan was remembered as bubbly and warm, chatty but a good listener who didn't dominate on-set conversations. She was a team player who radiated a sweet intelligence, saving her sterner, more ambitious self for those important on-set interactions with Patrick J. Adams.

In a show that became known as much for its fashion as its plot line, costume designer Jolie Andreatta's vision of Meghan's on-screen look was crucial. She later recalled: 'Rachel is classic, to the word, with a hint of rebellion thrown in. Her style is understated and her cute figure pulls it off perfectly.'

On Meghan's return from New York, Trevor took her to a beach resort in the Central American country of Belize for a vacation. It was there, amid the tropical greenery and the soothing waves, that he asked his girlfriend of six years to be his bride, slipping a princess-cut diamond solitaire onto her finger. Meghan was thrilled. 'They were both googly-eyed for one another,' recalls a friend. 'They were very much in love.'

Meghan was engaged to her long-time boyfriend and was in a pilot for which the omens looked good. There was serious talk of a TV series. At long last her Hollywood dream was coming true. As her half-brother Tom Junior told me: 'Meg was on her way up, marrying a guy with a production company and now making good money.'

All those on-set rumours turned into a joyous reality when, in January 2011, USA Network gave the green light for the first series. Shooting would begin on 25 April in Toronto. Finally, after years of auditions that went nowhere, roles that ended up on the cutting-room floor, and most disheartening, pilots that never got picked up, Meghan had a series. The only downside was that she would have to take a five-hour flight if she was to see her Hollywood-based fiancé. But since she and Trevor caught planes like others hailed taxis, the sacrifice was going to be worth it. They were both ambitious young people; if anything, Trevor more driven than Meghan. He understood that this was an opportunity that she could not miss.

Her joy, however, was tempered with sorrow. While she was preparing for the series, her mother phoned to tell her that

Alvin Ragland, her eighty-two-year-old grandfather, had tripped and fallen as a result of getting tangled with a dog lead while out walking his dog. He had hit his head on the pavement and died of his injuries on 12 March. Meghan remembered Alvin as a real character, appreciating his knowledge of antiques, an enthusiasm that inspired her own fascination with the finer things in life. In the family reorganization following his death, Doria inherited his single-storey green stucco house in what is known as the 'black Beverly Hills'. It was close to the University of Southern California where, in the late spring, Doria, now a mature student, would complete her Master's degree in social work. Her daughter was ecstatic, probably more effusive than her mother. She watched proudly as Doria collected her degree on a makeshift stage at one of the many graduation ceremonies taking place on the extensive campus in June. Given the difficulties of her mother's background, the trouble at her high school following the 1971 San Fernando earthquake and the casual jobs she had taken on to make ends meet, her achievement was a genuine personal triumph, an indication of her smarts and her determination.

❖

The first episode of *Suits* aired on 23 June, to generally favourable reviews and, more importantly, an enthusiastic audience. Cast, crew and the money men at the network were ecstatic, the producers thrilled that their gamble to cast Meghan opposite Patrick had paid off big time, the show's fans buzzing about the couple's on-screen chemistry.

Their off-screen chemistry was equally noticeable, almost uncomfortably so, according to guests at Meghan and Trevor's wedding, which took place in Jamaica in September 2011. The two actors had clearly developed a bond of familiarity that is invariably the corollary of working up close and personal for so long and so intensely. Patrick J. Adams has a different take on their interaction at that time. He later told writer Lesley Goldberg: 'In some ways, Meghan and I were the closest because we were the youngest people in the cast and both came in with the least experience. We grew up together over the course of the show.'

He might have kept his distance if he had known that she had been cast to play a calculating serial killer in an episode of the quirky crime show *Castle*, entitled 'Once Upon a Crime', which she filmed while *Suits* was on hiatus. As Princess Sleeping Beauty, Meghan's character plotted a complex series of murders with fairy-tale themes, having been cast for the part by her champion, Donna Rosenstein.

For Meghan, shooting her first series of *Suits* turned out to be more stressful than organizing her wedding. After choosing Jamaica Inn in Ocho Rios, an idyllic spot with balconies overlooking the sea, she had delegated the organization to an in-house wedding coordinator, who handled every detail of their destination wedding. Given the hectic lives she and Trevor were leading, it was a lifesaver. All she had to worry about was the guest list, choosing the flowers, agreeing to the menu – and packing a bikini or two. Oh, and her strapless white wedding dress.

Three weeks before their wedding Trevor made an obscure podcast where he talked about his career with two old friends,

Kristian Harloff and Mark Ellis. His breezy, self-deprecating manner – he told a story about how he was chastised by a senior agent at Endeavor for standing too far away from the urinal because he was afraid of getting 'splash back' on his favourite Italian Canale 'hero suit' – was very different to his bride-to-be who, as her former colleagues on *Deal or No Deal* observed, was always very self-contained and considered. *The Schmoes Know* podcast was live streamed, meaning that Trevor could be seen on camera swigging from an engraved hip flask – a gift from Meghan – during the show. She texted him to 'put that flask down, it looks incredibly unprofessional'. When one of the Schmoes suggested that they have Meghan on the show, Trevor interjected: 'She's a big deal, fuck off.' The podcast hinted at their personality differences, Trevor loose-lipped, unconcerned, carefree, a striking counterpoint to Meghan who was archly protective of Brand Meghan, always keen to project an air of sophistication and style.

She may have felt that at times Trevor was too brashly laid-back for comfort, especially now that her star was rising, *Suits* having been picked up for a second season. It was a cause for celebration but also uncertainty as, once more, the newly-weds would be long-distance commuters, seeing each other every two or three weeks, depending on whether Trevor had meetings or had arranged to see his family, who lived on Long Island. Their wedding would be a rare opportunity to let their hair down, and the couple were determined to enjoy a long weekend of parties, including beach wheelbarrow races, culminating with the twelve-minute wedding ceremony, which made the 'Hitched, Hatched, Hired' column of the *Hollywood Reporter.*

With the ocean as backdrop, the couple recited vows they had written themselves, promising to love and care for each other. One of Meghan's bridesmaids recalled: 'It was such a moving wedding. I started crying the moment I saw her in her dress.' Though the pair had officially married in Los Angeles in a brief civil ceremony, this was the real celebration for family and friends, complete with a rousing chorus of the traditional Jewish 'Hava Nagila' sung while the bride and groom were hoisted up in chairs held above their guests' heads.

On returning from their Jamaican celebration, Trevor and Meghan were able to spend more time with one another before shooting was due to begin once more in Toronto. It was just as well that she was enjoying a brief break, as her father was in need of her support. For the last few months, he had cared for his increasingly frail mother Doris Markle, whom he had flown from her home in Florida to his house in Los Feliz. As his home was close by the ABC TV studios where he worked, he was able to visit during the day to check that she was OK. Sadly, as her chronic forgetfulness slipped into dementia, that was no longer a practical option. The last straw was when she absent-mindedly left a pan on the stove, causing a small kitchen fire. He arrived home to find the fire department and paramedics at the scene.

The only option was to place her in a specialist facility, moving her into Broadview Residential Care Center, an affordable nursing home in Glendale, Los Angeles. Once the first season of *Suits* wrapped up, Meghan visited her as much as she could, making the twelve-mile drive from her cosy house on Hilldale in West Hollywood to see her grandmother. She read to her, brushed her hair, and did simple arts and crafts with her. As she slipped deeper into the gloaming of dementia, Doris did not recognize her son, Tom Senior, nor her grandson, Tom Junior. Yet her eyes would light up when she heard Meghan's voice and felt her comforting touch. 'With her dementia, grandmother got weird about me and dad, but was always OK with Meg,' recalls Meghan's brother Tom Junior. 'I saw the private side of Meghan, a genuinely caring, loving person. She had an amazing relationship with Doris even though she didn't know her that well.'

In October, Meghan and Trevor walked the red carpet at the Anti-Defamation League Entertainment Industry Awards dinner at the Beverly Hilton Hotel, the most high-level event she had ever attended. More importantly, she was Master of Ceremonies for the evening. She dressed for the part in a simple Stella McCartney velvet cocktail dress, while Trevor, beaming with pride, looked his usual slightly rumpled self. They mingled with other celebrities, and Meghan glowed. She was on her way.

Meghan continued to visit her ailing grandmother at the nursing home. Tom Senior and Junior could only be there on weekends, but Meghan came frequently during the week. With Doris fading fast, Tom Senior flew in his brothers to say their last goodbyes. She died on 25 November 2011, Trevor and Meghan present at her funeral. It was the first time that most of the Markles had met the TV producer. Meghan's brother remarked, 'She was completely head over heels and seemed really happy when I saw them together, despite the sad circumstances. They seemed extremely happy together.'

These family reunions were few and far between. The last time Meghan had seen her half-sister Yvonne, who had re-christened herself Samantha, was when she and Tom Senior made the trip to Albuquerque for the eldest Markle daughter's college graduation. 'She was lovely, very polite and sweet,' Tom Senior's first wife Roslyn told me about Meghan's visit. During the graduation ceremony, Meghan sat next to Samantha's pre-teen daughter Noel and made small talk with the girl, then posed for photos, smiling and trying to make everyone feel at ease.

It was the last time Meghan would see her Markle relations, the actor also leaving Trevor behind when she flew to Toronto to settle back into her new life, filming for nine months for the show's successful second season. Of course the couple Skyped and Facetimed, but it was wearing being apart, especially during the long grey, Canadian winter. She did her best to get the Californian vibe going in her rented house in Summerhill, lightening the wall colours and trying to convey a bright and airy feel amid the chilly gloom. Candles, leafy plants and, of course, white hotel-style bedsheets with a high thread count helped to bring a touch of Hollywood to Toronto.

It might have been cold outside, but it was hot on set, the budding if often-thwarted romance between Rachel Zane and Mike Ross fuelling *Suits'* growing success as much as the Machiavellian plot twists about a law firm and its clients. On screen, sparks flew between Rachel and Mike, enthralling viewers, especially after the second-season finale, which climaxed with their characters having heated sex in the fictional law firm's file room. Fans had become really invested in the fictional couple. Adams recalls a chance encounter with a Swedish hiker who had twisted his ankle on a backpacking trail in New Zealand. When Adams, who was on holiday, went to help, the young man forgot his injuries and told the actor how badly he wanted Mike and Rachel to 'figure things out'.

Their on-screen intimacy led to speculation that the pair had fallen into the trap of many co-stars: Elizabeth Taylor and Richard Burton, Angelina Jolie and Brad Pitt, Daniel Craig and Rachel Weisz. In fact, the Canadian-born Adams had fallen for an earlier female lead, Troian Bellisario – the daughter of producers Deborah Pratt and Donald P. Bellisario – who played opposite him in 2009 in the play *Equivocation*. They fell in love, but after a year they broke up, Bellisario going on to win a role in the first season of *Pretty Little Liars*. In a move that his *Suits* character Mike Ross would have approved of, Adams devised a cute way of winning back the showbiz heiress. He quietly took a bit part on *Pretty Little Liars* and then joined his surprised ex-girlfriend on set at the table read-through. His ploy worked, the couple reuniting and eventually becoming engaged in 2014 and marrying in 2016.

While the 'will they, won't they' romance between Rachel and Mike gave the show its sexual tension, it was the other man in Rachel's life, her father, a powerful rival lawyer played by African-American actor Wendell Pierce, who really caught the attention of some of the show's 4 million-strong audience.

As the story develops, we learn that Rachel, much to the disappointment of her successful and wealthy father, is stuck as a paralegal because she just can't pass the law exam, the LSAT. While her character has some daddy issues, it was Rachel Zane's bi-racial heritage that stirred controversy, with both African-American and white viewers confused that a girl who looked so white had a black father. One fan asked if she was adopted, while others were more hostile about the fictional paralegal's heritage. Even though the American president himself was bi-racial, the decision by the show's producers to cast a woman of mixed race as a modern-day equivalent of a conventional upper-class white woman helped move the dial a little with regard to racial stereotypes and traditional images of beauty.

As the show's popularity grew, Meghan and her colleagues were asked to build a following using social media in order to help with ratings. Even though she had never heard of Instagram, she found herself opening an account and posting photographs from her private life. What began as a chore turned into an enjoyable and highly addictive daily habit, the actor building up more than a million followers by the time she closed the account. Her first image on 24 May 2012 showed her *Suits* script from the episode 'Break Point', a copy of *Forbes*, the American business magazine, as well as liberal TV commentator Rachel Maddow's first book, *Drift*: *The Unmooring of American Military Power*, about the rise of presidential authority and the diminution of Congress. With her Instagram debut, Meghan was demonstrating that here was an actor with brains as well as beauty who was involved and engaged in the world around her. Subsequent posts would be less forthright, featuring her favourite food, engaging selfies, travels abroad and images of Toronto. It was a curated, very considered vision of her private world.

Her involvement in the outside world was not just through the distorting prism of Instagram. In February 2012, Meghan took part in a USA Network campaign against racism, appearing on screen in *Characters Unite*, an award-winning public service programme created to address social injustices and cultural divides. Wearing a T-shirt with the words 'I won't stand for racism' printed on it, she encouraged people to stand together against prejudice, while sharing her experiences of being a fly on the wall as white people told black jokes or made bigoted remarks.

Closer to home, the actor volunteered to help at a local Toronto soup kitchen for the homeless, the St Felix Centre, which was founded by the Felician Sisters. She also asked the *Suits* producers if, at the end of a day of filming, they would donate any leftover food from the craft service, the daily unlimited buffet of snacks designed to fuel the actors and crew through the shoots. They were happy to agree to her request, the *Suits* family also making a substantial cash donation to the homeless charity.

The cast and crew were also encouraged to bond, to be a family. It helped all round. A happy set was a productive set. The result was a tight-knit group, bicycling places and going out for drinks or dinner, playing board games and drinking whiskey, as one cast member recalled, 'into the wee hours'. The cast also holidayed together over Canadian Thanksgiving, Meghan bringing her Vitamix super-blender to whip up soups and cocktails for the group. It was during one of these group get-togethers that Meghan was inspired to take what turned out to be one of her favourite-ever holidays. During a casual conversation with her co-star Gabriel Macht, he told her that he and his wife loved campervan vacations. After listening to him wax lyrical about a trip to New Zealand, Meghan decided to follow suit. She and Trevor, too, hired a campervan and spent two weeks driving around New Zealand's sparsely populated

South Island. They went hiking over glaciers, visited wineries in Marlborough, and rented a beach house for a few days.

She vividly remembers the extraordinary night they pulled up at a campsite in Akaroa, a tiny village surrounding a dead volcano. As she later recalled when she talked to ZM radio in New Zealand: 'I was washing my hair and I hear something and I open the shower curtain and there is this thirteen-year-old boy who had crawled under the stall and was trying to steal my underwear. I grabbed my towel and I had shampoo in my hair and I yelled, "Where is your mother?!" I found his parents and they were mortified of course. And to this day, oh my God, that kid will be sitting at home going "that's the girl from *Suits*, I saw her naked!"' Now, of course, he will be able to boast that he saw a Hollywood princess in the buff. In spite of her encounter with this junior Peeping Tom, she voted the holiday one of the best trips of her life.

When she returned home, she discussed with Trevor the prospect of adding to their family. She wanted a dog. So, just before Christmas, she and Trevor found themselves gazing at a pair of six-week-old puppies at a pet adoption agency in Los Angeles. The pups had only recently been rescued from being put down at a dog shelter. One of the Labrador mixes was black, the other golden. As luck would have it, David Branson Smith, the screenwriter son of Sally Bedell Smith, who has written biographies of Princess Diana and Prince Charles, adopted the black puppy, whom he called Otto; Meghan took the golden puppy, whom she named Bogart. She had talk-show host and comedian Ellen DeGeneres and her wife, Portia de Rossi, to thank for the final decision. As Meghan was communing with the tiny pooch, Ellen tapped on the glass of the viewing area and yelled, 'Take the dog!' As Meghan recalls, 'So I brought him home because Ellen told me to.' Soon the adorable Bogart had ousted pictures of herself and her husband on her Instagram feed, the puppy overrunning the joint social media feed.

In February 2013 Meghan emailed David Branson Smith to say that she and Trevor 'always wondered if [Bogart] and his brother would recognize each other … Kind of a sweet thought.' Diaries were consulted and the two brothers had a reunion on the beach at Malibu. As Sally Bedell Smith recalled in the London *Sunday Times*: 'Otto bounded out of David's car straight towards Bogart. For the next hour they romped around like, well, long-lost brothers.' Meghan filmed and posted the reunion like a social media pro, exclaiming, 'Oh my God, how sweet, they're really the same size!' It was to be the dogs' only meeting, but two years later, in 2015, Bogart was joined by another rescue dog, a beagle mix that Meghan named Guy.

By then the other 'guy' in her life was long gone. Even though Trevor opened an office in New York – only an hour's flight to Toronto – to expand his business and to be nearer to Meghan and his own family, cracks began appearing in their marriage. What once endeared, now irritated. Meghan, a self-confessed perfectionist who was as fastidious as she was controlling, had tolerated Trevor's scattered approach to life for years. He was notorious for arriving late, his clothes rumpled, his hair dishevelled, and often as not with a new stain on his seersucker jacket. 'Sorry bro', was a constant refrain as he hurtled from meeting to meeting, always just behind the clock.

Meghan's home in Summerhill was a vision of order and crisply ironed perfection. When she flew back to their Los Angeles home after Trevor had been in solo residence for a few weeks, the sight that greeted her increasingly rankled. Though Trevor would consistently visit, he often felt like an outsider, his presence an irritating distraction.

Whether she wanted to admit it to herself or not, Meghan, who once said that she couldn't imagine life without Trevor by her side, was now building a new world for herself. As Toronto was becoming more her home than Los Angeles, the dynamics in their relationship subtly altered. She was her own woman now, earning a steady income, making new friends on set and off, no longer dependent on her husband's connections.

A $500 Vitamix blender symbolized the growing divide. She insisted that her favourite kitchen appliance from their West Hollywood home come with her to Toronto, packing it into the backseat of her car, which was being moved by truck to Canada, even though it would have been just as easy to buy a new one. It sat on the kitchen counter in the Toronto house, a material reminder that her home was no longer in Los Angeles.

While Meghan saw her star rising, her husband's career was treading water. During this time he produced *Amber Alert*, a low-budget thriller about a pair of reality-show contestants who spot a car containing a kidnapped child. Though it was an intriguing premise, the movie did little box-office business and garnered fewer favourable reviews. With no new projects in sight and with *Suits* on hiatus, Trevor took Meghan on a cycling vacation to Vietnam. It didn't help that he became sick with food poisoning as a result of Meghan sampling obscure local dishes like a female version of the TV globetrotter Anthony Bourdain. Their escape to exotic locales, which once provided a backdrop for their love, only served to highlight the distance between them.

He was not the only one experiencing the Meghan chill. Her friends in Los Angeles noticed the change in her now that she was on the way up. She no longer had the time for friends she had known for years, cancelling lunches at short notice or expecting them to rework their own schedules to accommodate the busy life of the rising star. A networker to her fingertips, she seemed to be carefully recalibrating her life, forging new friendships with those who could burnish and develop her career. New people like talented fashion stylist Jessica Mulroney, who worked with Sophie Trudeau, wife of the Canadian Prime Minister Justin Trudeau, and her TV-personality husband Ben, the son of the former Canadian Prime Minister Brian Mulroney, now came into her orbit, Meghan seeing them regularly at the newly opened Soho House in Toronto. As she was expanding her social horizons, her LA circle felt they were being left behind. While she might have been getting above herself, everyone expected Trevor to keep her feet planted on the ground.

Without anyone really noticing it, the couple were going their separate ways. In February 2013 Trevor went to the Oscars without Meghan, who had dreamed of attending the starry event ever since she was a little girl. Trevor's older brother Drew laconically wrote on his Facebook page: 'My brother at the Oscars tonight proving that they'll let in just about any hobo off the street.' It seems that Meghan was too busy filming to join him.

A few weeks later, on 8 April, 2013, Meghan fully embraced her part-time home when she went to watch the Toronto Maple Leafs beat the New York Rangers at the Air Canada Center. Not only was she watching the game, she was there supporting her friend Michael Del Zotto, nine years her junior, skate as a defenseman for the Rangers. Del Zotto played hard, incurring a two-minute time-out for high-sticking rival Nazem Kadri.

Two weeks later, on 21 April, Meghan was at Madison Square Garden to watch Del Zotto and his fellow Rangers defeat the New Jersey Devils, and was captured by photographer James Devaney casually dressed in jeans and grey scarf sitting alone. In a series of posts on Instagram, Meghan documented her hockey adventures, on one occasion posing with Del Zotto and her *Suits* co-star Rick Hoffman. A year later Del Zotto made headlines regarding his relationship with porn star Lisa Ann, best known for her parodies of former presidential candidate Sarah Palin. Lisa Ann publicly dressed him down, according to the *Toronto Star*, for pestering her to set him up on dates with other women while he was on the road. She outed his behaviour in a series of Twitter posts.

Whatever the nature of their friendship – representatives for both Meghan and Del Zotto emphatically denied to the *Sun* newspaper that they were in a relationship – by then the marriage of Trevor and Meghan was over. The sad news, in the summer of 2013, came as a bolt from the blue. Everyone in their circle was genuinely shocked, none more so than Trevor's parents David and Leslie who had embraced her like a daughter.

As her maid of honour Ninaki Priddy told writer Rebecca Hardy: 'I knew they fought sometimes, but it wasn't anything huge. The only obstacle was the distance because she was living in Toronto and Trevor was based in LA. But I thought they were manoeuvring through it. Trevor would take his work to Canada to be with her and run his office remotely.'

It was such a surprise for Trevor that, even at a distance of five years, he can barely contain his anger, the normally affable laid-back New Yorker switching gear from his usual 'Hi bro, how's it going?' to a cold fury when her name comes into the conversation. 'I have zero to say about her,' he said to enquirers. Trevor went from cherishing Meghan to, as one friend observed, 'feeling like he was a piece of something stuck to the bottom of her shoe'. A wealthy entrepreneur friend claimed that the marriage ended so abruptly that Meghan sent Trevor her diamond wedding and engagement rings back to him by registered mail. Another confirmed that the decision to end the marriage was made by Meghan and that it had come 'totally out of the blue'.

There were other consequences. The break-up also fractured her thirty-odd-year friendship with jewellery designer Ninaki Priddy. After listening to Trevor's side of the story, she decided she no longer wished to associate herself with Meghan. Exactly why is a close-kept secret. As she described it in the *Daily Mail*: 'All I can say now is that I think Meghan was calculated, very calculated, in the way she handled people and relationships. She is very strategic in the way she cultivates circles of friends. Once she decides you're not part of her life, she can be very cold. It's this shutdown mechanism she has. There's nothing to negotiate, she's made her decision, and that's it … The way she handled it, Trevor definitely had the rug pulled out from under him. He was hurt.'

Actor Abby Wathen, who had starred with Meghan in the low-budget movie *Random Encounters* in her pre-*Suits* days, had a different perspective on Meghan's break-up. She told the ITV documentary *Prince Harry and Meghan: Truly, Madly, Deeply*, 'We both went through divorce, so we bonded on that too. I was destroyed, but she was empowered. She took her power back. It wasn't the right relationship for her, so she moved on.'

Now footloose and fancy-free, Meghan spent more time exploring downtown Toronto. She could often be found, glass of wine in hand, at Bar Isabel, the tapas bar where the grilled octopus and garlicky roast potatoes threw her into a 'carb coma'. She also went into raptures about the pasta at Terroni's, the local high-end Italian deli chain, and enjoyed poutine, a dish that originated in Quebec in the 1950s, comprised of fries covered in gravy and cheese curds. According to Meghan, the best poutine squeaks when bitten into. On nights when she stayed at home, Meghan, who loves to cook, made vegetable soup in her beloved Vitamix or threw courgettes into the slow cooker with a little water and bouillon until it became what she called 'a filthy, sexy mush' that she would toss with pasta.

It was her fascination with food that got her a gig with *Men's Health* magazine. In 2013 they filmed an interview for their website, asking Meghan to give them the secret to a great burger and steak. It was sweet, unpolished and very natural; as a California girl, she said, she preferred fish tacos, but for a quick meal 'for her man', she would throw a steak on the grill. She also agreed to film a racier version of the same shoot. This video, which appeared two years later, showed Meghan riffing on her role on *Suits*, her hair in a bun, wearing sunglasses, a short leather skirt and power blazer. She unbuttons her sheer black top to reveal a spotted bra. 'Grilling never looked so hot', screamed the film title. As the steak smouldered so did Meghan. But there was a hesitancy in her eyes. She was playing up to the camera but she seemed uncomfortable, conscious that she was portraying herself as a sex object to be leered at by men. She thought she had left those days behind on the set of *Deal or No Deal*. As far as she was concerned, this wasn't a part she was going to play for much longer.

During the *Suits* break, Meghan took the female lead in a low-budget crime thriller called *Anti-Social*. The drama, which was based on a series of real-life robberies involving graffiti gangs, was filmed in Budapest and London. While the money men on the production were looking for nude scenes between Meghan and her co-star, Gregg Sulkin, who is ten years her junior, writer-director Reg Traviss stuck to his guns and refused to exploit his star. He later explained, 'It wasn't needed for the story.'

Meghan's stock and standing were rising with each season of *Suits*, which was now the highest-rated American television show in the demographic sweet spot: those aged between eighteen and forty-nine. In November 2013 she was invited to attend the red-carpet premiere of *The Hunger Games: Catching Fire*, in London's Leicester Square. Two days later, Meghan and male model Oliver Cheshire were hosting the high-profile Global Gift Foundation charity gala, which benefited the Eva Longoria Foundation and Caudwell Children charities. Not that she was a fan of the red carpet, finding the glamorous shuffle with other celebrities an ordeal. As she wrote in *Working Actress*: 'I loathe walking the red carpet. It makes me nervous and itchy, and I don't know which way to look. I just revert to this nerdy child that I once was. I hate it. I get off the carpet and have to shake it off. Sounds dramatic, but it's really nerve-racking for me.' As far as she was concerned she never wanted fame. Acting was the chance to make a 'great living' by playing 'dress up and working with awesome people.'

Nonetheless, while in London, Meghan, the consummate networker, hoped to raise her public profile by discussing the last six episodes of *Suits* season two with members of the press. *Mail on Sunday* reporter Katie Hind wasn't expecting much when she agreed to meet Meghan on a chilly night in November, just another up-and-coming actress looking for a mention or two in the press. From what she had read, Meghan's ambition was to become a politician and she had fallen into acting during a holiday from her work at the US embassy in Buenos Aires in Argentina.

As they drank a bottle of Prosecco at the rooftop bar of the Sanctum Soho hotel, the conversation turned to men and particularly, as Hind put it, to 'her keen interest in British men of a certain, well, standing'. To the reporter's surprise, Meghan took out her iPhone and showed her a picture of a handsome man on her Twitter account. 'Do you know this guy Ashley Cole? He follows me and he keeps trying to talk to me on Twitter. He's trying really hard.'

Katie kept her cool, replying, 'I bet.' Meghan continued to confide eagerly. 'He wants to go out on a date while I'm over here in London. What do you think? Do you know him?'

The reporter certainly knew of his reputation as both an England and Chelsea football player and the husband of Girls

Aloud singer Cheryl Cole; someone who had cheated on his wife with several women, who had in turn sold their stories to the tabloids. Once Hind had broken the bad news, the actor seemed somewhat deflated, possibly having anticipated that her visit to London might have spawned a new romance. 'Thanks, I appreciate it,' Meghan told the *Mail* reporter, adding, 'Some of my friends told me to stay away from him, too. I think I'll leave it.'

During the next three hours, Meghan continued to down glasses of the Italian sparkling wine as she and Katie, both thirty-two, discussed the difficulties of modern romance and of finding the right guy. Meghan admitted that she was newly divorced – her decree cited 'irreconcilable differences' – and was now single and ready to mingle.

The tipsy talk wound down and the two hugged goodbye, with Katie wishing Meghan good luck. 'Not that she'd need it,' the reporter commented wryly as she watched Meghan, who was unable to catch a cab, persuade the owner of the Sanctum to drive her the couple of minutes through the rain to her hotel, the Dean Street Townhouse.

7

The 'Aha' Moment

Feeling bloated and puffy-skinned, her black leather trousers a little too tight, Meghan, who had just returned from a 'carb heavy' holiday, was a tad out of sorts as she sat alongside her *Suits* co-stars on the dais at the five-star Langham Hotel in Pasadena. She looked out at the sea of television critics in front of her and seemed rather glad that her colleagues were fielding the questions from the Television Critics Association in a long-planned January conference. So far she had sat silently watching the back and forth, the discussion moving on to the shifting time slot, *Suits* being scheduled to move from 10 p.m. to 9 p.m. 'Will that affect the cursing?' asked one critic, referring to the show's liberal use of profanity.

Meghan popped alive and grabbed the question. She looked at the show's creator and executive producer, Aaron Korsh, and playfully rephrased the question: 'Is that going to change for us being at 9 o'clock — the shits and the dammits?' 'Shit, no!' responded Korsh. The audience laughed. This was classic Meghan: the good sport, the slightly naughty girl next door, the guy's gal. Her intervention had won the crowd. But it was no longer enough. She wanted to stretch her wings; she had things to say, points to make, that went way beyond the question-and-answer format concerning all things *Suits*. She was a well-travelled young woman with an appreciation of different countries, cuisine and culture. Meghan had a take on everything from Middle Eastern politics to make-up. Her role on *Suits* was, she felt, a launch pad to something more. She knew she was not yet exploiting her full potential. But in order to do that, she needed to wield more clout.

Her recent visit to London, for example, had yielded only a small mention in the *Daily Mail* and a photograph in the giveaway morning daily *Metro*. She had appeared on numerous red carpets since her work on the series began, but what started out as thrilling was now routine. She was still just a pretty face in the crowd.

Meghan realized that she had to do better, to expand her visibility. From the moment *Suits* became successful, she could see that her young audience, especially teenage girls, were listening to what she had to say. Her Instagram following was growing exponentially, but static pictures of her life, her food and her dogs didn't provide an outlet for her thoughts on the world at large. She had a genuine point of view about a kaleidoscope of topics; she just needed a vehicle to express herself.

Just a few days later, on 22 January 2014, she attended the annual Elle's Women in Television Celebration, her third appearance since *Suits* launched. Meghan felt that she had come home. She was inspired to be surrounded by so many creative and stimulating women, such as cooking and lifestyle celebrity Giada De Laurentiis and multi-award-winning actress Tracee Ellis Ross, who, like Meghan, was bi-racial. Unlike Meghan, Ross came from

Hollywood royalty; her mother was Diana Ross and her father music manager and industry executive Robert Ellis Silberstein.

Ross's career included a stint as a model, including walking the runway for Thierry Mugler, contributing as an editor and writer for *Mirabella* and *New York* magazines, and as the star of *Girlfriends*, a long-running sitcom, for which she had won several NAACP awards. Her new comedy, *black-ish*, in which she played a doctor and mother to four, was garnering rave reviews. Rubbing shoulders with Ross and others, listening to their can-do success stories, stirred the urge in Meghan to do more. The questions was: how to go about it?

The answer came indirectly and unexpectedly. In February 2014 DirecTV, the satellite television company, celebrated the Super Bowl with a huge televised pre-game party which they held the day before the big game itself. The spirited match of celebrity flag football, called DirecTV Celebrity Beach Bowl, was held in a large heated tent at Pier 40 on the Hudson River in Lower Manhattan. For the event, they created the world's largest indoor beach, trucking in more than a million pounds of freshly poured sand.

The band Paramore was scheduled to entertain the crowd and Food Network star Andrew Zimmern would broadcast live during half-time. Ever the good sport, Meghan joined model Chrissy Teigen, a former colleague on *Deal or No Deal*, and other celebrities, including former pro-quarterback Joe Montana, comedians Tracy Morgan and Tom Arnold, and celebrity chef Guy Fieri, in a beach game, which Meghan's team won.

After the show, Meghan won much more – a new, influential friend, tennis legend Serena Williams. At the time, Williams held seventeen world and US tournament singles titles and almost as many for winning doubles tournaments. More importantly, she had parlayed her fifteen-year career as a super-athlete into lucrative endorsements, including her own fashion line, and even some acting gigs. 'We hit it off immediately, taking pictures, laughing through the flag football game we were both playing in, and chatting not about tennis or acting, but about all the good old-fashioned girly stuff', Meghan later wrote. 'So began our friendship.'

What also impressed Meghan was how Serena had used online platforms to keep connected with and expand her fan base. She had an online clothing label as well as Instagram, Snapchat and Reddit accounts, and a regular newsletter, all pulled together on the serenawilliams.com website.

This was the light-bulb moment. Meghan had been mulling over a website for some time, and seeing how someone as busy and successful as Serena controlled her own site gave her confidence that she too could follow suit. Her thinking was reinforced by an approach from an e-commerce company, which offered to create an all-singing, all-dancing site with her name front and centre. At first she was excited by the idea. 'It will be your name, meghanmarkle.com, and we can run it for you,' they told her. Essentially, her name would drive consumers to the site. While there would be some created content, the aim was to sell clothing from which Meghan would receive a percentage of sales. She pondered their offer, then stood back for a moment and took a breath. As tempting as it sounded, the more she thought about it, it just didn't feel right. 'There was so much more I wanted to share,' she explained to friends. Meghan wanted a place where she could showcase her deeper self, where her voice would be heard, and where if there was e-commerce it would be thoughtful and ethical, rather than just marketing the latest fast fashion and trend. She wanted to stress the importance of giving back. Dumping a bucket of ice-cold water over herself on the Manhattan apartment roof of golfer buddy Rory McIlroy for the ALS Challenge and then posting on Instagram with the result wasn't quite enough, though it did raise money for a good cause: research into motor neurone disease.

For now, she left the website idea percolating in the background. With *Suits* on break, she flew to Vancouver in western Canada to appear in a Hallmark Channel TV movie called *When Sparks Fly*, in which she played Amy, a plucky reporter sent back to her bucolic hometown to write a human-interest piece about growing up as the daughter of fireworks' manufacturers. Her old boyfriend is about to marry her high-school best friend and suddenly Amy realizes that maybe the big city life isn't for her after all. It's a pleasing trifle and a pay cheque, but that is about it. The plot, concerning a difficult return home, was the polar opposite of her next excursion, a visit to her old college, Northwestern University.

If she needed any more proof that she had an audience that went beyond the confines of *Suits*, she only had to look at the line snaking around the Ryan Auditorium as 600 students shuffled forwards for a coveted seat to see Meghan and the rest of the *Suits* family.

Communication Studies freshman Nikita Kulkarni, who waited five hours for the event, was breathless with excitement. 'I didn't think it was real when people first told me about it. I thought people were messing with me. I was excited to have Meghan come!'

Meghan basked in the attention from the Northwestern students, comparing shared college experiences and discussing her character's development. She gave her adoring audience a tour of the mind of her alter ego, Rachel Zane. 'She's layered and humanized; even though she seems so confident, she really has all these insecurities and vulnerabilities, and I relate to that as a woman and I think the fans will too.'

After the chat she posed for photos, signed posters, and later she and fellow star Rick Hoffman, who plays Louis Litt, recorded a promo video for the Northwestern University Dance Marathon, a charity fundraiser in which Meghan had participated as a freshman.

This was the fourth stop of seven for the *Suits* university tour, which included the Universities of California at Berkeley and Los Angeles, the University of Arizona, Boston University, Harvard, and Columbia. It was a bid by the network and show's producers to reward their highly engaged collegiate audiences by treating them to a preview screening of the winter mid-season premiere.

Returning home, the website idea now moved to the front burner, as she contacted her friend, photographer Jake Rosenberg. A graduate of Ontario College of Art and Design, Rosenberg had started Coveteur.com six months after graduating with a degree in industrial design. While he loved photography, he was also enthusiastic about branding and design. During a photoshoot in 2011, he and fellow twenty-something stylist Stephanie Mark ended up creating a site devoted to snapshots of beautiful closets and snippets of subjects' homes. 'We thought it would be fun and interesting to see what it is really like in stylish people's homes and closets,' Mark told *Forbes* writer Susan Price. The pair did six photoshoots and posted them on their new site, which crashed due to the amount of traffic. They immediately realized they were onto something that might be profitable as well as fun.

'We would come back and talk about what we had seen, where this person we'd met was shopping, which restaurants and bars people were talking about,' says Mark. 'We realized we had all this content.' They expanded their coverage and, in 2013, redesigned the site to make space for advertising and advertorial, a blend of advertising and editorial. Rosenberg listened to Meghan's concerns about her proposed site. Over tapas and several glasses of wine, they discussed her vision for the site, which would essentially be an insiders' guide to travel, food, fashion and make-up with a leavening of more serious op-ed articles dealing with women's issues. Essentially, it would be a dash of Gwyneth Paltrow's blog, GOOP, with a soupçon of *Marie Claire* seasoned with Meghan's own style and focus.

Now with a vision in place, Meghan turned down the original company's offer to create a commercial 'Meghan Markle' site and decided to have a go on her own. First she hired a website designer. When she showed the results to Rosenberg, his sharp and practised eye immediately told him that this could be a problem.

'I beg you, please don't go down this path; use our graphic designer from Coveteur,' he told his friend. The result was TheTig.com, which featured Meghan's own elegant handwriting, and a logo with a wine drop as the dot of the letter 'i'. Meghan had chosen the name, The Tig, from an Italian wine called

Tignanello. It is a Sangiovese blend and the first Chianti made without white grapes – a wine born out of the vintner's desire to make his product stand out in a sea of reds. Meghan liked that idea. Standing out. She would drink to that.

For Meghan, Tignanello had a deeper meaning, representing that 'aha' moment when she finally understood what components went to make a good wine, to give it length, finish and legs. She wanted to carry that excitement of discovery into her website, writing: 'The Tig is a hub for the discerning palate – those with a hunger for food, travel, fashion and beauty. I wanted to create a space to share all of these loves – to invite friends to share theirs as well, and to be the breeding ground for ideas and excitement – for an inspired lifestyle.' Frothy, fizzy and fun, The Tig appealed to her fan base, who appreciated her elegant style and her classy persona. At the same time, she envisaged using The Tig to express her thoughts on more serious subjects, in particular giving attention to social and political issues that affected women.

Meghan, the aspirational girl next door, had created a site for other classy girls like her who wanted to join the party. With the help of Jake Rosenberg, fashion designer Wes Gordon, and Brett Heyman, designer of the acrylic purse brand Edie Parker who created a resin clutch with 'Ms Tig' for Meghan, the stage was set. Finally, she also followed the advice of her co-star Gina Torres, who had told her, using one of Meghan's long-time nicknames, 'Nutmeg, just leave room for magic.'

When filming started again, Meghan's busy days didn't leave a lot of time for magic. She would wake up at 4.15 a.m., down a cup of hot water with freshly squeezed lemon, and eat a bowl of oatmeal with sliced bananas and agave. Then she would let the dogs out in the back yard before driving her leased Audi SUV to the set, a maze-like replica of a law office, detailed down to the pink message pads and pens on secretaries' desks, with pivoting glass walls that allowed the cameras to shoot any angle without glare. The New York skyline was a backdrop, and the location scenes were shot in Toronto, with establishing shots from the B-roll of Manhattan to give a sense of place. After early-morning make-up and wardrobe, where clothes would be altered 'on the inhale' to give them their tightest, sleekest fit, Meghan would wait in her trailer for her scene to be ready.

With the birth of The Tig, Meghan had her hands full, making sure that the new arrival was fed, watered and coddled. It was a full-time occupation, staying awake until the early hours cruising Instagram for ideas about what was trending, interesting and timely; writing all the short, snappy content herself; and hustling anyone and everyone to get celebrities to answer the five questions that created the format for Tig Talk. Actor and singer Emmy Rossum got the ball rolling by saying that if she was down to her last ten dollars – one of the standard questions – she would sing in the street for money. Others, like fashion guru Joe Zee and model Jessica Stam, added their thoughts, while Meghan dragooned interior designer Natasha Baradaran to talk about her favourite city, Milan. She knew that big names drove traffic and would attract other celebrities to participate. One of the first people she wanted to have for Tig Talk was model-turned-entrepreneur Heidi Klum. She contacted everyone she knew, hoping to get the email or phone number for Klum or her assistant. In the end, Heidi responded, as did 'the Queen', who informed the actor that everything tasted better with a slug of vodka. Of course the Queen she was talking about was TV screen queen, Elizabeth Hurley, who plays the conniving and occasionally cruel Queen Helena in the E! show *The Royals*, a tongue-in-cheek take on the House of Windsor.

There were profiles of cool places to visit, interesting restaurants and innovative chefs. This last feature introduced her to a new love. For years she had been eating at The Harbord Room, a small restaurant in downtown Toronto that opened in 2007. It was run by handsome celebrity chef Cory Vitiello, who boasted that he cooked the best burger in town. The foodie in Meghan was intrigued.

Over the past seven years, Vitiello had made a name for himself both in and out of the kitchen. He had famously dated Canadian heiress and former politician Belinda Stronach as well as *eTalk*'s talking head Tanya Kim, before turning his attention to Canadian TV gossip reporter Mary Kitchen. Now with The Tig, Meghan had a way to get to know him better. Much better. For Meghan, life was looking rosy, but things were about to take a nasty turn.

❖

One evening, Meghan was curled up with her laptop, a glass of wine in hand, preparing for an evening finding stories and people to populate The Tig. Her methodology was to delve into other lifestyle blogs and online news sites, follow links for inspiration and then maybe poke around on Instagram using hashtags to guide her to potential Tig tales. First, though, she wanted to peek at the *Suits* pages on Facebook, Twitter, Reddit and USANetwork.com. The latest episode had a storyline featuring Rachel Zane front and centre and it was airing that night in America. She was curious to know the response to her character's dalliance with an old boyfriend. When Meghan took another sip of her red wine, she nearly choked as she scrolled through to the comments. 'You dirty bird!' 'I'm unfollowing you! How could you cheat on Mike?' 'Whore ...' And it just got uglier as the episode hit different time zones and aired right across the country. Meghan deleted the worst of the comments from her own page and Twitter feed and blocked the abusive users. As the night wore on, she was genuinely concerned, and not a little afraid, as more and more emojis of knives and guns appeared.

Fans weren't just angry at her character Rachel Zane for kissing her old boyfriend, Logan Sanders, played by Brendan Hines; they were furious at Meghan Markle. They believed that the actor was responsible for the storyline, not the scriptwriters. As she pondered just how fans could become so invested in a story, which was, after all, make-believe, the comments kept heating up. Now there were death threats. 'Meghan Markle, I wanna kill you. You slut.' This was out of control, as she later told writer Vanessa Pascale of *Miami Living*.

The next morning she went to see *Suits* creator Aaron Korsh. 'This has to stop,' she told him, adding that they had to scale this back. The producers and writers had always been good to her, incorporating aspects of her own personality into Rachel's character, making Rachel a foodie because Meghan enjoyed cooking and making her bi-racial because of Meghan's own family background. This time the lines were becoming uncomfortably blurred, with fans unable to tell the real Meghan from the fantasy of Rachel. Besides, Meghan wasn't that kind of girl. The storyline going forward had Rachel more actively attempting to seduce her old boyfriend as she turned her back on Mike. That plot development didn't feel right to Meghan, not least because it presaged a possible exit for her character, something for which she wasn't yet prepared. As she later told *Miami Living* magazine, she discussed her concerns about her character's change of direction with the show's creator, Aaron Korsh.

'I like Rachel, I like playing Rachel, I like what she stands for. And this feels really out of character,' she said earnestly. It was a bold move, telling the show's creator she didn't like the direction her character was going in. But she felt she owed it to the fans and to her own integrity to speak up. Plus, she had been frightened by the aggressive vitriol online and threats of violence.

Editor Angela Catanzaro, who had worked on the series since the beginning, agreed with Meghan, telling Korsh, 'I love Rachel, but if you put that scene on the air, I would never like her again. That's not the kind of woman I would like working with my husband.'

Korsh saw the wisdom in their words, and within an episode, Mike Ross and Rachel Zane's romance was correcting itself and gearing up to be back on track. Panic over. At least for the time being.

❖

Meghan stared at her phone in disbelief. The inbox of her email was filling up almost faster than she could read the subject lines. Her site, The Tig, was proving to be more popular than she had ever imagined. At this early stage every email went directly to her mobile phone and as Meghan quickly scrolled the ever-expanding list, one sender jumped out at her, the United Nations. It might just be a fundraising appeal, but what the heck? Meghan opened the message and read the contents with growing surprise. The United Nations were asking her to consider becoming involved in their new gender-equality programme, HeforShe. When Meghan dialled the number given in the email, the contact person at UN Women explained that they had read her short essay in The Tig on women's independence, which Meghan had published to coincide with America's Independence Day. She had begun by writing: 'Raise a glass to yourself today – to the right to freedom, to the empowerment of the women (*and men*) who struggle to have it, and to knowing, embracing, honoring, educating and loving yourself. On this day, and beyond, celebrate your independence.' She then went on to showcase the thoughts of Nigerian writer Chimamanda Ngozi Adichie.

While she was honoured by the approach, she also wanted to get an idea of what the project was all about, rather than blindly saying yes. 'I have a one-week break, can I come and intern at the UN in New York', she asked them, offering to bring them coffee and answer the phones. Within a few weeks surprised UN officials found themselves inducting Meghan into the bustling corridors of the New York-based institution. In truth, it was rather more than making the coffee. She shadowed Elizabeth Nyamayaro, head of the UN HeForShe movement to encourage men to support women in the quest for gender equality, and

Phumzile Mlambo-Ngcuka, executive director of UN Women. She also sat in on meetings at the World Bank, the Clinton Foundation and even the war room for the UN Secretary-General, Ban Ki-moon.

At the campaign's public launch, she was assigned a seat on the front row, as Harry Potter actor and UN Goodwill Ambassador Emma Watson made a rousing speech for men as well as women to join the HeForShe campaign. Watson noted that at the present rate of progress it would be seventy-five years before women were paid the same as men for the same work and that it would take until 2086 before all teenage girls in rural Africa receive a secondary education.

During the launch of the campaign Meghan experienced her very own 'Tig' moment when she watched the interaction between the former President of Finland Tarja Halonen and a UN staffer. 'Madame President, may I get you anything?' she asked. 'Would you like water or a pen?' Halonen smiled and replied, 'A lipstick.'

It was something that Meghan connected to. She saw no contradiction between a woman running a country and still wearing lipstick – she could be feminine and a feminist at the same time; as she later wrote, 'a breadwinner at work, and a bread baker with her kids at home'.

At that time, before Donald Trump had entered the race for the presidency, one of her other female idols was businesswoman Ivanka Trump, who had her own jewellery and clothing line. She was thrilled when Ivanka agreed to fill in her simple questionnaire for Tig Talk. More thrilled when she accepted her invitation to meet for drinks and dinner the next time Meghan was in New York.

Meghan gushed in The Tig: 'Don't get me started on her jewellery collection: the late-night "window shopping" I have done on my computer, snuggled up in my bed with a glass of wine, staring longingly at the beautiful designs. And there are the shoes, the home collection, the clothing, and the natural extension of her brand with a kids' collection – a smart choice given that she is now a proud mama ... When we have drinks, I will make sure I order whatever she does – because this woman seems to have the formula for success (and happiness) down pat.'

With well-known names like Ivanka Trump involved, her 'little engine that could', her nickname for her website, was gaining a head of steam. She was justifiably proud when her site was named Best of the Web in both *Elle* magazine and *InStyle*.

She was, though, in need of help to stoke the boiler. Every post on The Tig had to be cross-posted to Instagram, Pinterest and Facebook to increase traffic; luckily, there was an app for that. Even better, there was now a person, Judy Meepos. Meepos, then the deputy editor of the 'Tech, Yeah!' section of *InStyle* magazine, had received a lot of internet air kisses from Meghan in August when she had written a breathless profile of Markle and The Tig. Meghan decided to hire her in October 2014.

She was not only responsible for social media but also, as she says, 'wrote and edited daily postings, initiated collaborations and partnerships, and served as a market editor for posts and television appearances'. The popularity of The Tig and Meghan's Instagram account meant that after just six months her little engine was ready to earn its keep through e-commerce. She followed the lead of Jake Rosenberg and Coveteur in partnering with RewardStyle. com, an e-commerce site which, rather clunkily, billed itself as an 'invitation-only end-to-end content monetization platform for top-tier digital style influencers and brands around the world'. Or in plain English, a clever way of helping upmarket blogs make money.

The site RewardStyle was founded in 2011 by the then Amber Venz and future husband Baxter Box as a way for Amber to monetize her fashion blog. For a while their system worked like a dream. Bloggers created clickable links from their content that led directly to retailers and brands. If a reader clicked through and made a purchase, the blogger earned commission, creating a semi-passive income stream.

With The Tig in Meepos's capable hands, Meghan boarded a plane headed to Dublin where she had been asked to participate in the One Young World Summit, an international forum for young leaders of tomorrow. The biannual conference was the brainchild of two advertising executives, David Jones and Kate Robertson, the duo aiming to 'gather together the brightest young leaders from around the world, empowering them to make lasting connections to create positive change'. Organizer Kate Robertson felt that Meghan had something to say and was popular with the student-aged audience. Not only would she be discussing global issues with young people, but she would be rubbing shoulders with humanitarian celebrities like Mary Robinson, Ireland's first woman president, Sir Bob Geldof, and Nobel Peace Prize winner Kofi Annan. For her forum on gender equality she was with a high-powered panel that included lawyer Sabine Chalmers, General Electric senior Vice President Beth Comstock, digital pioneer Michelle Phan and film director Maya Sanbar. In the beginning, Robertson, who chaired the discussion, was worried as to whether Meghan would cope with a question-and-answer-style forum. She came away pleasantly surprised at Meghan's eloquence, saying, 'It wasn't your average actress stepping up and talking about gender equality. It was the real deal – very forthright, very confident and very un-celebrity.' Others in the audience were also impressed by her grasp of human rights and gender issues, as well as her approachability and warmth. Human rights lawyer Phiwokuhle Nogwaza told *People* magazine: 'She is really soft and gentle. She is friendly and very warm and engaging. It didn't feel like I was speaking to someone from one of the biggest shows on TV. It was like talking to a regular girl. She knew the problems in detail, which I found incredible. She is humble and really down to earth.'

She had, too, a real knack of mixing the glamour of celebrity with the commitment to her humanitarian work, she and her chef boyfriend Cory Vitiello flying to Florida in early December for Miami Art Basel, an offshoot of the Swiss original. The now annual event, started in 2002, attracts 77,000 visitors a year, and the place to see and be seen was her usual stomping ground, Soho House.

Meghan was excited. While she wasn't that into art, preferring fashion, food and wine, she welcomed the opportunity to network with a wider range of members and guests who were arriving at the Soho Beach House, a repurposed vintage hotel on the sand. She tried not to gawk as rap mogul Russell Simmons and actor and activist Rosario Dawson strolled by, or to take too much interest when Goldie Hawn's daughter Kate Hudson waved at friends from a terrace. She felt she had truly arrived. She had worked hard, she was on a top-rated show, and her blog was considered one of the best on the web. Miami Art Week, or at least the Soho Beach House version of it, would be hers.

Her great friend, Markus Anderson, Soho House membership director, casually dressed in flip-flops and shorts, wandered over to say 'Hello' and brief them on the next few days of dancing, cocktails and luxurious beauty treatments. This was the life. A Sapphire gin gift basket awaited Meghan and Cory in their room, along with a fully stocked drinks bar. The celebrity tent would have a full selection of tropically themed gin drinks. And then there were the sparkling wines and champagnes …

Markus Anderson is a great fixer and mixer. He has an instinct for putting strangers together who he thinks might gel. At lunch he placed Meghan next to Bahrain-born fashion designer Misha Nonoo. At the time she was an up-and-coming designer known as much for her marriage to art dealer Alexander Gilkes, friend of Princes William and Harry, as for her maverick designs. Meghan and Misha got along famously, lunchtime drinks extending into evening cocktails. During the course of the afternoon they got to talking about her new collection, which was going to be unveiled at New York fashion week. Meghan would be on break from *Suits*. She would be there.

❖

Hours later, Meghan was once again on a plane, this time headed for Spain, one of five countries she was due to visit on a whirlwind tour. This time there were no luxury hotels or smart cocktails. Instead, Meghan was taking part in the United

Service Organization holiday tour, visiting American military bases in Spain, Italy, Turkey, Afghanistan and England. Joining Meghan were eight-time USO tour veteran and country star Kellie Pickler and her songwriter husband Kyle Jacobs, comedian Rob Riggle, *Glee* co-star Dianna Agron, former Chicago Bears linebacker Brian Urlacher, and Washington Nationals pitcher Doug Fister, as well as the chairman of the Joint Chiefs of Staff, Army General Martin E. Dempsey and his wife, Deanie.

When the travelling troupe, who were joined by USO President J.D. Crouch and his wife Kristin, met at the Joint Base Andrews passenger terminal in Maryland on 5 December, Deanie Dempsey told the assorted celebrities. 'Embrace this experience. You will be so proud of our service members and their families.' Meghan was excited and a little apprehensive. Not only would she be flying aboard Air Force Two, specially commissioned for this tour, she would be meeting thousands of service members and their families during the trip. While she had done fan meet-and-greets before, it had never been on this scale or at this intensity.

After arriving in Rota, Spain, Meghan and her USO group toured the USS *Ross*, an Aegis missile-equipped destroyer. Then they performed before an audience of two thousand service personnel and their families in a hangar on the base. Meghan, in a blue hardhat, posed with servicemen before going into her routine. She knew that she, Kelly Pickler and Dianna Agron were carrying on a time-honoured tradition, following in the steps of stars like Marilyn Monroe, Bob Hope and Jayne Mansfield who had entertained the troops, providing a sweet taste of home, a reminder of why the troops did their jobs. Now things were rather different. There were women in the military and families on the bases, so goodbye cheesecake, hello folksy and funny. On stage she did one of her routines, giving a light-hearted talk about *Suits* before showing off her five-inch heels as Pickler and her band performed signature song, 'Red High Heels'.

The USO tour group repeated their act in Vicenza, Italy, to soldiers of the 173rd Airborne Brigade and US Army Africa before heading to the air base at Incirlik, Turkey. Even though the base was several hundred miles from the battles raging in neighbouring Syria, the atmosphere was tenser, security tighter. Meghan smiled and tried to say more than 'thank you' as she passed out cupcakes to the several hundred who gathered to watch Pickler and Jacobs perform country hits, and the troupe do various comedy sketches.

The next morning the USO performers and their 'chaperones' gathered on the tarmac to head to their most challenging gig, Bagram airfield in Afghanistan. This was the most isolated outpost, home to 40,000 military personnel and service members. 'Bureaucrats, administrators, logisticians and thousands of International Security Assistance Force civilian contractors live at Bagram air base,' said British photographer Edmund Clark. 'Unless you go out on patrol, you exist only on base.'

Surrounded by fencing and barbed wire, reinforced by sandbags, with ground-penetrating radar used to make sure enemy fighters don't use tunnels to break into the coalition base, Bagram was relatively safe. Except for the occasional Taliban rocket that made it over the walls.

Meghan and fellow performers joined service members for a holiday meal before they took to the stage. Meghan turned her back to the audience and snapped a quick selfie with the uniformed military members, then went into her inspirational speech, 'I've never wanted to be a lady who lunches; I've always wanted to be a woman who works ...'

Once again cupcakes were passed out, then, as fighter jets and C-130 transport planes taxied outside, Meghan and the others posed with groups of service members in front of a netting-draped wall. While the celebrities put on their practised smiles for the cameras, the troops could barely muster a grin between them. Unlike the stars who had swooped in for a couple of days, they had months more of mind-numbing boredom punctuated by bursts of frenzied action to look forward to. It was a poignant interaction.

Their final stop in Cambridge, England, was a perfect way to decompress. Before their final show, airmen at the base gave the USO troupe a tour of the military hardware at their command, including F-15E Strike Eagles and CV-22 Ospreys, a helicopter–plane hybrid. Meghan spent her time chatting with families, paying special attention to the children. That evening, the Dempseys hosted a thank-you gathering for the USO performers at a Cambridge pub, The Anchor, with the performers in turn warmly thanking the Dempseys and the USO for the privilege of being able to entertain the troops. Before the evening ended, the chairman of the Joint Chiefs of Staff serenaded the group. 'If only we could have gotten him to do that in Bagram!' someone joked.

That was to be Meghan's first and last USO tour. She expressed her feelings in an Instagram post, where she showed a picture from the tour and then a heart-felt caption: 'In gratitude to our troops, and the opportunity to thank them personally for their sacrifice and service. Such an honor and feeling very, very blessed.'

8

Seeing Both Sides Now

She had her passport. Check. Her bag of homeopathic remedies. Check. Her vaccines, including hepatitis A and B, typhoid, rabies and tetanus, were up to date. Check. She had super-strength mosquito repellent. Check. A bag of long-sleeved light clothes. Check. Meghan was ready for a very grown-up journey, embarking on her first-ever fact-finding mission on behalf of the United Nations. Though her visit to Rwanda in the heart of Africa was to focus on issues surrounding gender equality, it was also a chance for United Nations officials to run the rule over the *Suits* star, to see if she was able and willing to make the commitment as a goodwill ambassador for the international organization. A UN official pointed out that Meghan's involvement as a gender-equality advocate was at the level of an informal collaboration.

In early January 2015, when she landed in Kigali, the Rwandan capital, her first stop was to be introduced to the nation's female parliamentarians. Almost a week of meetings had been scheduled to discuss the role of women in the nation's democracy and the challenges facing Rwanda going forward. Time and again the point was made that only when women were treated equally, in the home, at school and in the workplace, could they enjoy rich, fulfilling lives and give back to the community. The under-representation of women in the top jobs, a feature of life not just in developing countries but across the world, was an issue that always concerned her. At the time, the UN was celebrating the fact that Rwanda was the first, and at the time the only, country to have a female majority in the nation's parliament, with almost two-thirds of the seats taken by women.

It was a great step forward, Meghan complimenting Rwandan President Paul Kagame. 'We need more men like that,' she said.

Though Kagame has his critics, this was a truly remarkable turnaround for a country which, just twenty years earlier, had suffered an appalling genocide. The figures were astonishing, with approximately one million people killed, most brutally hacked to death with machetes, and two million displaced into refugee camps. Meghan travelled to see the other side of Rwanda herself, the actor and her UN team travelling by van to Gihembe refugee camp, the sprawling collection of huts studded into the lush green hillside now home to 17,000 people who had fled the violence in the neighbouring war-torn Democratic Republic of Congo. She wanted to speak to the women at the grassroots, find out how they coped with a life that was meant to be temporary but had become permanent. Inevitably, every visit by a celebrity, even if the local population has no clue who they are, attracts a crowd, Meghan posing happily with dozens of curious and excited local children.

As she travelled back over the bumpy dirt road, past the grazing goats and the lush green fields, she idly checked her emails, amazed that the signal was better here than in some parts of Toronto and Los Angeles. While she bounced along the track she learned that she had been invited as a guest to the BAFTAs, the British Academy film awards which take place a few weeks before the Oscars themselves.

Her management company told her that she would be sponsored by a high-end jewellery company that would fly her directly from Kigali to London, where she would be whisked into hair and make-up before being poured into a gown. 'No,' screamed her gut. It had always been a dream to attend the BAFTAs, but she couldn't shift emotional gears that quickly, from the purpose-driven work she had been doing all week in Rwanda to the polished glamour of an awards show. There would be other BAFTAs, other red carpets. But for now there was only Rwanda. As she later wrote: 'This type of work is what feeds my soul.'

Of course she was not the first, nor will she be the last, celebrity to struggle to reconcile the air-kissing superficiality of Hollywood with the stark reality of life for so many in the developing world. Oscar-winning actor and UNHCR special envoy Angelina Jolie is a vivid example of a star who manages to straddle both worlds. The more she became involved with her humanitarian mission, the more she had to learn to switch off and switch on. Just like acting. But in real life.

Shortly after her return from Rwanda, Meghan was front and centre for New York Fashion Week in February. She was now on the front row, watching the models at the show of her fashion mentor Wes Gordon, but she was also photographed reviewing Misha Nonoo's stylish collection. The theme was Meghan's *cri de coeur*: the empowerment of women. Nonoo had the models

153

do their hair themselves, pulling it back into ponytails with a minimum of product and as many bobby pins as they liked. 'It just set the tone,' Meghan enthused.

She was still raving about the collection when she appeared on Joe Zee's streaming fashion programme on Yahoo! Style. The duo went back years, from the time they first met in 2011 drinking and shooting the breeze until late into the night. What Joe liked about Meghan was that she was decidedly un-Hollywood; she appreciated people other than herself.

❖

In between the glitz and the glamour, her advocacy for UN Women continued, and she undertook further meetings at the World Bank and the Clinton Foundation, learning more about the facts and figures of gender bias in the developing world and, for that matter, her own country. While she had always had a thoughtful side, these days her friends noticed that she seemed more considered, more seasoned and more appreciative too of the advantages she had been given and the opportunity she had to make a difference. In the days when she was scrabbling to gain a foothold on the slippery ladder of success, her time was taken up not with causes but with endless auditions, simply trying to make a living. Such ambitions had seemingly been left behind when she graduated from Northwestern. But now, her acting success coupled with her voice on The Tig had opened up doors and brought back memories of the little girl who had written letters of complaint about sexist advertising and a young woman who had aimed for a job in the State Department.

She travelled to London to support Emma Watson in her HeforShe initiative, the Harry Potter actor holding a live Facebook event to engage her fans in the campaign. Then it was Meghan's turn to take centre stage in front of a friendly but awe-inspiring audience. Meghan took a deep breath and focused. She was about to hit a personal milestone. Her mother and friends were there to support her in front of global luminaries like United Nations Secretary-General Ban Ki-moon, UN Women Executive Director Phumzile Mlambo-Ngcuka, actor Patricia Arquette, her own mentor at the UN, Elizabeth Nyamayaro, as well as Hillary Clinton. (Ironically, the same day, Clinton overshadowed Meghan's appearance with her comments about her controversial use of a private email server during her tenure as Secretary of State.)

On 10 March, a day that she will always remember, Meghan was about to speak before the United Nations as the newly appointed UN Women's Advocate for Women's Leadership and Political Participation.

Understandably, Meghan's voice sounded a little higher, as the normally nerveless actor opened her speech: 'I am proud to be a woman and a feminist, and this evening I am extremely proud to stand before you on this significant day, which serves as a reminder to all of us of how far we've come, but also amid celebration a reminder of the road ahead …'

She told her story of the LA riots, her schoolroom, Ivory dish-washing liquid, and the chauvinist little boys at her school; of how she wrote to Procter & Gamble, women's rights lawyer Gloria Allred, journalist Linda Ellerbee, and Hillary Clinton. The putative presidential candidate smiled at that. Meghan spoke inspiringly of how her letter made a difference and how she felt that she had helped, in her small way, to make the change.

She took aim at the weak representation of women in the world's parliaments, citing data showing that the number of women lawmakers had increased by only 11 per cent since 1995. 'Eleven per cent in twenty years. Come on. This has to change,' she said to applause.

As Meghan concluded, UN Secretary-General Ban Ki-moon led the standing ovation. It was quite the accolade, one that would resonate as her speech was played in numerous classrooms around America and the world, inspiring and provoking a new generation of young girls to make a difference.

'Meghan Markle has helped raise global attention to gender equality issues,' said a spokeswoman for UN Women. 'UN Women trusts and hopes that in her new and important public role she will continue to use her visibility and voice to support the advancement of gender equality.'

She appeared to have it all; she was a young, articulate campaigner with a tasteful, on-trend website and a successful TV career. Curiously, her speech to UN Women seemed to be the high-water mark of her involvement with the international organization. Once they officially appointed her as an advocate, it seems that her charity work on their behalf tapered off considerably.

Nonetheless, the invitations to represent the issues she cared about or to discuss them on chat shows now started to come in thick and fast. And so it was only natural for her to be asked to host the Women in Cable Telecommunications 2015 signature luncheon. Maria E. Brennan, WICT's chief executive, explained the choice, saying: 'Meghan is a sterling example of someone who not only plays a strong female character, she is one in real life.'

Chat-show host Larry King invited her back on his show – previously she had talked *Suits* with Patrick J. Adams – to discuss her role as a women's rights advocate. Meghan was proving her skills at diplomacy, deftly deflecting Larry King's question about which country had the worst record on gender equality by saying that we have to take into account cultural context.

Hand in hand with her humanitarian work were the undoubted perks of being a glamorous TV star. As her celebrity status rose, so did her price tag. She was learning that she could charge a fee just for turning up. Turbo-charging these opportunities for her was Kruger Cowne, a speaking, branding and hosting agency with headquarters in Chelsea in central London and offices in Santa Monica.

The agency, founded in 1999, represents a whole range of celebrities such as Virgin boss Richard Branson, Cher and Sir Bob Geldof as well as charities like One Young World, which Meghan had represented. The skin-care line Clarins and the Pakistani poet Fatima Bhutto were also clients who were frequently name-checked by the actor. Meghan's rate? Twenty thousand dollars and upwards per appearance.

She had entered a glorious, gilded world, Meghan previously writing about her rapidly shifting day-to-day existence in her anonymous blog, *Working Actress*. 'I work long hours, I travel for press, my mind memorises. My mind spins. My days blur. My nights are restless. My hair is primped, my face is painted, my name is recognized, my star meter is rising, my life is changing.'

In March, just before her speech to the United Nations, she found herself on the island of Malta in the Mediterranean. The visit, sponsored by *Elle* magazine, was a chance for her to discover a bit about her roots – and to enjoy some of the island's fabulous but oft-neglected cuisine. Malta held a special place in her heart; her paternal great-great-grandmother Mary Merrill, the daughter of Mary Bird, a former housemaid to the British royal family, and a British soldier, had been born here, and she was eager to know more.

She went by ferry to the tiny island of Gozo, tasted the famous Goz cheeselet (a traditional filled flatbread and pastry dish), then, after returning to the main island, she explored the Casa Rocca Piccola in Valletta and viewed the Caravaggio paintings at St John's Co-Cathedral. During her week-long stay, she fell in love with Maltese cuisine. Meghan threw herself into her cooking lesson with chef Pippa Mattei, Malta's equivalent to Martha Stewart, at her home in Attard. Given that Meghan liked to emphasize that, as a California girl, her experience with farm-to-table cuisine was hardwired, here was an opportunity to see the Maltese version. Mattei took her shopping for produce and to the local fish market, then gave her a lesson in pasta and pastizzi making, followed by a meal in Mattei's garden.

For the girl who conjured The Tig from her favourite tipple, no visit to Malta would have been complete without a comprehensive wine tasting, the actor visiting the Meridiana wine estate for a leisurely afternoon exploring fruity reds and tasty whites. As Maltese wines rarely, if ever, reach the shores of America, this was a real treat. She didn't discover much more about her Maltese ancestry – but at least her taste buds had a holiday to remember.

Her visit to Malta was a solo trip, even though her chef boyfriend would have been inspired by the variety and distinctiveness of the local cuisine. Like Meghan, he was being kept busy, on the verge of starting a new venture, FLOCK Rotisserie and Greens, a restaurant specializing in roast chicken and salad. The chef admitted that he had been testing a fair bit of roast chicken on Meghan, Cory working virtually round the clock running three restaurants.

He was also in front of the camera, too, taping episodes of *Chef in Your Ear* for Food Network Canada, which were due for broadcast in December 2014. Taking a leaf out of Meghan's philanthropy playbook, he volunteered for Kids Cook to Care, a programme for youngsters who were taught how to make home-cooked meals by celebrity chefs. The idea was to ignite their understanding of proper cooking techniques and the importance of serving the community.

With his filming and restaurant commitments, he was unable to join Meghan on her next exotic jaunt – to Istanbul, where she, together with actor Eddie Redmayne, 'Fifty Shades' actor Jamie Dornan and singer Paloma Faith were on hand to celebrate the opening of the latest enclave of Soho House.

It was another glamorous interlude in her busiest and most successful year to date. The profile high of her UN speech was matched by an invitation to become the face for one of Canada's oldest and most respected retailers, Reitmans. What was more, the ninety-year-old store chain wanted her to curate her own clothing line. Not only was her face going to be on billboards and on TV all over Canada, she was going to influence how women dressed.

It was a marvellous opportunity, though when she first mentioned the overture to savvy friends they scoffed at the idea of involving herself with a retail brand that was so fuddy-duddy. 'Oh, that's where my mom would buy her jeans in the eighties,' they chorused. Meghan was not so sure. As she was American she didn't have the same knee-jerk reaction towards this venerable retailer as her Canadian friends. At meetings with store executives, Meghan brought a fresh eye. 'There are pieces here that are so cool that if you're going to re-energize it, I'd be happy to be a part of that,' she told fashion writer Jeanne Beker. They planned an advertising campaign starring Meghan wearing trimmer, slimmer, hipper Reitmans clothing. In one commercial, Meghan is filmed walking into an elegant restaurant where two ladies who lunch eagerly give the TV star the once-over. One exclaims, 'So stylish', while the other asks what she is wearing. They then try to crawl over the back of the booth to get a closer look at the label in her shirt. Catching them in the act, Meghan smiles and says: 'Ladies, it's Reitmans.' Another showed Meghan, all crisp business, slick high heels and tight jeans, speaking on her mobile as she strides out into the street. As the camera follows her down the street, she notices herself in the store's glass window. Her cute alter ego in the reflection preens and wiggles for the camera before blowing her other half a kiss. Cue her slogan for the brand: 'Reitmans. Really.'

Not only was she the brand ambassador: she worked hard on a capsule collection to be launched in spring 2016. Meghan was thrilled, reflecting on the days when she was a little girl and how she had sat with her mother at her clothing store, A Change Of A Dress, on La Brea in Los Angeles. In those far-off days, Doria had taken her daughter to fabric warehouses where she had walked along the aisles of fabrics. Now she had the opportunity to create her own fashion line. Meghan and the design team sketched out ideas, played with swatches, examined the zippers and fit of sample pieces. As she later remarked: 'I'm super involved with the design process, and I'm sure that it drives them crazy. But how could I not? It has my name on it.'

First off the runway in the Meghan Markle Collection were four distinct dresses: the Soirée, Date Night, the Sunset maxi-dress and 'a little white dress', the Terrace. Once she had approved the designs it was a fingers-and-toes-crossed moment for the actor, anxious that her fans and the wider public should appreciate her efforts. As she wrote in her blog: 'I toiled over design and print, I shared my thoughts on everything and I ended up with a limited collection of pieces that reflect facets of my personal style that I think you'll love.'

All the dresses sold for under a hundred dollars each, revealing the budget-conscious nature of the creator, who boasted that she was the one who shopped on the sale rack. 'I've always been the girl flipping through the hangers trying to find the best deal.'

Of course, that's not quite true. When her designer friend Misha Nonoo invited her to join her at the 2015 CFDA/Vogue Fashion Fund awards in New York in early November she was thrilled to wear one of the pieces from her collection. It was a short liquid metal dress that combined with a plunging deep V-neck to make it a showstopper, photographers clamouring for a snap of the TV star.

On top of all of this, Ms Markle was also now the central character in a chick-lit novel, *What Pretty Girls Are Made Of*, written by her 'bestie from the westie' Lindsay Roth, who was such a frequent visitor to her Toronto home that the spare bedroom was christened 'Lindsay's Room'. It had taken Roth five years, and copious glasses of wine, to craft the jaunty novel based on the exploits of her heroine, Alison Kraft. From when she had been a little girl, all Alison had ever dreamed of was being an actor. Too bad that after years of auditions she doesn't have the stellar career she envisioned. After some soul searching she looks for other jobs and ends up working for a make-up guru.

It was, of course, a thinly disguised portrait of Meghan during her lean years in the noughties. Lindsay had all the research material she needed, not just from Meghan's lips but from the blog, *Working Actress*, about the ups and downs of life for a struggling wannabe, which Meghan is now credited with writing between 2010 and 2012. Meghan loved the book, posting effusive Instagrams touting the fluffy tome. Naturally, she was at the summer launch party, afterwards taking her pal to an ice hockey game. Not only did Lindsay give her actor friend a shout-out for helping her explore 'what "pretty" is': she sent a copy of her amusing trifle to Kate Middleton at Kensington Palace, her accompanying card informing the duchess that in her eyes she was the definition of 'prettiness'.

Lindsay then proudly posted the pro forma thank-you note from the Duchess of Cambridge's office online. She never for a second contemplated meeting the future queen at Windsor Castle after her best friend married Prince Harry. If she had suggested that plot to her publisher they would have laughed her out of their New York offices.

In actual fact Meghan *was* about to get married, but neither to Prince Harry nor to her boyfriend Cory Vitiello. She was due to walk down the aisle with badass lawyer Mike Ross in the climax to season five of *Suits*. Filming was scheduled for 13 November before the show wrapped up for the Christmas break. As she read the script, Meghan thought that if she was getting married, at the very least she – or Rachel – wanted a say in the style of the wedding dress. As she later told *Glamour* magazine, she contacted *Suits* costumier Jolie Andreatta and her friend, wedding stylist Jessica Mulroney, for inspiration. The three women met at the Toronto outpost of New York-based bridal store Kleinfeld's. The store, which boasts 30,000 square feet of bridal wear in Manhattan, and even has its own show on TV, *Say Yes to the Dress*, has a much smaller outlet at The Bay. 'I need something that will be comfortable and won't wrinkle, that's classic and sort of fairy tale,' explained Meghan. Jessica pulled out an Anne Barge full-skirted V-neck with Swiss dot netting. Meghan tried it on. 'It screams Rachel!' she exclaimed.

'We need the dress in two days,' said Jolie. 'Can we do this?' In the original script, Mike and Rachel were finally going to get hitched. However, after producer Gabriel Macht and series creator Aaron Korsh reviewed the scenario they decided it would be more plausible if Mike went to jail and told Meghan's character, a sobbing Rachel Zane, that he cannot marry her – at least not yet. This was the cliff-hanger for the series five finale, which was broadcast in March 2016.

After filming her emotional scenes, Meghan flew to a place about as cold, if not colder, than Toronto. The California girl headed to Iceland to see the Northern Lights, along the way discovering the town of Elves, Álfabærinn, where she couldn't resist posting a photograph on her Instagram site. From admittedly knowing little about the inner workings of the web, Meghan was now a social media junkie, posting cute selfies, wry observations – New Year's resolutions were to run a marathon, stop biting her nails, stop swearing and relearn French – and intelligent essays on her burgeoning social media accounts.

In the eighteen months since it had launched, Meghan had assiduously used The Tig to promote what she felt was important and beautiful: a charming photograph of Doria on Mother's Day, a recipe for beet pasta with arugula pesto, suggested reading lists, her favourite picture by artist Gray Malin, or a shot of her eating a raw urchin as she stood in the warm Caribbean surf. Meghan was relentless, diligent and disciplined about creating daily content. She brought in guest writers like PR guru Lucy Meadmore to write about a trip to Costa Rica, her yoga coach Duncan Parviainen and her *Suits* co-star Abigail Spencer. There was, though, a serious underpinning to all this gauze; in an essay entitled 'Champions of Change' Meghan wrote passionately about race relations, retelling the family story about the prejudice they suffered during a road trip from Ohio to California. 'It reminds me of how young our country is,' she told her readers. With its mix of serious and frivolous, girly and gritty, The Tig had the feel of an upmarket woman's magazine but in Meghan's distinctive voice. As she said, 'It's my outlet to say my own words and to share all these things that I find inspiring and exciting, but also attainable.' It was bringing home a little bacon too. Through her online shopping link and the promotion of brands such as Birchbox, a subscription beauty box brand, she was now making money off the venture. 'I would never take ads,' she said. 'Or sell a $100 candle. Obnoxious.'

There were times she had to remind herself not to give in to the compulsion to photograph and share every last detail of her life. She had to remember to enjoy real life as it happened. As Warren Beatty, the then-boyfriend of Madonna, said of the star when she was making the documentary *Truth or Dare*, 'she doesn't want to live off camera, much less talk'. He made that withering remark in the days before social media ran rampant. Now Meghan was one of a generation who, if they were not careful, would only define their existence through social media.

The real world, though, kept intruding. In February 2016 the actor flew to Kigale in Rwanda once again to undertake charity work.

Before she left she celebrated Valentine's Day, not with Cory, but with friends in New York's West Village. It had become a pattern, both of them being ambitious people, and neither willing to give the time – or effort – to nurture a meaningful relationship. He was immersed in his restaurant chain and television career as a celebrity chef, Meghan in her world as an actor, humanitarian and fashion personality. By the time Meghan boarded the plane to Kigale, it was clear that the writing was on the wall for their two-year relationship.

This time her visit to Africa was arranged, not by the United Nations, but by World Vision Canada, an Evangelical Christian humanitarian aid charity. Their sister organization, World Vision, based in the United States, hit the headlines the previous year with their decision not to hire Christians in same-sex marriages. It was a policy position quickly disavowed by their independent Canadian neighbour. The charity's mission statement reads: 'Motivated by our faith in Jesus Christ, World Vision serves alongside the poor and oppressed as a demonstration of God's unconditional love for all people. World Vision serves all people, regardless of religion, race, ethnicity, or gender.'

On the surface it was an odd choice, especially as Meghan had rather trodden water with United Nations Women and had nothing in the diary in relation to her role as UN advocate. However, World Vision Canada were eager to harness her celebrity to promote their work in the developing world, notably bringing clean water to rural villages. Whatever misgivings she may have had, she accepted their invitation to see their work in Rwanda. It was an enthusiastic meeting of minds, recalled Lara Dewar, WVC chief marketing officer. 'She's remarkably approachable. She was very open to a conversation about the kinds of causes that moved her and that she would like to learn more about.'

This was a very different kind of visit to her UN-sponsored trip where she met female parliamentarians and discussed how they could best promote women's issues in a mainly rural nation. Her tour this time was much more traditional, top-down benevolence, Meghan watching a well being completed in a village and then helping turn on the mechanism that drew the water to the surface. All the while her friend, fashion photographer Gabor Jurina, captured the scenes.

Though her visit did not directly focus on gender equality, Meghan quickly grasped the concept that a community's access to clean water keeps young girls in school because they aren't walking hours each day to find water for their families.

Later, after taking part in a dance lesson, she visited a school in the Gasabo region and met twenty-five students whose access to a clean-water pipeline, installed by World Vision Canada, had transformed their lives. She sat with the children as they painted with water colours using water drawn from the well, their paint-dipped fingers creating images of their dreams and futures.

When she returned to Toronto she staged a charity art sale, using the children's art as a basis for what she named The Watercolour Project. The invitation-only function, held on 22 March at the LUMAS gallery in downtown Toronto, was hosted by Meghan and raised more than $15,000, enough to bring clean water to an entire rural community. Applauded as World Vision's newly minted global ambassador, she told the sixty-strong audience, 'Access to clean water allows women to invest in their own businesses and community. It promotes grassroots leadership, and, of course, it reinforces the health and wellness of children and adults. Every single piece of it is so interconnected, and clean water, this one life source, is the key to it all.'

Meghan was now the official face of the organization, short snappy videos of her appearing on the charity website, on their financial statement, their promotional material and their online profile. Unlike the United Nations, where Meghan was one of many celebrities working to promote important issues within the organization, here Meghan was the figurehead of this Christian charity, one of Canada's largest.

❖

Meghan spun and posed in front of the white backdrop as her friend Gabor Jurina snapped away. Video was also rolling, capturing behind-the-scenes action as Meghan modelled the four dresses in her first capsule collection for Reitmans. Then she dashed home to write copy about the collection for The Tig.

She waxed rapturous over the Los Angeles-inspired maxi-dress, trilled over the Rachel Zane-esque little black dress, and gushed about the white flouncy dress with an asymmetrical hem. The maroon Date Night dress made Meghan feel 'fashion-y and Frenchie'. The day before the 27 April launch of her collection, Meghan hastened to New York to the taping of the finale of Fashion Fund, a *Vogue*-sponsored event where designers battle it out to win sponsorship and funding for their line. She was mixing and matching with fashion luminaries, the perfect lead into the launch of her collection. Meghan was also travelling alone. In news that shocked none of her friends, she and Cory decided to go their separate ways. Nonetheless, the break-up still had an effect, a friend of Meghan's remarking that she felt down, vulnerable and hurt by the split. Though there were hints that Cory was seeing other women, the root of the issue was the plain fact that neither side was prepared to make any commitment.

No matter. The next day she put on a brave face and enjoyed a glass of champagne as she attended the unveiling of her first-ever fashion collection at Reitman's flagship store in Toronto. It was an immediate hit.

The collection virtually sold out on day one. Eat your heart out Kate Moss. Meghan was thrilled, especially as the company were so enthused about sales that her second capsule collection, to be released in the autumn of 2016, was a done deal.

The actor barely had time to finish her glass of bubbly before she was one of the celebrity guests at a luncheon to honour ten game-changing women under the age of twenty-five. Meghan, along with Olympic athletes and successful internet start-up founders, was designated a mentor for the finalists at the fifty-ninth anniversary of the College Women of the Year. Now a grizzled veteran, Meghan was asked about the most common misconception about college girls. 'You realize there is so much depth, there is so much incredible inspiration, and that young women are thinking outside of the box in a way that we haven't seen before. It is the biggest sign that we are in good hands, that our world is going to be just fine, and that these are the women who are going to be the players changing the game.'

She wasn't so confident of the future a couple of weeks later when she agreed to appear on Comedy Central and join a panel discussion on Larry Wilmore's *The Nightly Show*.

With the presidential election just six months away and Republican candidates dropping like flies, Donald Trump looked like the front runner. On the night she appeared, his endless attacks on Fox News anchor Megyn Kelly, calling her 'sick' and 'overrated', had finally engendered a response from the Republican-leaning channel. In a statement backing Kelly they said, 'Donald Trump's vitriolic attacks against Megyn Kelly and his extreme, sick obsession with her is beneath the dignity of a presidential candidate who wants to occupy the highest office in the land.'

Wilmore asked his guests, 'Do you think the momentum surrounding Mr Trump could be stopped?' Meghan joined in the banter with the host and his correspondents, laughing wryly,

'It's really the moment that I go; we film *Suits* in Toronto and I might just stay in Canada. I mean come on, if that's the reality we are talking about, come on, that is a game changer in terms of how we move in the world here.'

A few minutes later she jumped in to make other points, 'Yes of course Trump is divisive. Think about just female voters alone. I think it was in 2012, the Republican Party lost the female vote by twelve points. That's a huge number.' She went on to label Trump a 'misogynist' and suggested that voting for Hillary Clinton was made easier because of the moral fibre of the man she was up against. 'Trump has made it easy to see that you don't really want that kind of world that he's painting,' she argued.

It would not be long before Trump's long shadow would affect her life in ways that she could never have contemplated.

9

When Harry Met Meghan

Sometimes timing is everything. If Meghan Markle had met the man standing before her, casually dressed, hand outstretched in greeting, a couple of years earlier she would have likely smiled, made friendly small talk and moved on. Prince Harry would not have impressed – except as an anecdote to tell her friends.

Of course she would have noticed his ginger hair and beard – her father, half-brother and former husband Trevor Engelson are all strawberry blondes – and that at six foot one inch he is not far off her father's height, although skinnier and fitter with the rangy, loping gait of a young man who's spent a lot of time in the great outdoors. But Meghan would have found the early Harry hard work, something of a lost soul.

Looking back, Harry would be the first to admit that, during his twenties, his life had descended into 'total chaos', the prince struggling to process the black cloud of grief that had enveloped his life since the moment he had been awakened from his bed in Balmoral in the summer of 1997 and told that his mother, Diana, Princess of Wales, had died in a car accident.

Though millions of tears had been shed as people around the globe watched the prince, then only twelve, walk behind his mother's coffin in the televised funeral, only he had been left to pick up the pieces of his life. Not even his brother Prince William, sober, pragmatic and sensible, had been able to reach him at times.

Without a mum, without a steadying, nurturing influence in his life, Harry had gone off the rails. He became notorious as an angry drunk who lurched out of London nightclubs, ready to lash out at the loathsome paparazzi who dogged his every footstep. For years he was carefully protected by highly paid public relations professionals who smoothed over his public escapades. So when, in February 2004, Harry was branded a 'national disgrace' and a 'horrible young man' by influential columnist Carol Sarler over his late-night shenanigans, Prince Charles's communications director Paddy Harverson swung into action.

Harry flew to Lesotho and was photographed with a little orphan called Mutsu Potsane, Harry speaking of his deep shock about the impact of AIDS on the country. The trip was followed up by royal aides helpfully releasing a letter he wrote to patients in a hospital unit dealing with the victims of rape and abuse. It was a classic public relations exercise, utilizing Harry's evident personal qualities – an easy-going manner, fundamental decency and a sense of fun – together with his mother's humanitarian legacy to project a different narrative about a young man best known for his nightclubbing.

For many years this was the go-to template for the prince, any night-time indiscretions more than compensated for by his charity work and his life as a professional soldier, serving for a time in Afghanistan before training to fly Apache helicopters. In Prince Harry's world there has always been someone to do the sweeping-up. When he dressed up in a Nazi uniform for a Colonials and Natives fancy-dress party shortly before Holocaust Memorial Day in 2005, his minders accepted that it was a 'poor choice of costume' but insisted that there was no malice in his decision. Similarly, when he was caught on video referring to a fellow officer cadet at Sandhurst as 'our little Paki friend' and another as looking like a 'raghead' (a pejorative term for an Arab), once again his PR minder Paddy Harverson came to the rescue.

If Meghan had been in his life at that time, she would not have been impressed by his casual racism. Nor were others. 'He was a very lost young man,' a former royal official told me. 'Harry was deeply troubled, unhappy and immature, imbued with the slanted, quietly racist views of those from his class and background.'

Perhaps the low point in Harry's party lifestyle came in 2012, when he was pictured cavorting naked in a Las Vegas hotel room during a game of strip billiards with a bunch of strangers, some of whom had camera phones and helpfully uploaded his antics for the startled world to watch. 'Too much army and not enough prince,' was his rueful response.

In spite of the uproar, by and large the prince retained the affection of the public, who instinctively sympathized with the emotional difficulties he and his brother had gone through with their parents' bitter divorce and their mother's untimely death. The difference between them was William's more grounded temperament and, later on, his having the support of a sensible and stable wife to see him through the dark nights of the soul. The younger brother found a curious respite from his demons and a sense of purpose during his time in the Army. He is not the first, nor will he be the last, young person who has been given direction and discipline by the military.

There was one episode in particular that had a profound impact on the course of his life. At the end of his first tour of duty in 2008, on a flight home from Afghanistan he travelled with the coffin of a dead Danish soldier, which had been loaded on board by his friends, as well as three British servicemen, all in induced comas, who were being transported with their missing limbs, wrapped in plastic. That flight set him on the trajectory that would culminate in the Invictus Games.

'The way I viewed service and sacrifice changed forever,' he recalled in his speech to open the 2017 Invictus Games.

'I knew it was my responsibility to use the great platform that I have to help the world understand and be inspired by the spirit of those who wear the uniform.'

The prince's idea was to combine his royal connections, his lifelong interest in the armed forces, and his passion for humanitarian causes into one focused event. The Invictus Games are an international multi-sport jamboree in which sick, wounded or injured servicemen and women compete in a variety of sports such as indoor rowing and wheelchair basketball. In September 2014, after a year of planning and meetings, the first games, which involved three hundred Army personnel from around the world, were held in London. The games were a triumph, giving the prince, who was due to leave the Army in 2015, new focus and impetus. He was fully committed to using his unique position to help and encourage those who were at the sharp end of modern warfare, veterans who had been damaged and injured but who were prepared to fight on, albeit on a basketball or tennis court. The Invictus Games were the making of Harry. 'Since then he has become the man he is today,' observes a former royal courtier. 'It has not been an easy process. He has become more open and developed into someone who genuinely cares about social issues.'

The experience opened up something in Harry, and increasingly, he became happy to talk about his personal hopes and dreams, too. His conversations, public and private, were peppered with talk of the princely problem of finding a partner, of settling down and raising a family. It was clear that he had reached a crossroads in his life and that his days of sowing wild oats were coming to an end. As the rest of his friends were settling down and starting families, it seemed that Prince Harry was in danger of becoming the last man standing. He had seen his brother enjoying the simple joys of family life and wanted that experience for himself.

At a birthday party in February 2016, he told TV presenter Denise van Outen, 'I'm not dating and for the first time ever I want to find a wife.' It became a familiar refrain. Three months later, when he was in Orlando, Florida, for the Invictus Games, he again brought up the subject of love and marriage during an interview with the *Sunday Times*. 'At the moment my focus is very much on work but if someone slips into my life then that's absolutely fantastic. I am not putting work before the idea of family and marriage. I just haven't had that many opportunities to get out there and meet people.'

The difficulty of finding someone 'willing to take me on' was an issue that was always at the back of his mind every time he met someone new. Were they attracted to him for his personality or his title? As one of his friends pointed out, 'You have to be a very special kind of girl to want to be a princess.'

❖

As Meghan Markle nestled back in her seat in preparation for landing at Heathrow Airport, she had love and marriage on her mind. The actor was returning from a long weekend on the Greek island of Hydra, once home to the lugubrious poet and singer Leonard Cohen. It had been several days of wine, red mullet, hummus and incredible yoga moves as Meghan, her best friend from college, Lindsay Jill Roth, and Lindsay's bridesmaids discussed wedding dresses, veils, flowers, the past and the future. Meghan's relationship with celebrity chef Cory Vitiello had ended recently, withered on the vine as both their lives became busier and busier, and Meghan relished time away from Toronto and the house they had shared there.

As maid of honour to Lindsay, who since leaving Northwestern had embarked on a career as a TV producer and novelist, Meghan had taken her role very seriously, organizing the bachelorette party on this beautiful Greek resort island rather than some raucous downtown club. 'There is something wholly cathartic about being able to turn it all off – to sunbathe with no one watching, swim, eat copious amounts and toast to the day', she wrote in her blog, The Tig. The mini-vacation was a triumph, as was her earlier surprise invitation asking Lindsay to

Toronto where she had arranged a wedding dress fitting at the upmarket Kleinfeld Hudson's Bay bridal boutique (where she had previously shopped for Rachel Zane's wedding dress) with the help of another of her great friends, Jessica Mulroney, who worked in public relations for the bridal shop. Lindsay, who was marrying a British actuary, ended up falling for a wedding gown from fashionable Lebanese designer Zuhair Murad, who has dressed many of Hollywood's elite, including Taylor Swift, Beyoncé and Katy Perry.

Having executed her duties as the impeccable maid of honour, Meghan arrived in London looking for a little self-promotion – and a few fun days socializing.

With more than six million Twitter followers, a morning breakfast show, and a plethora of high-profile celebrity friendships, media royalty Piers Morgan was a favourable catch for an up-and-coming soap actress seeking her name in the headlines. After all, her week-long visit to London was mainly to promote the upcoming season of *Suits* and to dress to impress at Wimbledon, where her sponsor Ralph Lauren held (centre) court.

With the two of them already Twitter buddies, having enjoyed an energetic back and forth online, Meghan contacted Piers on 29 June while she was seated in the stands watching her friend, tennis legend Serena Williams, at Wimbledon. She suggested they meet. They arranged an early evening drink at his local pub, the Scarsdale Tavern in Kensington. Piers was a *Suits* aficionado, but this was the first time he had met 'Rachel Zane' in the flesh. He recalled in the *Mail* online: 'She looked every inch the Hollywood superstar – very slim, very leggy, very elegant and impossibly glamorous.' Or as the landlord put it, 'a stunner'.

As she sipped a dirty Martini, they chatted about *Suits*, her background, her days as a briefcase girl, gun control in America, her passion for calligraphy, women's rights, and her one-time ambition to be a TV presenter. Piers was duly flattered and impressed. 'Fabulous, warm, funny, intelligent, and highly entertaining,' he later recalled. 'She seemed real, too; not one of those phony actress types so prevalent in California.'

At eight o'clock, she left for her dinner date at the private members' club 5 Hertford Street, amid a flurry of texts, observing that she was recently single, 'out of practice' with the dating scene and trying to fend off 'persistent' men.

Was Meghan leaving a media prince to meet the real thing? Though Piers has a track record as a celebrity Cupid – I was at the lunch where he first introduced Paul McCartney to Heather Mills, whom he later married – it is doubtful a woman as socially careful and perkily camera-ready as Meghan would have downed a couple of stiff Martinis before meeting the Queen's grandson.

❖

Professionally, the reason for her visit to London in the first place was to promote the new season of *Suits* and designer Ralph Lauren. Her big day was 30 June, so she had to be bright-eyed, bushy-tailed and ready for another afternoon of dazzling smiles – and the odd glass of champagne.

With her networking hat on, Meghan was working closely with Violet von Westenholz, a Ralph Lauren PR executive, who had organized her '*Suits* Day' and her marketing efforts on behalf of the RL fashion brand. 'How much more could I adore this gem', an effusive Ms Markle wrote of her new 'bestie'. It's worth noting that not only is Violet a well-connected fashion maven but her father, Baron Piers von Westenholz, an upmarket interior designer, is a friend of Prince Charles, while her sister Victoria was once seen as a possible match for Prince Harry.

For years Violet and Victoria joined Princes Charles, William and Harry on their annual skiing trips to Switzerland. While she has been modest about her matchmaking skills – 'I might leave that for other people to say,' she told the *Daily Telegraph* – it seems likely that she set up Meghan and Harry on their famous blind date, timed to coincide with his return from a First World War commemoration in France.

Meghan has always been very careful to emphasize that they met in July, insisting that *Vanity Fair* magazine, which had published a flattering article about her, print a correction when they indicated that the couple first met in May 2016 in Toronto.

If Violet had the royal connections, then Meghan's friend, Canadian-born Markus Anderson, the brand ambassador for the exclusive Soho House, who had just returned from a holiday in Madrid with Meghan, was on hand to rustle up a private room at the members' only club for an intimate evening away from prying eyes.

The scene was set, Cupid's arrow was aquiver, the stars, as Harry observed during his engagement interview, were aligned. Not that Meghan had much of an opinion about the man she was about to meet. When she was asked, during a TV quiz, to choose between William and Harry she appeared nonplussed and the presenter had to encourage her to choose the prince who was still single. Meghan, it appeared, preferred the actor Dennis Quaid, in any case.

So it seemed that Harry had his work cut out. That said, Meghan was meeting a very different Harry from the young man who made a profession of falling out of bars. On 1 July, he had just returned from France where he had joined the then prime minister David Cameron, Prince Charles, the Duke and Duchess of Cambridge and other dignitaries at a service to commemorate the hundredth anniversary of the start of the Battle of the Somme, the bloodiest day of warfare in British history. At an evening vigil for the fallen, Harry had read 'Before Action', a poem penned by Lieutenant W.N. Hodgson, who died in action on the opening day of the battle. The event had been a sombre and moving reminder of the enormity of that day. And Harry returned in sober spirits.

Meghan was meeting a grown-up, a man with focus and resolve, a sense of who he was and what he could achieve. She had asked her friends before their meeting if he was kind and nice; the answer lay in his blue eyes. As they say in the movies, they had each other at 'hello'. She was immediately sensitive to him, aware that this was a man who, beneath the banter and the surface chatter, was looking for a safe harbour. The question she asked herself after that first intoxicating meeting was: could she provide it – and all that entailed?

They were mesmerized by one another, Harry enthralled by her beauty, sophistication and perceptiveness. She understood him as a man, not a title. In that subtle one-upmanship of a first date he realized that while his grandmother might be the Queen, Meghan had given a speech at a United Nations forum.

As he subsequently confessed, he realized that he would have to up his game.

At the end of the evening, they said their goodnights and went their separate ways, he to Nottingham Cottage at Kensington Palace, she to a room at the Dean Street Townhouse in Soho. Both were buzzing. As she relived that fateful evening in her mind, she perhaps wondered if she had been too eager to accept his invitation to meet again the following day. Stay classy, Ms Markle.

As Harry later confirmed, the couple enjoyed back-to-back dates, making every minute matter before she had to fly back to Toronto on 5 July to continue promoting the new series of *Suits*. The normally self-contained actress was smitten. Unable to keep her feelings contained, her Instagram account gave away just a little; on 3 July she posted a picture of two 'Love Hearts' sweets that bore the simple message: 'Kiss me.' Next to the photograph Meghan posted: 'Love Hearts in London.'

She had taken even herself by surprise. When Harry asked if she would be interested in joining him on safari for a few days in August – mere weeks after their first meeting – she found herself saying, 'Yes, please.' Diaries were consulted, days were agreed, plans were made. She had to pinch herself. Here she was about to travel halfway round the world to spend five days in a tented camp in the middle of nowhere with a man she had met twice. It was a side to herself that she was just discovering.

The last full day she had in London she spent at Wimbledon, where she sat in the players' box along with *Vogue* editor Anna Wintour and her niece. As she was watching her friend Serena Williams thrash Russian Svetlana Kuznetsova, it began to rain. Meghan was wearing a simple but expensive black suede Ralph

Lauren dress, so Anna, ever the fashionista, offered the actress her woollen cardigan so that the suede would not be stained by the water while they waited for the roof to roll across. Once play resumed, Anna recovered her cardigan and Serena eased her way through to the last eight.

Though she was nursing the biggest secret of her life, Meghan was focused on the action, standing to applaud her friend's outstanding play. However, courtside photographers were more focused on *Vogue*'s Anna Wintour and Kate Middleton's sister Pippa than Meghan. She was placed under the heading 'incidental people' by one photographic agency. Not for much longer.

'Gutted to be leaving London,' Meghan told her army of Instagram followers before she boarded her flight to Toronto. It would be some months before even her close friends realized exactly why the parting was so bittersweet. As she sipped a glass of champagne on board the flight, she would have had time to ponder the preposterous course her life had taken. But not that long. Hours after she had landed, her life continued its dizzying pace. She barely had time to make a fuss of her rescue dogs, Bogart and Guy, and check in with the design team at Reitmans about her upcoming winter capsule collection, before this one-woman perpetual motion machine was on her travels again, flying to New York and Boston to continue the promotional tour for *Suits*.

In Boston she posed for pictures and made a video for *Good Housekeeping* magazine, while for NBC's *Today* show she discussed her recipe for a grilled Caesar salad before talking about the plot developments in the new series.

During her publicity tour she realized how little she knew of her boyfriend's home country. On 12 July she took part in a light-hearted quiz on the Dave TV channel. She had gamely tried, and failed, a series of questions about Britain, looking perplexed when asked what 'apples and pears' meant in Cockney rhyming slang. (Answer: stairs.)

Meghan was also amazed by the national animals of England, Scotland and Wales, complaining, 'Am I supposed to know that?' She pointed out that even the British camerawoman did not know that a lion was the national animal of England. 'You don't know that,' she said.

She was delighted to discover that the national animal of Scotland is a unicorn, saying, 'No! Really? It's a unicorn! We're all moving to Scotland.' When she realized that a dragon is the national animal of Wales, she said, 'Are these real right now? It's a dragon. Lions and unicorns and dragons, oh my.'

On 4 August, she was in New York for her thirty-fifth birthday, where she stayed in the five-star St Regis hotel in midtown in preparation for her friend Lindsay's big day. 'Happy birthday to the most kind, generous, wickedly smart and gorgeous (inside and out) #maidofhonor a girl could have!' Lindsay posted on Instagram. Intriguingly, on her birthday a bouquet of peonies, her favourite flowers, were delivered to her hotel suite. A princely offering perhaps?

Certainly something was going on in Meghan's heart. 'I am feeling so incredibly joyful right now', she wrote in The Tig. 'So grateful and content that all I could wish for is more of the same. More surprises, more adventure.'

She was by no means short of adventures. In mid-August, after the Roth wedding, she left behind the elegant butler service at the storied St Regis in New York and flew to Rome, where she joined her friend Jessica Mulroney. They planned to embrace *la dolce vita* in some style, checking into the equally civilized Le Sirenuse hotel on the Amalfi coast in Italy.

With breathtaking views of the Bay of Positano it is hard not to feel that this is but an anteroom to paradise. Typically, Meghan publicized every detail of their four-day stay, even giving the holiday the hashtag #MJxItaly. They lounged around the pool, strolled into the market square and took pictures of their breakfast under the heading: 'Eat Pray Love'. Meghan, who had had a couple of weeks to ponder the impending safari with Prince Harry, gave an indication of her romantic feelings when she held up a red leather-bound volume, entitled *Amore Eterno* (Eternal Love), and photographed it under the light of a full moon. It was, she said, given to her by friends as a good omen.

At the end of their stay she kissed goodbye to Jessica, one of only a handful of friends who knew the secret of her next destination, and prepared for her thirteen-hour flight to Johannesburg.

❖

There may have been a slight raising of eyebrows inside the royal palaces when the news percolated through that Prince Harry was taking yet another girlfriend on a safari holiday to Botswana.

Those who monitor these things would have noted that this was his seventh holiday in Botswana with the fourth female companion to join him for a few romantic nights under the stars in a southern African hideaway. The young man certainly had style.

And he was not the only prince of the realm to fall headlong in love with the delights of the African continent. Another Harry, his great uncle, the Duke of Gloucester, enjoyed a torrid affair with the famous and married aviatrix Beryl Markham during a visit to Kenya in 1928. The duke's elder brother, the Prince of Wales, later and briefly King Edward VIII, took his mistress, Lady Thelma Furness, on safari while her husband camped nearby. 'This was our Eden and we were alone in it', she wrote breathlessly. 'His arms about me were the only reality, his words of love my only bridge to life.'

There is something about the vast plains, the never-ending skies, the daily struggle for existence, that seems to bring out the passionate and the spiritual in a prince. Prince Charles has passed on his more mystical appreciation of southern Africa to both of his sons. His message to William and Harry was that the exploration of the outer world allowed a deeper engagement with the inner world, a chance to seek truth in their surroundings.

Charles's own guide was the South African philosopher Laurens van der Post, who encouraged the future king to find peace in the vast featureless wilderness of the Kalahari Desert. During a visit in March 1987 Charles and van der Post travelled to the desert by Land Rover, slept under canvas and chatted around a camp fire, listening to the sounds of the desert while marvelling at the brilliant night sky. On the third day they came across a herd of zebra that stretched across the flat horizon. It was such a magnificent and imposing natural wonder that Charles found himself moved to tears. Nowhere else on the planet gives such a vivid reminder of the ineluctable rhythm of life – and of death – than the African plains.

Perhaps with these thoughts and reflections in mind, Prince Charles invited Prince Harry to join him on a five-day visit to South Africa, Swaziland and Lesotho. It was just two months after Harry's mother had died in a Parisian underpass. Harry was still struggling to come to terms with her loss and his father thought that time away from England would help the healing process.

Accompanying Harry, who was then thirteen, was his 'surrogate mum', Tiggy Legge-Bourke, who had been an official companion to the young boy during his parents' separation; also his schoolfriend Charlie Henderson and Mark Dyer, a former equerry to the Prince of Wales. While Harry's father undertook official engagements, the young prince was taken on his first South African safari. It was the beginning of a lifelong love affair.

After touring some of the famous battlegrounds such as Rorke's Drift from the famous Zulu war of 1879, the prince met South Africa's first black president, Nelson Mandela, and the Spice Girls, who were then at the height of their popularity and had travelled to South Africa to perform in a charity concert.

It was six years before he enjoyed a return visit, the prince, then nineteen, spending two months of his school gap year in the impoverished kingdom of Lesotho, the land-locked country which suffered from one of the highest HIV-AIDS infection rates in the world. Initially it was seen by many as a cynical public relations exercise to restore the prince's stained reputation. Not as far as Harry was concerned. Moved by the plight of the children and with his mother's memory clearly in mind, Harry joined forces with the country's Prince Seeiso, who had also lost his own mother. In 2006 they set up the Sentebale charity to help children suffering from

AIDS to lead fulfilled and productive lives. The Sentebale charity – the name means 'forget me not' – was so popular and, thanks to the prince's involvement, became so well known outside the nation's boundaries that it expanded into neighbouring Botswana. Harry has energetically supported it ever since. In 2008, he recruited his brother to take part in a thousand-mile cross-country motorbike trek across South Africa's Eastern Cape to raise money for Sentebale and other charities supporting disadvantaged children. 'It's not just a bimble across the countryside; we're expecting to fall off many a time,' Harry told the BBC before they set off.

Alongside his visits to help conservation projects as well as his charity work for Sentebale and official duties, Harry made Africa his favourite holiday destination – especially when trying to impress a girlfriend. Before Meghan, he had taken TV sports presenter Natalie Pinkham, Zimbabwean-born Chelsy Davy, and actor Cressida Bonas on safari. Botswana was the preferred destination. As his biographer Penny Junor observed: 'Africa is the one place on earth where Prince Harry can be truly himself. He describes Botswana as his "second home". He is not a prince under African skies. He is just Harry.'

The problem with these romances was that once he arrived back in Britain, the HRH tag got in the way of building an honest, workable commitment. Harry's previous serious relationships with Chelsy Davy and Cressida Bonas floundered because they couldn't cope with being in the spotlight. As Harry's first serious girlfriend, Chelsy bore the unwelcome media attention for seven years. During their on–off relationship that lasted from 2004 to 2011, the feisty blonde was often described as the love of his life.

She became part of the royal set, and was invited to the weddings of Prince William and Kate Middleton, and of Princess Anne's daughter Zara Phillips and rugby player Mike Tindall. The trainee lawyer admitted that she found it difficult to cope with the pressure. 'It was so full on – crazy, scary and uncomfortable,' she later revealed at the launch of a jewellery range in June 2016. 'It was tough being chased down the road by photographers. I was trying to be a normal kid and it was horrible.' These days, she enjoys a 'calm' life making jewellery.

Actress Cressida told a similar story. She put her career on hold during her two-year romance with the prince. Though nervous of the paparazzi, she did agree to join him at a public charity event at Wembley Arena in north London. In a telling exchange, she felt that as an actress she was being defined by a 'famous man' rather than by what she had achieved herself. 'Yeah, I think it's that thing of being pigeonholed,' she complained during an interview on Radio Four's *Woman's Hour*. 'Especially in this country [Britain] I find people are very quick to put you in a box or put you in a corner.'

Others girlfriends such as lingerie model Florence 'Flee' Brudenell-Bruce, former girlfriend of Formula One racing champion Jenson Button, seemed to enjoy the limelight – but not Harry's roving eye. For his part he complained, as have princes down the ages, about the difficulty of finding a partner who wanted him for himself. As one of his friends observed in the *Sunday Times*: 'He's always wary in case women throw themselves at him to make a name for themselves. And often the sincere ones who love him for who he is don't want to live in the goldfish bowl that is the royal family for the next fifty years.'

But despite the obstacles, it doesn't appear to have been too much of a hardship, the prince enjoying romances, confirmed or suspected, with a veritable galaxy of beautiful, successful women, among them, actors Sienna Miller and Margot Robbie, TV presenter Poppy James, Brazilian socialite Antonia Packard, and German model Anastasia Guseva. The list is by no means exhaustive. Just a few weeks before he met Meghan for the first time, he was seen 'dirty dancing' with a pair of brunettes and downing shots at Jak's bar in west London. Though his headline antics had been curbed, his new-found maturity remains tempered with a healthy dose of mischief.

10

Into Africa

In the month of August, as far as the public and media were concerned, Harry was taking yet another trip to Africa. The prince was scheduled to spend several weeks in Malawi helping to protect elephants from poaching before travelling to Botswana to work on measures to save the dwindling rhino population. He had taken part in a similar effort the previous year in Namibia. As well as his charity work, he was to be a guest at the 6 August wedding of his cousin George McCorquodale to Bianca Moore at Netherwood, a wedding venue, in KwaZulu-Natal, South Africa. Unfortunately, the social occasion ended up eclipsing his good works, the *Sun* newspaper describing how the prince and his friends, all the worse for wear, were said to have stripped a younger cousin naked during a drunken late-night session of high-jinks. Under the headline 'Jäger Lout Harry Strips Wed Guest', a fellow reveller was quoted as saying: 'Harry was on his best behaviour during the wedding but afterwards he went pretty wild. Everyone was laughing, having a good time.'

For all the banter and horseplay, Harry had something more meaningful on his mind. Later that month, after working with herds of elephants in Botswana, he was scheduled to meet

Meghan at Johannesburg Airport in South Africa to join her on the flight to Maun Airport in northern Botswana. The final leg of their journey was a bouncy ride along a series of dirt roads in a rugged four-by-four off-roader. At a roadblock, the couple had to get out of their vehicle and walk across a disinfectant mat, a precaution to prevent diseases from the outside world getting into the vast game reserve. When they arrived at the exclusive tented camp known as Meno a Kwena, or 'teeth of the crocodile', they were greeted by breathtaking views across the dark-blue waters of the nearby Boteti River, meandering along the valley below them. It was a magnificent natural paradise, with herds of elephants, zebra and wildebeest cooling off in the waters. A casual visitor would never know that for nearly twenty years the river had been dry and had only come back to life in 2008 when millions of gallons of water came gushing through from the Okavango Delta due to a shift in the tectonic plates.

Situated halfway between the delta and the spectacular Central Kalahari Game Reserve, the camp has nine luxurious guest tents, all with ensuite bathrooms equipped with solar-powered hot-and-cold-running showers.

It is run by conservationist David Dugmore, an old friend not just of Harry but also of his brother and father. He and his brother Roger, who organizes mobile safaris, were guests at William and Kate's wedding in 2011. At the forefront of dealing with the conflict between wildlife and cattle farming, Dugmore's views have helped shape the thinking of the princes towards conservation. He has a radical plan to make Botswana the biggest conservation project in the world by creating a trans-frontier park in which animals can freely migrate between the Okavango and the Kalahari.

Doubtless he discussed the latest developments with the prince, while giving a conservation primer to Harry's American girlfriend.

However, they had not come thousands of miles to learn about conservation. Their days and nights under canvas in the middle of nowhere were a chance to get to know one another without any distractions. That meant, for once, the chattily effusive Ms Markle maintained radio silence on her social media accounts, the normally prolific web maven going dark between 21 and 28 August.

Conversationally, Harry, who has spoken about his ambition to be a safari guide, was on home turf, the old Africa hand well able to impress Meghan with his local knowledge of the bush and the dynamic relationship between indigenous tribes and the native flora and fauna. After all, what is there not to love about a man who spends his holidays saving elephants and rhinos?

Though Meghan had been to Rwanda on behalf of World Vision Canada, she had never experienced anything so remote and uncomplicated. Sipping a glass of decent red wine by the pool at Le Sirenuse in Positano simply did not compare with watching the vast herds roaming the plains, a 'sundowner' cocktail in hand.

When the sun finally did go down, after a meal of chicken or game stew, they drank in the shimmering carapace of the stars above them. And when they retired for the night, they were lulled to sleep by the chirping of the yellow-throated sand grouse and the melancholy call of zebra at the water's edge. At dawn they were awoken by a chattering chorus of birds, noisier than usual as it was their mating season.

During the days, the couple were able to choose from walking tours or day-long safaris deep into the Kalahari Desert. Along the banks of the river, crocodiles are a common sight, while sharp-eyed visitors can occasionally see lions and cheetahs. After a dusty safari the couple could relax in the natural rock swimming pool overlooking the river – crocodiles excluded.

It was here, in this natural idyll, that the couple cemented their relationship, both of them realizing that they had found something special. As Harry later described: 'It was absolutely amazing to get to know her as quickly as I did.'

In spite of the looming difficulties of distance and busy diaries, by the end of those magical six days they knew that their blossoming love affair was too precious to waste. As Meghan later told the BBC: 'I think that very early on when we realized we were going to commit to each other, we knew we had to invest the time and energy and whatever it took to make that happen.'

Luckily, they had a template in Meghan's friend, the recently married Lindsay Roth, who had managed to juggle executive producing *The Real Girl's Kitchen* for the Cooking Channel in New York while dating London-based Gavin Jordan, an actuary for Ernst & Young. Their long-distance relationship had thrived and even ended in marriage – as had many others in Harry's circle.

However, with due respect to Harry's male friends, none of them would qualify for the position of one of the world's most eligible bachelors. Harry had taken that gig – together with all that entails in terms of media, and public, fascination with his life. And as tricky as a long-distance relationship was, they had other considerations to bear in mind. Paramount among them was secrecy. Meghan and Harry needed their romance to be private, at least long enough for them to decide honestly if their relationship was going to succeed in the long run – or whether it was a feverish summer fling that would not endure the winter chills and inevitable absences.

They faced obstacles that just don't occur in most relationships; Meghan had to ask herself if she was in love with the man or the position, and if she loved the man could she cope with the position? She might be a popular actress and used to being recognized in public, but that was nothing compared to the scrutiny she would be under should she choose to go the distance with Harry. Mid-range celebrity boyfriends like chef Cory Vitiello were one thing, royalty was quite another. Could she take it? And for that matter, could her family and friends?

For his part, Harry had fallen for a (slightly) older, bi-racial divorcee from California. He didn't need any reminding of the chaos and bitterness caused by the last American to marry a member of the royal family. When King Edward VIII fell for Wallis Simpson, the twice-divorced woman from Baltimore, he abdicated the throne rather than give her up.

Long after Edward VIII had gone into self-imposed exile, divorce remained the great No No inside the royal family. In the 1950s, Harry's great aunt, Princess Margaret, the Queen's sister, had agreed, after much pressure from the Church and politicians, to walk away from her relationship with another divorcee, the late king's equerry, Group Captain Peter Townsend. Her life was never really the same again.

Of course, his father Prince Charles had married his mistress

Camilla Parker Bowles in Windsor in 2005 after leaving a decent interval following the death of Diana and that of his disapproving grandmother, the Queen Mother, who died in 2002. That union signalled a permanent retreat from the moral position the royal family had clung to during the bitter run-up to the abdication.

There was much history for Meghan to learn and absorb. Far more than dragons, unicorns and lions! Though he was instinctively protective towards her, Harry wanted Meghan to understand clearly what she was getting into and make her own choices. Hopefully in his favour. He was much more the anxious supplicant, worried that the price of fame could be his future happiness. Like clambering into the unheated plunge pool at the Meno a Kweno camp, it was best if her introduction into his world was 'pole, pole'. (Slowly, slowly.)

The trick was in planning and timing. Many long-distance couples apply the twenty-one-day survival rule – to make sure that they see one another at least every three weeks. Harry and Meghan managed every fourteen days. Jet lag – not the paparazzi – became their main enemy. Meghan would often arrive in Toronto and go straight to the set of *Suits* and start filming. As she later recalled in the couple's engagement interview: 'I think we were able to really have so much time just to connect and we never went longer than two weeks without seeing each other, even though we were obviously doing a long-distance relationship … we made it work.'

When they compared diaries before they parted it was clear that, if anything, Meghan was the busier of the pair that autumn, what with her TV filming commitments, promoting her new fashion collection on behalf of Reitmans, her blog and humanitarian work. Even before Harry came into her life she was often up till the small hours scouring the internet for inspiration for The Tig. Now she was going to be stretched even further.

Upon his return to London, Harry was soon back in the royal routine. After celebrating his thirty-second birthday on 15 September on the Queen's estate at Balmoral in the Scottish Highlands, he undertook engagements in Aberdeen on behalf of the Diana Princess of Wales Memorial Fund, the charity set up in his mother's name that recognizes young people who have made a difference to their communities.

Meanwhile, in the last weekend in September, Meghan travelled to Ottawa, the Canadian capital, to attend her second One Young World Summit. The non-profit organization had Meghan's resounding endorsement: 'They are delegates who are speaking out against human rights violations, environmental crises, gender equality issues, discrimination and injustice. They are the change.' Meghan, who had already spoken at the Dublin conference in 2014, joined other inspirational counsellors, notably Mary Robinson, the former Irish President, Canadian Prime Minister Justin Trudeau, as well as actor Emma Watson, and fellow Kruger & Cowne clients, including former UN Secretary-General Kofi Annan, poet and activist Fatima Bhutto, and singer Cher. As a sign of her standing, Meghan was asked by *Vanity Fair* photographer Jason Schmidt to pose alongside Mary Robinson, Fatima Bhutto and Saudi activist Loujain al-Hathloul, with the Ottawa Parliament building as a backdrop.

Left: Meghan visited New Mexico with her father when her older half-sister, Samantha Markle Grant, graduated from the University of New Mexico with a degree in criminology. During the trip she met her father's first wife, Roslyn Loveless, and Samantha's daughter Noel Rasmussen. Their meeting, in 2008, was one of the last times Meghan would see her half-sister.

Below: Meghan and her mother, Doria, in Jamaica during Meghan's destination wedding weekend in 2011.

Left: Meghan has become a fixture at New York fashion week. At the Tracy Reese show in September 2013 she wears one of the designer's painterly print dresses.

Below: Meghan's last small role before she was hired for *Suits* was playing an attractive FedEx delivery girl, opposite the leering comedian Jason Sudeikis, in the comedy *Horrible Bosses*. During filming she met her dream actor Donald Sutherland.

Above: Meghan mans the phone at a fundraiser for the 2013 annual Charity Day, hosted by brokers Cantor Fitzgerald and held each year to commemorate their friends and colleagues who perished in the 9/11 terrorist attack.

Below: Meghan at the sprawling Bagram Airfield in Afghanistan during her 2014 goodwill tour. From left to right: Washington Nationals pitcher Doug Fister, Meghan Markle, comedian Rob Riggle, country music performer Kelly Pickler, actor Dianna Agron, and retired Chicago Bears linebacker Brian Urlacher (far right).

Above: Meghan on board the USS *Ross* on 6 December, 2014, with former Chicago Bears linebacker Brian Urlacher (left) and Washington Nationals pitcher Doug Fister as part of a USO holiday tour.

Below: At the 2014 One Young World Summit, held in Dublin, Ireland, Meghan was invited to speak on gender equality and human rights.

Above: Meghan co-starred with Christopher Jacot in the 2014 Hallmark Channel movie *When Sparks Fly* during a break from filming *Suits*.

Right: Meghan and her boyfriend celebrity chef Cory Vitiello attending a fashion event during the glitzy Miami Art Basel show, which was held in December 2014.

Above: On their second trip to Botswana in 2017, Prince Harry and Meghan celebrated her thirty-sixth birthday when they briefly stayed at the Meno a Kwena camp before driving their hired car on an eight-hour journey to Victoria Falls, one of the natural wonders of the world.

Previous page: Meghan with Misha Nonoo at the Twelfth Annual CDFA/Vogue Fashion Fund awards, 2 November, 2015, in New York. Meghan is wearing a dress from the designer's collection.

During a visit to Wimbledon in 2016, Meghan wore an expensive black suede Ralph Lauren dress when she watched her friend Serena Williams on court. When a brief rain shower disrupted the match, fashion guru Anna Wintour, who was also in the players' box, loaned Meghan a sweater to protect her dress.

Above: On 10 March, 2015, Meghan delivered a highly regarded speech before the United Nations Women organization as the newly appointed UN Women Advocate for Women's Leadership and Political Participation. Her mother, Doria, and Hillary Clinton were in the audience as Meghan recounted taking on Procter & Gamble over a sexist advertising campaign when she was just eleven.

Below: Meghan's last trip for World Vision Canada was to India, in January 2017, where she promoted education for young women, stressing the importance of menstrual supplies and separate toilet facilities to encourage school attendance.

Left: Chic and stylish, Meghan arrives at an AOL Build forum in downtown New York to discuss her role as a paralegal in the hugely popular legal drama *Suits.*

Below: Meghan, with Prince Harry's mentor Mark Dyer and wife, Amanda, watch the prince play polo at the Audi Challenge on 5 June, 2017. A former equerry to the Prince of Wales, Dyer arranged Harry's gap-year trip to Lesotho and was instrumental in assisting the prince to establish Sentebale, an HIV/AIDS charity focusing on children who suffer from the deadly disease.

Left: Meghan's mother, Doria Ragland, joined her daughter and Prince Harry at the closing of the Invictus Games in Toronto. With her arrival, it meant that the engagement announcement was only a matter of weeks away.

Below: When Meghan and Prince Harry officially attended the Invictus Games together on 25 September, 2017, they caused a media frenzy. Photographers were instructed not to move when the couple, who walked hand in hand, arrived at the Toronto stadium. They put on quite a show, stroking each other's arms, whispering to each other, and chatting with families of competitors.

Left: Prince Harry and Meghan pose for photographers in the Sunken Garden at Kensington Palace after their engagement was announced on 27 November, 2017. The Sunken Garden was one of Princess Diana's favourite spots.

Below: Prince Harry and Meghan Markle visit Nottingham on their first official joint royal engagement on 1 December, 2017. She appeared relaxed, if a little nervous, as she went into the royal handshaking mode and made conversation about the weather.

On Christmas Day, Meghan attended St. Mary Magdalene Church in Sandringham with her future in-laws. This was a break with tradition, as only couples who were married or single family members attended the royal family's holiday gathering. As the Queen left the church to return to Sandringham House, the royal ladies, including Meghan, dropped a brief curtsy. While her future sister-in-law Catherine Middleton dropped a perfectly relaxed curtsy, Meghan's was much more wobbly, a sign that practice was needed.

The next royal generation: Catherine and William, the Duke and Duchess of Cambridge, with Meghan Markle and Prince Harry after church on Christmas Day, 2017. The royal quartet are now known as the Fab Four, the nickname used for the pop group The Beatles.

Above: Meghan greets a crowd of well-wishers in Brixton, in south London, while visiting community radio station Reprezent 107.3 FM on 9 January, 2017.

Below: Prince Harry, Meghan Markle and Catherine Middleton, then six months pregnant, at 'Making a Difference Together,' the first annual Royal Foundation Forum in London in February 2018. Since Meghan joined the royal family in November, more than a million fans have clicked on royal social media sites.

Inside the conference centre, Meghan, speaking without notes, told a women's equality forum about the time she had confronted the creator of the *Suits* TV show concerning the fact that the scriptwriters were sketching too many scenes that opened with her character, Rachel Zane, emerging naked from a shower dressed only in a towel. It was sexist, it was unnecessary, it was stopped. Her complaint came years before the rebellion about the way women were treated by Hollywood, in the light of the Harvey Weinstein scandal, and the subsequent #MeToo campaign. For all her own professional difficulties, she admitted to feeling humbled, nervous and rather emotional when she introduced activist Luwam Estifanos, who had bravely escaped a life of slavery in Eritrea and now works to end that government-sponsored practice in her home country.

Meghan's exposure at the conference was a reminder to Harry, if any were needed, that he was dating a very special woman. A keeper, as they say.

She arrived in London shortly afterwards for a reunion with the prince. As the watchword was privacy, they stayed at his modest grace-and-favour home, in the grounds of Kensington Palace. Best remembered now as the place where thousands of people laid flowers in the summer of 1997 in memory of Diana, Princess of Wales, the palace is probably the most exclusive village in Britain, home to an assortment of royals, including the Duke and Duchess of Cambridge and their children, courtiers and retired staff. Like any village, it feeds on a diet of gossip and rumour, but for the most part what happens inside Kensington Palace stays inside Kensington Palace.

If Meghan was expecting to be sleeping in a palace, she was sadly disappointed; Harry's home of Nottingham Cottage was smaller than her own place in Toronto – and with lower ceilings. It had been the home of Prince William and Kate while the capacious apartment 1a Clock Court, the former residence of the late Princess Margaret, was being renovated. Cosy and neat, the cottage, known as 'Notts Cott' by residents, boasts two bedrooms, two bathrooms, two reception rooms and a small garden. In summer it has the feel of being in the heart of an English country village, which perhaps explains why the first thing Harry did when he moved in was to instal a hammock in the garden.

It had the virtue, also, of being private and secure, the exits and entrances watched twenty-four hours a day by armed police. It is here, as schedules permitted, where they began living together, quietly, secretly, unobtrusively. Meghan recalled: 'I don't think that I would call it a whirlwind in terms of our relationship. Obviously there have been layers attached to how public it has become after we had a good five, six months almost with just privacy, which was amazing.'

Fortunately for Meghan, the palace is also in the centre of an extensive park which meant the actress was able to go jogging – mobile meditation as she calls it – along the tree-lined avenues or stroll on Kensington High Street to go shopping. It will doubtless have given her a kick to know that when she went into Whole Foods, the American-owned supermarket, which shares a building with journalists from the *Mail* newspaper group, she was operating under the radar.

Not that Kensington Palace was a home away from home. It was a culture shock. Not just the security but the rather utilitarian way the royals live. Take, for example, food. As a rule the royal family eat to live rather than live to eat, watching their diets so that they remain the same shape and weight. 'Bloody organic,' said Prince Philip to palace chef Darren O'Grady one day when confronted with a basket of his eldest son's home-grown produce.

When Harry was growing up, a treat was to be taken to McDonald's by his mother for a hamburger. For the most part, he was brought up on institutional food at his boarding schools and then, during his Army career, fed with whatever was available, especially when he was based in Afghanistan. He was raised in a family where traditionally, even on formal occasions – when palace chefs pull out the culinary stops – everyone stopped eating once the Queen finished. When she put down her cutlery it was a signal for all the plates to be cleared away. Hardly the recipe for a calm digestion.

Though all members of the royal family have their dietary quirks, none seemingly enjoys the act of cooking – though Prince Philip does like a barbecue when in Balmoral. Meghan, though, comes from the other end of the foodie chain; she loves cooking, exploring new foods and experimenting with fresh flavours. During the first few months of their romance, Meghan's blog, The Tig, enthused over recipes for pumpkin fondue, spiced broccoli and hempseed stew, poached pear in orange, spelt Anzac biscuits, and red wine hot chocolate. As she likes to sample her recommendations, Harry will have been the royal guinea pig.

Meghan also extolled the virtues of a 'holistic plant-based food delivery service', complete with brand ambassadors who were 'experts, influencers and leaders in the wellness world'.

Maybe it was wise to have kept Prince Philip out of the loop on that one.

Just as Meghan encouraged a helping of culinary adventure, so she dramatically changed the contents of Harry's fridge. Meghan never leaves home unless she has hummus, carrots, green juice, almonds and chia seed pudding in the fridge. When California met Kensington there was only going to be one victor in the dietary smack-down. As one observer noted: 'Americans like to change their men in many small ways.'

They were, however, hardly prisoners of the palace. As Harry doubtless told himself, if his mother could keep her long-time romance with heart surgeon Hasnat Khan a secret, then he could do the same with Meghan. They enjoyed a quiet trip to see the musical *The Lion King* and visited Princess Eugenie, the Duchess of York's daughter, and her soon-to-be fiancé Jack Brooksbank at her apartment at St James's Palace.

'Eugenie and Meghan have become firm friends, bonding over a shared love of art, dogs, and late-night macaroni cheese suppers', one friend of the couple later revealed. 'Eugenie loves Meghan to bits and believes she is perfect for Harry.' The prince also carefully introduced her to his closest friends, notably Hugh van Cutsem and Rose Astor, and his schoolfriend Tom 'Skippy' Inskip and his wife, flame-haired Lara Hughes-Young. One of the first to run the rule over his brother's latest was Prince William, Harry and Meghan frequently visiting the duke and duchess and their children, Prince George and Princess Charlotte, in their neighbouring home at Kensington Palace.

They also visited the gastropub The Sands End, in south-west London, which is owned by Harry's 'second dad' and mentor

Mark Dyer. Dyer was utterly delighted that Harry had found a 'good sort' after so many years of drift and occasional debauch. It probably helped that Mark is married to Texan heiress Amanda Kline, who was able to give Meghan recommendations for mundane but vital matters for an actress, such as hairdressers, nail bars and beauty salons.

'Meghan loved her from the start,' observed a friend of the Dyers. 'She is a compatriot and terribly kind and jolly — and Harry trusts the Dyers implicitly.'

One weekend Harry and Meghan headed to the Cotswolds, staying at the Oxfordshire farmhouse run by Soho House. It is a seriously stylish hang-out for metropolitan hipsters who want to road test their designer wellies. Every night a cocktail cart visits the various rooms and wooden cabins, dispensing Martinis and, in Harry's case, aged Scotch whisky. While staying at Soho Farmhouse, the club's founder Nick Jones introduced Meghan to musician Richard Jones, husband of singer Sophie Ellis-Bextor, whom Meghan had met at the opening of Soho House in Istanbul in 2015. A keen amateur pilot, he said to Meghan, 'Let me show you how to fly a plane.' As he later told the *Daily Mail*: 'She jumped at it. I took her up with me and she loved it. She was great, a natural, and we flew over the Cotswolds.'

On 11 October she boarded a rather larger conveyance than Richard Jones's single prop and flew from London to Atlanta, Georgia, where she was guest speaker at a blogging conference aimed specifically at millennial women who want to network and learn how best to use digital space. In a thirty-five-minute discussion on stage with Create and Cultivate founder Jaclyn Johnson, she passed on her own pearls of internet wisdom and made it clear that she planned to expand The Tig. By now her baby had grown into a toddler that needed constant feeding. Her brand, which she described as 'aspirational girl next door', needed help, someone who could instinctively know how to channel Meghan and satisfy The Tig's growing appetite. Clearly she wanted to be able to balance her site with her private life, but had not yet given serious thought to how her royal romance would change things.

During the taped conversation, she also gave her adoring audience a window into the whirlwind that was her world, admitting that she had arrived from London the previous night and, after the conference, was flying to Toronto to film three episodes of *Suits* for the show's sixth season. Her talk left the audience impressed by her candour and smarts. 'Charming, intelligent and unafraid to let her guard down, Meghan is the definition of the modern woman,' noted Jaclyn Johnson.

Once Meghan had finished filming it was Harry's turn to join her in Toronto. Unlike Meghan, who's normally the camera-ready girl sitting in business class in her jeans or chinos and black tailored blazer, a cashmere scarf on her shoulders, quietly reading *The Economist* while listening to Petit Biscuit or Christine and the Queens on her designer headphones, Harry is the boy in a beanie, travelling head down, avoiding eye contact. Fortunately, unlike London, Paris and New York, there is no paparazzi culture in the Ontario capital, so life was more relaxed for the couple, and once again they were able to continue with their relationship outside of public or media scrutiny.

Apart from an SUV containing plain-clothes police which was parked unobtrusively on her tree-lined street in the affluent neighbourhood of Seaton Village where she now lived, there was no obvious sign that a member of the royal family had come to visit.

With its wooden floors and light painted walls, Meghan's open-plan property has the feel of Southern California, a trick that is hard to pull off on a dull October afternoon in Toronto. Unlike Nottingham Cottage's relatively utilitarian interior, the rented property is suitably luxurious, with a cinema room, a high-spec kitchen-diner, three bedrooms and two bathrooms. Her rescue dogs, Bogart and Guy, had the run of the house and, despite having a kennel outside, the pair often slept on Meghan's king-sized bed. When Harry came to stay, doubtless she dressed them in the Union Jack jumpers she bought to amuse her boyfriend.

Meghan would also throw barbecue parties for friends who were in the know, such as Jessica and Ben Mulroney, on a small decked area, or they would go to Soho House for drinks.

Housed in an elegant Georgian building in the west of the city on Adelaide Street, the club provided the cosy corners and intimate bars where the couple could escape with Meghan's closest friends. Here they could enjoy the Italian-style cuisine or venture onto the rooftop terrace for panoramic views of the downtown skyline.

For much of the time they just hung out, Meghan cooking dishes fit for a prince, mainly pasta and her signature roast chicken. At Halloween, the eve of Meghan's collection for Reitmans hitting the stores, they met Princess Eugenie and Jack Brooksbank, who were over in Canada on holiday, at Soho House for supper, before Harry donned a mask and went trick-or-treating with his girlfriend.

It was a fun and carefree evening, but their days of secrecy and privacy were coming to an end. Meghan and Harry were about to be unmasked.

11

A Very Public Affair

On a briskly chilly but blue-skied day at the end of October 2016, Camilla Tominey, the royal editor of the *Sunday Express*, was cheering on her young son Harry in a Sunday league football match. Much to his mother's delight, young Harry, aged six, was on the score sheet.

Some hours earlier his mother had scored too, breaking the biggest royal story of her career. Under the headline HARRY'S SECRET ROMANCE WITH A TV STAR, and billed as a Royal World Exclusive, she told her readers that Prince Harry was 'secretly dating a stunning US actress, model and human rights campaigner'. Her story went on to detail the romance between the Queen's grandson and *Suits* actress Meghan Markle. It quoted a source as saying that Harry was the happiest he had been in years.

Her editor, Martin Townsend, was equally happy, so thrilled with the royal exclusive that he shared it with the *Daily Star Sunday*, sister paper to the *Sunday Express*.

The story was gold dust. And Camilla was absolutely confident of her source. For once the newspaper decided against placing a courtesy call into the press office at Kensington Palace.

The fear was that the palace would put out a statement, thus spoiling their scoop.

It was just like the old days of Fleet Street, the one-time newspaper capital of Britain. Normally, Sunday newspapers have a gentleman's agreement whereby they swap their first editions so that if a rival has missed a story, they have a chance to catch up for later editions. Not this night. Townsend decided to deliberately delay printing the first edition of the paper so that none of his rivals were in a position to match their scoop. Late on Saturday night, frantic calls from journalists were being made to Kensington Palace when word spread that the *Express* had landed 'a big one'. Camilla's agitated competitors were met with 'No comment' by the duty press officer. Off the record, Prince Harry's communications director, Jason Knauf, an aggressive American, was reluctantly admitting that the article had a ring of truth about it.

Within minutes of the *Sunday Express* story breaking, social media went into meltdown as bloggers, royal enthusiasts, *Suits* fans and online newspapers worldwide spread the news. Overnight Meghan Markle went from being a moderately well-known actress to one of the most famous people on the planet.

When the story became public, Harry was staying with Meghan in Toronto. After he took a call from Jason Knauf to tell him their cover had been blown, he and Meghan poured themselves a glass of wine and toasted each other. But the celebration came with a sober warning, Harry telling Meghan, 'Our lives will never be the same again.'

At least they no longer had to hide from the world. Nor was the actress going to lose her mischievous sense of humour over this dramatic development in her life. Just hours after the story broke she posted a cryptic photo on her Instagram site of two bananas cuddling, with the caption 'Sleep tight xx'. The photograph, which showed the bananas 'spooning' – lying next to each other like a pair of spoons – attracted thousands of 'likes' from her followers, who quickly realized what she was alluding to. One user posted 'Princess Meghan Markle' while another wrote: 'Is this a message for your red-haired Prince?'

Equally tongue-in-cheek was another photo she posted showing a cup of English breakfast tea and a jigsaw, perhaps indicating how the couple were spending their time indoors. But their light-hearted attitude did not last long.

❖

There is a famous scene in the movie *Notting Hill* where Julia Roberts, who plays a glamorous American actress, opens the front door of the home of her bookseller boyfriend, played by Hugh Grant, to be confronted by a baying pack of photographers and reporters. Roberts promptly slams the door and heads inside. That's probably how Meghan felt when, dressed in a long coat, a beanie hat and dark glasses, she ventured out of her front door and made her way through the mob of media into a waiting Dodge van, which then whisked her to work on the set of *Suits*. Harry had somehow managed to make his escape earlier and had caught a flight back to London.

Meghan might have been a veteran of promotional panels, forums and podiums, but nothing could have prepared her for the sonic boom, the shock wave, of publicity that hit her.

Within the space of a few days, much of the print and digital media had painted her as a 'gold digger' whose 'torrid sex scenes' from *Suits* were featured on porn sites. One story suggested that Prince Harry was responsible for breaking up Meghan's relationship with chef Cory Vitiello, another that the prince had inundated her with texts until she agreed to meet for a date.

Under the headline 'Harry's girl on Pornhub', one tabloid helpfully reported that she featured on the adult site, where she could be seen 'stripping off and groaning', straddling her co-star Patrick J. Adams in an office, as well as mounting him on a sofa. 'It also includes close-ups of her crotch and her lacy bra – and has been viewed more than 40,600 times.' Another porn site superimposed Meghan's head onto the body of a glamour model.

Commentators had a field day. Columnist Rachel Johnson, sister of British Foreign Secretary Boris Johnson, described Meghan's mother, Doria, as a 'dreadlocked African-American lady from the wrong side of the tracks'. She continued, 'If there is issue from her alleged union with Prince Harry, the Windsors will thicken their watery, thin blue blood and Spencer pale skin and ginger hair with some rich and exotic DNA.' 'Prince Harry could marry into gangster royalty – his new love is from a crime-ridden Los Angeles neighbourhood,' claimed another article. The story suggested that Meghan's mother lived in a high-crime neighbourhood surrounded by 'bloodbath robberies and drug-induced violence'.

The stories acted as the call of a hunting horn for a torrent of racist abuse from online trolls. In a matter of days, Meghan experienced racism and sexism on a level beyond any she had come across before. While she had been discussing and writing about such issues for the last few years, nothing came close to the onslaught. It was neither pleasant nor accurate, Meghan the campaigner, the humanitarian and the woman being reduced to a two-dimensional caricature. As biographer Sam Kashner wrote: 'Criticism of Markle has been snob-ridden, racist and uninformed.'

It was reminiscent of the gleeful horror that greeted Prince Andrew's romance with American actress Kathleen 'Koo' Stark when it was revealed that she had starred in an erotic film which involved a tender lesbian shower scene. But back then there was no internet. This time around, Twitter, Facebook, online forums and comment sections gave the whole world and its worst side the platform to 'join the conversation'.

While Meghan was sympathizing with her mother, who found herself accosted by photographers every time she went out, as well as by confused friends wondering what they should say to the media, other members of her own family added to the tumult.

Her half-sister Samantha (previously named Yvonne) appeared particularly keen to share the limelight. Describing Meghan, whom she had not seen for years, as 'selfish', Samantha accused her of being a shallow social climber with a 'soft spot for gingers'. Samantha, who suffers from multiple sclerosis and is wheelchair-bound, went on to say in an interview with the *Sun* that her half-sister's behaviour was 'not befitting of a Royal Family member', berating her for shunning her family after she became famous. She observed that her half-sister had been changed by Hollywood before announcing that she would be writing a book about Meghan and her family with the title 'The Diary of Princess Pushy's Sister'.

Then Meghan's young half-nephew Tyler Dooley, the son of Tom Markle Junior, weighed in, announcing that Meghan was blissfully happy and that the actress was 'hurt' and 'stung' by his aunt's accusations. If nothing else, these scattered comments gave a sense of the dysfunction at the heart of Meghan's family.

The coverage was Harry's worst nightmare come true. Meghan had made the mistake of falling in love with him. Now she, her family and her friends were destined to suffer. Through it all, neither Harry nor Meghan had made any statement. Kensington Palace also remaining tight-lipped. But the media bedlam could not continue for much longer. Perhaps the deciding story was the one that appeared under the lascivious headline, 'Fancy a Quick Puck Meg', in which it was suggested that Meghan's marriage to Trevor Engelson had collapsed because she had become close to Canadian ice hockey star Michael Del Zotto. While Del Zotto and his agent categorically denied the suggestion, Harry decided to act. He contacted his brother, who had faced similar hysterical coverage during his courtship with Kate Middleton. They chewed over the problem and though William was cautious about issuing a statement, especially as it would confirm Meghan was Harry's girlfriend, he felt that matters had gone too far for them to remain silent. Unlike their father, William and Harry are not of the old royal school whose motto was: 'Never complain, never explain'. They have a track record of aggressively using the law to seek redress against intrusive photographers and other media outlets that invade their privacy. Harry went so far as to suggest hiring a retired Scotland Yard protection officer to watch over Meghan, who thought the idea 'charming but unnecessary'. That didn't stop the *Suits* producers from hiring their own heavies to protect their valuable asset, increasing security on set and accompanying her to and from work.

Amid these media histrionics their communications secretary Jason Knauf drafted a lengthy statement that addressed Harry's concerns and complaints. There was no hiding the anger and distress that suffused the bulletin, the voice of a young man trying to protect the woman he loved – and preserve their future together. On 8 November, Kensington Palace formally released the extraordinary statement. It acknowledged that there would be curiosity about the prince's private life, but the past week 'has seen a line crossed'.

> His girlfriend, Meghan Markle, has been subject to a wave of abuse and harassment. Some of this has been very public – the smear on the front page of a national newspaper, the racial undertones of comment pieces; and the outright sexism and racism of social media trolls and web article comments.
>
> Some of it has been hidden from the public – the nightly legal battles to keep defamatory stories out of papers; her mother having to struggle past photographers in order to get to her front door; the attempts of reporters and photographers to gain illegal entry to her home and the calls to police that followed; the substantial bribes offered by papers to her ex-boyfriend; the bombardment of nearly every friend, co-worker and loved one in her life.
>
> Prince Harry is worried about Ms Markle's safety and is deeply disappointed that he has not been able to protect her.

It is not right that a few months into a relationship with him that Ms Markle should be subjected to such a storm.

He knows commentators will say this is 'the price she has to pay' and that 'this is all part of the game'.

He strongly disagrees. This is not a game – it is her life and his.

While the prince's statement helped calm the hysteria, his formal confirmation that Meghan was indeed his girlfriend meant that all media outlets, not just the British tabloids, now saw Meghan as a possible royal bride. Picture editors around the world scoured their back catalogues for shots of the latest royal-in-waiting. A photograph of her modelling a wedding dress for a scene from *Suits* was manna from heaven.

Her now official proximity to the royal family became the new agenda, several newspapers wrongly reporting that Meghan had helped Harry celebrate his thirty-second birthday at Balmoral, and that during her time in the Scottish Highlands she had even met Prince Charles, who found her 'charming'.

Though the story was incorrect, they were on the right scent. Meghan was indeed now an accepted part of the royal furniture – as senior journalist Richard Kay, who had been a close friend of Diana's, discovered when, on 10 November 2016, he popped out of his office to buy a sandwich for his lunch.

As he strolled down busy Kensington High Street he could scarcely believe his eyes when he spotted Meghan walking along the road, holding two bags filled with produce from the Whole Foods Market store.

He followed her back to Kensington Palace and saw her

waved through security into the grounds. It was an obvious sign that the relationship between the actress and the fifth in line to the throne was 'serious'. Kay observed: 'The timing of Miss Markle's visit is hugely significant, not least because it appears she was in the UK when Harry publicly declared his love for her.'

What was even more telling was the fact that Meghan had spent only two days with Harry before flying back to Toronto to resume filming of *Suits*. Now that *was* commitment, the actress taking the trouble to see her boyfriend before he embarked on an official two-week tour of the Caribbean.

On the tour, he would be representing the Queen at independence anniversary celebrations in Barbados, Guyana and Antigua. It was a test of his mettle – and he knew full well that his grandmother would be monitoring his progress, as it was one of his first overseas tours to represent Her Majesty. It would prove to be an official tour of more import than he realized at the time.

Among many other activities, he took an AIDS test with superstar Rihanna in Barbados, observed a minute's silence for Fidel Castro in St Vincent, and played cricket in St Lucia.

Harry managed to remain cool when, at a reception for 300 guests, Antiguan Prime Minister Gaston Browne suggested that he and Meghan should return to the island for their honeymoon. 'I believe we are expecting a new princess soon. I want you to know that you are very welcome to come on your honeymoon here', he was reported to have said. Harry was later introduced to a group of scantily clad models with the words: 'Whatever is done here, stays here. So don't worry.' The prince said nothing, but afterwards told aides he found the incident 'pretty distasteful'.

Not that Meghan was worried. He was in constant touch with her via Skype, reporting back on the progress of his solo visit. He was given full marks by the trailing media, royal editor Camilla Tominey commenting: 'With his American girlfriend Meghan Markle putting a spring in his step, it's fair to say Prince Harry has rarely been on better form.

'Comfortable in his own skin and completely at ease with the spotlight being shone on his official duties as the Queen's representative overseas, he has truly come of age.'

Though the attendant media were assured that the prince was heading back to London, it was a red herring. Instead, Harry took a 1,700-mile detour to spend a few precious hours holed up in Meghan's rented house in Toronto. Her followers had the first clue that Harry was on his way when Meghan posted a picture of herself wearing a necklace with 'M' and 'H' as well as a snap of her beagle, Guy, in his Union Jack jumper. For the first time, a grand royal passion was being played out before the eyes of the world on social media. Not that such access would last for long.

Within forty-eight hours the prince was flying back to London. He had just time enough to take a shower before he was on parade in the City of London answering phones and joking with callers for an annual charity fundraiser, where his charity Sentebale was a recipient.

Harry then joined his friends for a shooting weekend at Oettingen Castle in Bavaria, Germany, before he was reunited with Meghan, who came for a week-long stay at Nottingham Cottage in early December.

They bought their first Christmas tree together, the staff at the Battersea garden centre Pines and Needles giving them a bunch of mistletoe for good luck. For the most part they managed to elude the watchful paparazzi, the couple wearing matching blue beanie hats to obscure their faces. They walked through the theatre district, where they saw the slapstick comedy *Peter Pan Goes Wrong* and sometime later the brilliantly staged *The Curious Incident of the Dog in the Night-Time*, based on Mark Haddon's novel.

Much as they would have liked to spend Christmas together, royal tradition put a spoke in their plans. Every year the extended royal family gather at Sandringham, the Queen's 20,000-acre estate in Norfolk. Girlfriends and boyfriends are excluded.

They did, however, see in the New Year together at Nottingham Cottage, before flying on 2 January to the remote town of Tromsø in northern Norway on the edge of the Arctic Circle to see the dazzling and awe-inspiring aurora borealis or Northern Lights.

Even if the happy couple were not quite ready to make a formal commitment to one another, they and others had to anticipate the future. In his mind, *Suits* creator Aaron Korsh decided that Meghan's private life now overshadowed her character Rachel Zane. For her sake it was best to write her out of the hit series. As he later told the BBC: 'I had a decision to make because I didn't want to intrude and ask her: "Hey what's going on and what are you going to do?" So collectively with the writers we decided to take a gamble that these two people were in love and it was going to work out.' As Harry's previous actress girlfriend Cressida Bonas had discovered, there was a high professional price to pay for dating a prince. If Harry and Meghan's romance had petered out, Meghan would have been out of work. It was a high-stakes romance with consequences for her career with every passing week.

Indeed, for how much longer could a potential princess be seen cuddling up to her screen lover, Patrick J. Adams, Meghan's hand placed suggestively on his knee? When Adams was asked by a fan what it was like 'making out on screen with a potential future English Princess', he replied deadpan: 'The same as it was before she was a potential future Princess.'

That said, both Meghan and Adams had by now appeared in more than a hundred episodes of the hit show. As far as he was concerned, it was time to hang up his role on *Suits*. Even if Meghan had felt the same way, her personal life took this professional decision out of her hands.

As Adams later told the *Hollywood Reporter*: 'There was this natural sense that we both knew that the time had come for both of us. It went unspoken and we just enjoyed the hell out of the last few episodes that we got to shoot. We both knew that we wouldn't be coming back. It made every one of our scenes that much more special. We had a great time. We could laugh through it. Even the things that might have frustrated us about the show, they became things that we could have a good laugh about and compare notes on just how crazy this thing had become.'

For as long as she was in the show, the producers were ready and willing to use her royal connections and new-found celebrity – that February she was ranked fourth in the most eligible dinner guests by *Tatler* magazine – to boost ratings.

One trailer promoted the characters as 'almost royalty', while another featured a scene from a previous season of Meghan in a wedding dress.

Others had the same idea. A gritty British crime movie *Anti-Social*, originally released in 2015, was repackaged as a 'special edition' and featured Meghan's name prominently in the publicity. In the movie she played fashion model Kirsten and was seen emerging from a shower dressed in a towel, drinking champagne and kissing an on-screen lover. A number of Trevor Engelson's friends, who knew that he had always been reluctant to cast Meghan in his productions, now teased him mercilessly, telling the Hollywood producer that he could have made a fortune repackaging his movies if Meghan had featured in the original. 'He got a lot of flak,' a friend told me.

Meghan herself had some serious commercial decisions to make. Her blog, The Tig, had meant the world to her. She had watched it grow from a modest one-woman show to a brand that represented her very civilized, refined, yet adventurous view of life. It was aspirational, frothily feminine, but always with a serious point, be it about gender equality or human rights. The Tig was, as she always said, the little engine that could. Now she realized that her blog couldn't go on as it had in the past as long as she remained within the royal orbit. Her pictures, comments, recommendations and thoughts would be taken out of context and associated with Prince Harry or the royal family or both. She was no longer Meghan the blogger, she was one-half of a partnership where the man she wanted to spend the rest of her life with was fifth (now sixth) in line to the throne. Different rules applied. For all her possible protestations and doubts, she conceded that if she was going to go forward with the prince, she would have to severely modify the contents of The Tig.

This was to be her first major reality check. If matters became more formal, in the shape of an engagement ring, then she would have to rethink the entire existence of her online identity. A friend said, 'She's trying to figure out how to scale back what she puts out there about her life, including her social media and website. If she had to leave all that she's doing for the relationship to work, she would without hesitation.'

But it was much harder than it sounded. In January 2017, for instance, with her global ambassador hat on, she flew to India on behalf of World Vision Canada. The five-day visit was intended to focus on child poverty and specifically on why teenage girls from slum communities dropped out of school. The answer partly lay in the fact that when girls at school begin menstruating there are no facilities in the local schools to help them cope with this perfectly natural change in their bodies. Ashamed, they stay away from school. It is a hidden issue, one which Meghan felt could be easily solved with the proper use of resources. She felt comfortable taking on these issues, telling an audience in Atlanta before she left that humanitarian work made her life feel more 'balanced'. Her new-found international celebrity enabled her views to find a wider audience, her essay on her visit to Delhi and Mumbai to discover why periods affected the potential of millions of teenage girls appearing in the March edition of Time magazine.

Her humanitarian work, though, was a ticklish issue. While the palace may not have objected in principle to the causes she espoused, they were not undertaken under the umbrella of the royal family. In short, she was acting as a freelance operation within the corporate royal 'firm'.

There was bound to be a conflict. In her own mind, Meghan had to square the intellectual and emotional circle. The Tig was designed to empower women and encourage gender equality. Yet she accepted that the mushrooming interest in her blog and Instagram had little to do with her work and more with the fact that she was dating a man who was in his position of authority and influence simply by dint of birth. The irony was not lost on Meghan. She is no fool, realizing that in the long run her association with Prince Harry would give her a megaphone with which to articulate the issues that she held dear. The price was giving up her baby. In early March 2017 she said a sad farewell to her thousands of Tig followers: 'After close to three beautiful years on this adventure with you, it's time to say goodbye to The Tig,' she wrote. 'What began as a passion project (my little engine that could) evolved into an amazing community of inspiration, support, fun and frivolity. Keep finding those Tig moments of discovery, keep laughing and taking risks, and keep being "the change you wish to see in the world".'

Her Instagram, which had more than a million followers, went the same way, one fan, Jennifer Oakes, writing: 'Never mind the people who would see you remain single forever, with marriage comes sacrifice (both sides).'

Not everyone was so understanding. Shortly before she closed down her popular and influential website, her half-sister Samantha launched another broadside: 'There is so much more to focus on in the world than shoes and handbags,' she tweeted.

'Meghan Markle needs to practise what she preaches or change her speeches.' Samantha's belated criticism, just as the site was about to close, indicated how out of the family loop she was.

Within days of kissing a fond farewell to her online community, Meghan was given a classic lesson about life in the royal goldfish bowl. In early March, Harry and Meghan made their separate ways to Jamaica for the three-day wedding festivities of his close friend Tom 'Skippy' Inskip and the Hon. Lara Hughes-Young.

Harry met Meghan at the airport and drove her to the exclusive Round Hill Hotel at Montego Bay, where they were booked into a $7,000-a-night villa. They changed into their swimwear, Harry in a pair of green swim trunks, Meghan into a dark-blue bikini topped off with her trademark white fedora. They kissed and cuddled as they paddled in the warm Caribbean water. Suddenly Harry's mood turned dark. It was nothing to do with Meghan. It was the presence of paparazzi photographers, their long lenses focused on the couple. Even Meghan's consoling arm around his shoulders did little to calm him down. Although the British media did not publish the offending pictures, several European magazines as well as websites had no such qualms.

Following his media spat, the next day Harry was one of fourteen ushers for the Hughes-Young Inskip wedding in the Hopewell Baptist Church. He was in a jauntier mood while Meghan, who wore a patterned floral $2,000 Erdem dress, was noticeably affectionate and loving throughout the ceremony.

Pastor Conrad Thomas, who conducted the service, said afterwards: 'Harry and Meghan held hands and I will never forget their radiant smiles. They looked so happy together. I told him, "It's your turn next, Sir."'

At the evening reception, guests, including the Duchess of York and her daughter Princess Eugenie, feasted on jerk chicken and lobster washed down by rum cocktails and champagne. Unfortunately, Harry knocked over a tray of drinks as he did a 'Michael Jackson moonwalk' on the dance floor.

'He was going backwards as "Billie Jean" blared out when he banged into a waitress carrying a tray of drinks and sent them flying,' said an onlooker.

'Harry gasped, looked shocked and put his hands on the waitress's shoulders and apologized.'

It was a temporary blip in an evening of drink, dancing and jollity, Meghan and Harry on the dance floor or in each other's arms – or both. Love was definitely in the air.

After the raucous party, Harry took Meghan to the exclusive Caves Hotel in Negril for three precious days alone. Afterwards, their long-distance commute continued, Meghan flying back to Toronto but returning to London a week later. Her absences from Canada were now so frequent that she had to hire a dog sitter to look after Bogart and Guy.

That said, soon it was Harry's turn to arrive on her doorstep, spending Easter at her home. He had other reasons for being in the city – in September the Invictus games were due to take place, and he had many meetings to attend and numerous agendas to go through. Top of the list on his personal agenda was a firm decision for Meghan to be by his side at some point during the games. Veteran reporter Phil Dampier quoted a royal source as saying: 'Harry wants everything out in the open and for the days of skulking around avoiding photographers to be over. He wants to show Meghan off as his future wife. The Games, which he has put his heart and soul into, will be the perfect platform to do that.' Dampier was on the money.

At long last, after nearly two unconventional years of courtship, four months in private, the rest in public, the romance between Harry and Meghan hit a traditional groove. Meghan drove to Coworth Park in Berkshire on 6 May to watch her boyfriend play polo. It is something of a royal rite of passage. Some of the best – and most affectionate – photographs ever taken of Princess Diana were when she attended polo matches involving Prince Charles. Kate Middleton, too, was always keenly on point when Prince William got in the saddle. It was no different when Meghan, who was accompanied by Mark Dyer and his wife Amanda, arrived at the ground. She dutifully clapped and smiled as she followed the back and forth of this most un-spectator-friendly of sports. Fellow attendees at the charity match, which raised funds for Sentebale and another of Harry's charities, WellChild, included Oscar-winning actor Eddie Redmayne, former ballerina Darcey Bussell and actor Matt Smith, who plays Prince Philip in the hit Netflix series *The Crown*. The crowning joy, as far as the serried ranks of photographers were concerned, would be to see the prince kiss his girlfriend.

Harry made them all wait. It was the following day, after playing in a match with Prince William, when Harry gave the cameramen what they wanted – he kissed Meghan in the car park. Game on.

Once again, Meghan flew home, only to return just a week later to attend Pippa Middleton's wedding to financier James

Matthews on 20 May. So as not to overshadow the bride's big day, Meghan stayed away from the wedding ceremony at St Mark's Church in the village of Englefield, Berkshire. After the service, Harry drove back to London to pick her up and then took her to the reception at the Middleton family home in the village of Bucklebury near to the church.

The evidence had been piling up all year and by now it was clear that it was only a matter of time before she was walking down the aisle herself. An informal strategy was emerging to clear the way for their own announcement. It had started with the closure of Meghan's various social media sites, including The Tig and her Instagram account, continued with the decision to involve Meghan with the Invictus Games and, of course, was followed by that kiss at the polo match. These days when she arrived at Heathrow Airport, often as not Harry was waiting on the tarmac and was able to whisk her through the VIP mini-terminal. So when Meghan attended a *Suits* convention in Austin, Texas, though she dodged questions about her future, most of her fans reluctantly conceded that this season would probably be her last. When Meghan admitted that the sex scenes she had done in the past seemed 'weird now', it appeared as if the writing was on the wall for her character, Rachel Zane.

A couple of weeks later, in mid-July, Meghan opened the door of her Toronto home and greeted Sam Kashner, the best-selling biographer of *Furious Love* – his dissection of another power couple, actors Richard Burton and Elizabeth Taylor. From the moment he arrived at her front door, bookies no longer needed to take bets on a royal marriage. The bespectacled scribe was there on behalf of *Vanity Fair* magazine not only to savour the pasta she had bought specially from the fashionable Italian deli Terroni's, but to imbibe her life.

It was an extraordinary development. Traditionally, royal brides-to-be are Sphinx-like, blushing furiously, ducking away from photographers, smiling politely but not saying a word. It is the uniting thread that links Lady Diana Spencer, Sarah Ferguson, Sophie Rhys-Jones and Catherine Middleton. They know the consequences. In the days when Diana's sister Sarah was dating Prince Charles, she was cast into the outer darkness the moment she chatted to royal correspondent James Whitaker about her relationship.

For Meghan to be giving an interview before any engagement announcement was a royal first, all the more so as she would not have gone ahead without the agreement of Prince Harry, his private secretary Edward Lane Fox, and their communications director Jason Knauf. Nor was she making anodyne remarks about fashion and *Suits* with the odd aside about her royal romance. No, Meghan was telling her true story – in her own words. She was emphatic, no dithering around the issue.

'We're a couple,' she told Kashner. 'We're in love. I'm sure that there will be a time when we will have to come forward and present ourselves and have stories to tell, but I hope what people will understand is that this is our time. This is for us.

'It's part of what makes it so special, that it's just ours.

'But we're happy – personally I love a great love story.'

Just so he got the point, she emphasized, 'We're two people who are really happy and in love.'

There was one troubling sentence amid the startlingly open declaration of love and commitment. 'I'm still the same person that I am and I've never defined myself by my relationship.' Perhaps not in the past. But certainly in her future. *Vanity Fair* would not have given her a prized cover with the bold-face headline 'Meghan Markle: Wild about Harry' if she had been simply an actress on a mid-range TV drama. The clue was in the title. His title. Whether or not she wanted to embrace the idea, in the future her considerable influence, her ability to make the change, will rest on something that goes against some of her core beliefs, namely women gaining power, not through their own endeavours, but because of whom they marry.

That was a conundrum to ponder another day. For the moment she was going where the internet signal was weak, Botswana, as she and Harry celebrated her thirty-sixth birthday. The prince was so happy to be returning to his second home that he even gave a thumbs-up to waiting photographers when he was reunited with Meghan at the airport. His gesture sent the media rumour mill churning. As journalists did not know that Meghan and Harry had already visited Botswana, and as William had proposed to Kate in Kenya in 2010, the obvious conclusion was that, during this trip, Harry would get down on one knee. The holiday was romantic enough, the couple once again staying at the Meno a Kwena camp before driving their hire car on the eight-hour journey to Victoria Falls, one of the natural wonders of the world.

During their visit they stayed at the privately owned Tongabezi Lodge by the Zambesi River, where they were enticed with sunset cruises, romantic Sampan (a flat-bottomed boat) dinners and early-morning game drives. They even had their own valet to cater for their every whim.

At the end of the holiday, though speculation was at fever pitch about a royal engagement, Meghan made herself scarce when Princes William and Harry, together with the Duchess of Cambridge, made an important pilgrimage. On 30 August, the day before their mother was involved in the fatal car crash in Paris, William, Harry and the Duchess of Cambridge marked the twentieth anniversary of Diana's death with a visit to the White Garden at Kensington Palace, which had been specially planted with her favourite flowers. They then met representatives of charities supported by the late princess.

The drumbeat of marital speculation grew ever louder, especially when it was learned that in early September Meghan had returned the Audi she leased while living in Toronto, innocently stating that she was 'moving to London in November'.

The critical test was the Invictus Games, which began in her adopted city, Toronto, on 23 September. Harry's own venture had grown into a mini-Olympics featuring 550 competitors from 17 countries taking part in 12 sports. It was hardly surprising that he chose that week for Meghan to make her debut on the world stage as a potential royal bride. Just before the Games began, Harry visited the set of *Suits* with Meghan, who introduced him to her co-stars, the scriptwriters and the crew.

'Meghan showed him around set. Everyone was so excited. He's incredibly supportive of her work,' a member of the cast was quoted as telling *Hello* magazine.

At the opening ceremony in the Air Canada Centre, Harry sat with America's First Lady Melania Trump, Canadian Prime Minister Justin Trudeau and Ukraine's President Petro Poroshenko. As was widely anticipated, Meghan was in the crowd accompanied by her friend, Canadian-born Markus Anderson, who had previously been so instrumental in helping arrange Meghan and Harry's first date. Wearing a purple dress and matching leather jacket slung over her shoulders, Meghan seemed comfortable and relaxed. Though she was not in the VIP section, the presence of a Scotland Yard bodyguard sitting near her was a sign that her days on the outside were numbered.

She listened intently as Harry told the audience of competitors, their friends and families, 'You are all winners and don't forget that you are proving to the world that anything is possible.'

As Toronto sweltered in a heatwave with temperatures nudging 35°C (95°F) the burning question was: when would they be seen together?

Two days after the opening ceremony, a posse of photographers who were snapping the wheelchair tennis match between Australia and New Zealand were approached by a Kensington Palace press officer.

Without naming Harry or Meghan, she whispered to them, 'When they arrive, stay in your seats and don't move out of them. If you do they will leave.'

A few minutes later the waiting press pack watched with eyes bulging as, hand in hand, Meghan and Harry walked in to Nathan Phillips Square and sat down at the side of the court. In the choreography of their romance, this was a showstopper. They laughed and joked, stroked each other's arms, whispered sweet nothings and chatted to the families and friends of the competitors. When Meghan was handed a bottle of water, Harry advised her to put it on the floor and not drink it in view of the cameras. Pictures of celebrities drinking can look awkward and clumsy.

Meghan had her own agenda. Instinctively attuned to the semiology of fashion, it was entirely deliberate that she teamed her ripped blue jeans with a loose-fitting shirt designed by her great friend Misha Nonoo called 'the husband shirt'. Naturally, the white shirt, which Meghan had once described on her blog as 'my very favourite button-down', sold out within minutes. That her handbag was made by the ethical brand Everlane also sent out a message; what she wore mattered.

In the past, Meghan's half-sister had accused Meghan on Twitter of being embarrassed of Samantha because she was in a wheelchair. In another tweet she mentioned that she was a military veteran, a suggestion that left her mother Roslyn perplexed. 'Samantha is not a veteran,' she told me. 'She joined the Army but left after her four-week boot camp because she spent most of her time in sick bay.'

But no one was going to rain on this parade.

The enthusiastic crowd enjoyed another sideshow with the arrival of former US President Barack Obama along with former Vice President Joe Biden and his wife Jill. The former world leaders were mobbed by cheering spectators as word spread of their arrival. Harry and his American guests looking totally relaxed as they cracked jokes and posed for selfies with members of the crowd.

During his whistle-stop visit to the city, former President Obama joined Harry at a city-centre hotel where a suite of rooms had been rigged up into a makeshift radio studio. The prince conducted a twenty-minute interview with the former president about life after the White House, their relaxed chat becoming the centrepiece of Harry's debut as a guest presenter on BBC Radio Four's the *Today* programme in late December.

As the games came to an end, Harry told the cheering crowd, 'You have delivered the biggest Invictus Games yet, with the most incredible atmosphere, making our competitors feel like the stars they are.'

At the closing ceremony, Harry gave Meghan a kiss on the cheek as they watched Kelly Clarkson, Bryan Adams and legendary rocker Bruce Springsteen play the games out. Standing beside them in the VIP enclosure was Meghan's mother, Doria Ragland, who had flown from Los Angeles to see her daughter and, it was now universally assumed, to run the rule over her future son-in-law.

It was time to dust off the morning suit.

12

Tea With Her Majesty

I t was the most important audition of Meghan's life. No rehearsal, no script, no second takes. This was live and improvised. When she was driven through the gates of Buckingham Palace on an overcast, drizzly Thursday in October in a black Ford Galaxy with darkened windows, the actress was about to give the performance of her career. Even though she has often said that she is not a woman who gets nervous, she could be forgiven for being a tad dry-mouthed. She was about to meet the Queen for afternoon tea. Gulp. Of course she had Prince Harry by her side, holding her hand, telling her it would be fine, just be yourself. Still, it was tea with the Queen of England.

There was a touch of cloak and dagger about the affair, which did little to quell the nerves. The Ford Galaxy nosed in so close to the Sovereign's entrance that Harry, Meghan and their Scotland Yard bodyguard were able to slip inside unnoticed.

They were then escorted along the seeming miles of red carpet to the Queen's private sitting room that overlooks the palace gardens by Constitution Hill. So discreetly did they arrive and depart that even senior palace servants were unaware of their visit until a few days later.

If truth be told, Meghan had quietly anticipated this moment. A few months before she had taken a secret excursion to Rose Tree Cottage, a little slice of England nestling in Pasadena in the suburbs of Los Angeles. It sells a plethora of British goodies but the centrepiece of owner Edmund Fry's emporium is the serving of afternoon tea. Meghan has visited several times, not only to buy English gifts but to take afternoon tea. Perhaps there had been just a little rehearsing, after all.

In a city dominated by coffee and to-go cups, Rose Tree Cottage brings a soupçon of English refinement. It is where Meghan learned to crook her finger as she held her cup and saucer and sipped her Earl Grey.

Necessary skills to remember as she dropped a curtsy to her future grandmother-in-law. However, the offering of thinly sliced sandwiches of cucumber and egg mayonnaise, the selection of small scones and cakes, and Her Majesty's own Queen Mary blend of tea, with the option of coffee for the American visitor, tell only part of the story.

Afternoon tea is a chance for the Queen to catch up on the Upstairs gossip from her ladies-in-waiting, the Downstairs chatter from her senior servants, and to see members of her family. In times past, Princess Diana – when she hadn't brought the boys with her, which wasn't often – used these informal occasions to tackle the Queen over her eldest son's affair with Camilla Parker Bowles. As she sipped her tea, the princess was looking for sympathy. Vainly, as it turned out. The topic was much too emotionally unsavoury for her regal mother-in-law, so the matter was dropped.

Though the encounter with Ms Markle and Prince Harry was much less fraught, there was still an air of tension about the occasion. This was perhaps inevitable. As fifth in line to the throne the prince had to obtain his grandmother's formal permission to marry. It was by no means a foregone conclusion. She could say no. She'd done it before. Then what?

For centuries the royal Houses of Europe have been defined by bloodline and breeding. In Queen Victoria's day, English princes and princesses could only marry their German counterparts. That changed during the First World War when in 1917 George V not only changed the family name to Windsor but allowed his offspring to marry English aristocrats. Down the decades even this edict has been considerably diluted.

For the most part, the Queen's brood have married commoners. An Olympic horseman, an equerry, a photographer, the daughter of the royal polo manager, a public relations executive, have all joined the royal family without a title between them. Only Lady Diana Spencer was from a traditionally aristocratic family. And look where that got them. The House of Windsor has been sustained by commoners – not by blue-bloods. In fact the same could be said of most of the royal Houses of Europe. And while divorce had long been a sticking point for the royals, Harry's own father had knocked that particular issue on the head when he married Camilla Parker Bowles.

Any possible uncertainty about the outcome of this meeting lay not with Meghan, but with the man she wanted to marry. He was the one who had been, if not on trial, then under close scrutiny.

If he had come to see Grannie a few years earlier when he had an unenviable reputation as an angry drunk with poor judgement, it would have been doubtful that the Queen would have agreed to him marrying a divorced American actress. 'It would have been a grim, unhappy confrontation,' a former senior royal official told me. Just as it was when she had to put her foot down in 1955 over her sister Margaret marrying Group Captain Peter Townsend, who was divorced. If anything, Harry's transformation over the last few years has, together with the popular union between Prince William and Kate Middleton, secured the future of the monarchy. Harry's impeccable behaviour when representing the Queen abroad and his commitment to the Invictus Games have been shrewdly watched and assessed by the Sovereign. As a courtier told me, 'The Queen trusts her grandsons. She has confidence in them in a way that she never has had with her eldest son. They have really established themselves as being in touch with the public. William and Harry have star quality, believable and authentic heirs to the monarchy.'

The final seal of approval came from the Queen's corgis. This normally irascible breed were friendly and welcoming when Meghan entered the Queen's sitting room. As Prince Harry said, somewhat ruefully, 'I've spent the last thirty-three years being barked at; this one walks in, absolutely nothing.' They lay at her feet and wagged their tails. 'Very sweet,' Meghan later told interviewer Mishal Husain.

During their one-hour meeting, Meghan witnessed at first hand the genuine respect and love Harry feels for his grandmother. 'She's an incredible woman,' she said afterwards.

With a flurry of barks and a final curtsy, Harry and Meghan bade their farewells, swiftly leaving the palace before the royal gossip factory was able to get into gear. Job done.

Not quite. Meghan still had to speak to her elusive father and bring him up to speed. Since his retirement, Tom Senior had become more reclusive, heading to Mexico where he had bought an apartment in the popular beach town of Rosarito, ten miles south of the American border. He changed his mobile phones frequently and even moved on from one apartment because the widow of the recently deceased owner was becoming 'too friendly'.

When she finally reached her father, she told him her news, warning him that the media would try and speak with him when the engagement was announced. He had already spoken with Prince Harry, so he knew what was coming down the pike. At some point, Harry had asked the voice at the other end of the phone for permission to marry his daughter. Not quite as traditional as tea with the Queen had been, but then there was not much about this romance that conformed to the conventional royal playbook.

❖

With both families alerted, it was time for the happy couple to take a public bow, their engagement announced at 10 a.m. on Monday 27 November 2017. The news was released from Clarence House, the home of Prince Charles and the Duchess of Cornwall, Harry's father expressing his 'delight' at the engagement. The bulletin continued: 'His Royal Highness and Ms Markle became engaged in London earlier this month. Prince Harry has informed Her Majesty the Queen and other close members of his family. Prince Harry has also sought and received the blessing of Ms Markle's parents.'

Within minutes, dozens of reporters, photographers and TV crews assembled outside Kensington Palace for a photo call at the Sunken Garden. At two in the afternoon, on a bitterly cold, windy day, the happy couple emerged and walked arm in arm down to the side of the pond. Harry looked more nervous than his bride, Meghan stroking his arm reassuringly. They answered a couple of shouted questions, the prince telling the throng that he knew she was the one the first time they met and describing himself as 'thrilled, over the moon'. Meghan smiled and said they were 'so very happy'.

As they walked away, Meghan rubbed his back as if to say 'well done', the couple returning arm in arm back to the palace for a twenty-minute interview with BBC reporter and campaigner, Mishal Husain. The forty-four-year-old mother of three, who had been named Broadcaster of the Year at the 2015 London Press Club Awards, first caught Meghan's eye for her campaign to win equal pay for women working at the BBC, and she and Harry handpicked her to undertake their engagement interview.

The televised conversation began with the couple describing the moment the prince proposed, saying that they were in Nottingham Cottage, roasting a chicken, when he got on one knee and asked her to marry him. 'Just an amazing surprise, it was so sweet and natural and very romantic' said Meghan, who confessed that she said 'Yes' before he had finished the proposal. They recalled that they had met one another through a mutual friend on a blind date in July 2016, and after two back-to-back meetings Meghan had agreed to join him on a safari holiday in Botswana. At the time Harry had never heard of *Suits* or the

Californian actress and she admitted that she didn't have much of an idea about Harry.

This had helped rather than hindered the development of their love affair. As Meghan observed: 'Everything that I've learned about him I learned through him as opposed to having grown up around different news stories, or tabloids or whatever else. Anything I learned about him and his family was what he would share with me and vice versa. So for both of us it was just a really authentic and organic way to get to know each other.' It helped to cushion the shock they both experienced with the level of media interest once the romance became public.

Nurturing their relationship had been their priority, the couple describing how they had made a promise from the start to make their long-distance relationship work. 'It was just a choice, right,' said Meghan. 'I think that very early on when we realized we were going to commit to each other; we knew we had to invest the time and the energy and whatever it took to make that happen.'

It helped to navigate the bumps in the road that virtually from the start the couple saw themselves as a 'team' with a shared vision of how they wanted to make a positive difference in society. Their mutual commitment was, Meghan observed, 'what got date two in the books'.

She recalled: 'One of the first things we started talking about when we met, just the different things that we wanted to do in the world and how passionate we were about seeing change.'

As with his brother's engagement interview, the spirit of their late mother hovered over the occasion. On that November day in 2010 the focus was on Diana's own engagement ring, which

William had carefully carried with him before he proposed to Kate Middleton during a holiday in Kenya. This time, small diamonds from her jewellery collection decorated Meghan's engagement ring, which was dominated by a conflict-free diamond from Botswana, the country where they fell in love. They were incorporated into Harry's design so that Diana would be there to 'join us on this crazy journey'.

Just as William had said in his own engagement interview, Harry too felt his mother's absence on these special days. The prince was clear about how she would have responded to her American daughter-in-law. 'They'd be thick as thieves, without question; I think she would be over the moon, jumping up and down – you know, so excited for me.'

Certainly there was a real sense of destiny for Harry about his romance with Meghan. As he admitted: 'The fact that I fell in love with Meghan so incredibly quickly was sort of confirmation to me that everything – all the stars were aligned, everything was just perfect. It was this beautiful woman just sort of literally tripped and fell into my life, I fell into her life.'

Meghan's engagement interview was worlds away from the shy, blushing days of Lady Diana Spencer and Prince Charles, and his comment 'whatever loves means', which skewered his romantic reputation forever. Different, too, from the more formal and conventional affair when Prince William and Kate Middleton faced the cameras. Then a visibly, and understandably, nervous Kate deferred to William in her responses. Not this time. Meghan was warm, affectionate and supportive, more at ease with the media than her royal fiancé. 'A breath of fresh air', was a common view.

The rapturous reception of the news of the engagement suggested that this indeed was a popular match and that the country, beset by Brexit angst, still loved a good romance. Naturally the Queen and Prince Philip were 'delighted', especially as the match cemented the monarchy's acceptance for generations to come. Prince William and the Duchess of Cambridge were 'very excited', while the Duchess of Cornwall described Meghan as a 'star'. 'America's loss is our gain,' she said.

Prime Minister Theresa May commented that the engagement marked a 'time of huge celebration and excitement', while Barack and Michelle Obama wished them 'a lifetime of joy and happiness together'. The king of Twitter, President Trump, remained silent about the first American since 1937 to marry into the royal family. Meghan's parents said they were 'incredibly happy' for their daughter, while her TV father, actor Wendell Pierce, gave Harry his blessing.

As for her screen lover Patrick J. Adams, he joked on Twitter: 'She said she was just going out to get some milk.' He later added his genuine thoughts: 'Your Royal Highness, you are a lucky man and I know your long life together will be joyful, productive and hilarious.' There was one victim in a day of smiles and laughter. While Meghan had been able to bring Guy, her beagle, to London to live with her, her second dog, Bogart, a Labrador Shepherd mix, was deemed too old to travel. He had been sent off to spend his final days with Meghan's friends.

There were other forfeits, too. Following the public announcement, Meghan resigned from her position as global ambassador for World Vision Canada and stepped back from her involvement with gender equality and women's empowerment in organizations like United Nations Women and One Young World. Now she was inside the palace walls she had to play by their rules.

Politics, in particular, was firmly out of bounds. Meghan has previously used her celebrity status to back Hillary Clinton, lament Brexit and attack Donald Trump as 'misogynistic' and 'divisive'. Such strident opinions will be muted by palace protocol that aims to prevent royals, not always successfully, from publicly expressing views on political figures, parties and issues.

Her communications secretary Jason Knauf told around a hundred journalists who arrived for a briefing at Buckingham Palace that, after touring the country, Meghan's withdrawal from her existing humanitarian work would give her a 'clean slate' to judge where best to invest her time and talent. It will be a struggle and a test for a woman who has grown used to enjoying a public platform. As a friend of Meghan's told me, 'She is going to bring a lot of diversity and new ideas, new ways of doing things. She is not just going to blend into the royals.'

During their engagement interview, Prince Harry hinted at the future direction the royal couple may take, working with young children in Commonwealth countries where Meghan's mixed-race heritage will be a positive asset. In April, the Commonwealth Heads of Government Meeting, known as CHOGM, took place, giving Harry the chance to introduce his bride-to-be to some of the Heads of State of the fifty-two countries in attendance in central London. It was a primer for Meghan's future role inside the royal family – and her first taste of a State banquet at Buckingham Palace.

A royal insider said, 'Prince Harry will definitely have a role to play, and now he is marrying Meghan Markle, CHOGM would provide the perfect opportunity for her to find out more about the Commonwealth.' She had her first glimpse in mid-March when she attended a Commonwealth Day service at Westminster Abbey in the presence of the Queen and other members of the royal family.

Amid the back and forth about her future royal career, there has also been talk of family matters, Harry saying in their engagement interview that the time for children would be 'in the near future'.

Though Meghan upon marriage will be conferred with the appellation Her Royal Highness and become a duchess – the smart money was on Sussex – she planned to retain her American citizenship at least for the time being. This means she will still be eligible to pay American taxes. In parallel, she is going to apply to become a British citizen, a process that can take up to three years. The application culminates in a quiz about British history and culture. Given her poor performance in that television quiz back in July 2016 – where she was tested on Cockney rhyming slang and the national animals of the British Isles – few thought she would do well.

She would not be the only one. After all, a YouGov survey showed that when the quiz was given to a group of Brits, half of those under the age of twenty-four flunked the exam. Some respondents thought that Hawaii was part of Britain and that National Insurance was used to pay for supermarket home deliveries. Other questions on the £50 test, such as what is Vindolanda (a Roman fort south of Hadrian's Wall) and the

Statute of Rhuddlan (the annexation of Wales to England), left even social historians baffled.

There were other life changes as well. As she and Harry were going to marry in St George's Chapel at Windsor Castle under the auspices of the Church of England, Meghan, whose father was born Episcopalian and mother Protestant, had to be baptized and confirmed before the May celebration. Her former religious studies teacher at Immaculate Heart, Maria Pollia, had no doubts that Meghan will 'utterly astound and delight' clerics from the Church of England when she undertakes her studies in preparation for her induction into faith. 'She will understand the liturgy and sacrament, not to mention demonstrating the depth of her theological appreciation.' Her prediction was spot on, Meghan forming a close bond with the Archbishop of Canterbury Justin Welby who conducted a private forty-five-minute baptism ceremony at the Chapel Royal in March. Among those present, who watched as the Archbishop poured holy water from the River Jordan over her head, were the future Defender of the Faith, Prince Charles, and the Duchess of Cornwall.

From the beginning, the couple were determined to have control over the wedding day itself. As their communications director Jason Knauf said, 'The couple of course want the day to be a special, celebratory moment for their friends and family. They also want the day to be shaped so as to allow members of the public to feel part of the celebrations too and are currently working through ideas for how this might be achieved.

'This wedding, like all weddings, will be a moment of fun and joy that will reflect the characters of the bride and groom.

Prince Harry and Ms Markle are leading the planning process for all aspects of the wedding.'

It will have relieved Tom Markle Senior to know that the royal family were paying for the flowers, the reception, the service and the music. He or Meghan would only have to shell out for her dress.

It was like a rebirth: a new religion, a new country, a new culture, a new language (sort of) and certainly a new career. In making a new beginning with the man she loved, Meghan was also giving up a lot. She could never again wander down to the shops without a bodyguard, never take her dog Guy for a walk on her own, never tell the world about a passing thought or fancy on Twitter or Instagram. In short, her life would never be the same again.

Almost overnight she and Prince Harry were the most famous couple on the planet and 'Meghan Markle' became the most googled name of 2017. She had been blessed with a gift, a gift that would challenge and fulfil her, giving her the kind of access and influence she'd never dreamed of. Her next test would be how to use that gift wisely.

13

The Billion-Dollar Bride

The moment Meghan Markle said 'Yes', you could almost hear the cash registers singing. Within minutes of committing to the royal family, the recently retired actor spawned a one-woman industry to rival any Hollywood blockbuster.

Everything from the coat, dress and boots she wore for her engagements, to her eye shadow, nail varnish and sweaters – even her cute turned-up nose – was copied, imitated, advertised and sold. She was big business, very big business, the fairy dust of royalty boosting fashion brands, tourism and even plastic surgery. The white wool coat, by Canadian company Line the Label, which she famously wore on the day of her engagement announcement, sold out within minutes, leaving eager customers no option but to add their names to the 400-strong waiting list. It was relaunched the following spring when it had been renamed 'The Meghan'.

Meghan-mania gripped the nation, newspapers printing special supplements about the life and times of Britain's newest 'Mega Star', to steal the *Sun*'s headline. In a declining industry, the hope was that Meghan, like Diana before her, was the new golden goose who could lay profitable circulation eggs.

Step aside Kate Moss, there was a new queen of the High Street in town. Everything Meghan touched or wore transformed lives – and bottom lines.

The niche sunglasses firm Finlay and Co. was able to open a shop in Soho, central London, on the back of a surge in sales after she wore their shades on her first public outing with Prince Harry in Nottingham. The company sold £20,000 worth of glasses within twenty-four hours thanks to Ms Markle's Midas touch.

Again, when she carried a £500 tote bag produced by a small Edinburgh-based company called Strathberry, stocks ran out within an hour.

Strathberry co-founder Leeanne Hundleby couldn't believe her luck. A couple of weeks before, acting on impulse, she had sent Meghan a selection of handbags and was thrilled to see her product given the royal seal of approval. 'It's just amazing for us, it really is the greatest,' said a company spokesman. 'It was a fantastic surprise and we are really excited. We're suddenly incredibly busy.'

For Meghan, her induction into the royal family was an opportunity to influence her new army of fans by wearing the labels of ecologically and ethically minded designers, as well as companies that have a philanthropic element in their business ethos.

She had previously used her blog The Tig to promote such brands as Conscious Step – a socks company that plants twenty trees for every pair sold – as well as The Neshama Project, a California-based jewellery business that donates a percentage of profits to Innovation: Africa. She had always known that being with Harry would give her a megaphone and, even if she was having to step back from her charity work while her future was being ironed out, she was determined to use it and communicate the messages that mattered to her in any way she could.

Careful and considered, Meghan is completely aware that anything she wears, be it make-up, clothes, a new hairstyle or jewellery, has an impact. She has to think strategically. During her days on *Suits* she got used to being looked at and discussed. But this was a whole new level of scrutiny. She has the personality to cope, describing herself as someone who likes to think things through, to pause before she jumps in. As she admits, 'I give things a lot of thought and I try to be as sensitive and thoughtful as possible to how it'll make someone feel.'

For example, during her visit to Cardiff she carried a bag by DeMellier, a British label that funds life-saving vaccines through their sales, and wore a cruelty-free coat by Stella McCartney, an animal rights activist as well as a top-line designer. As Meghan once noted on her blog: 'It's good if you are fabulous but great if you do something of value to the world.' Not everyone was impressed. Columnist Amanda Platell snarked, 'There's a thin line between doing good and signalling how virtuous you are. We may live in an age of social media, but the Windsors are NOT the Kardashians.'

Whether she wants to or not, Meghan has become a one-woman walking, talking advertising board, everything she wears pored over and then sold online. Websites such as Meghan's Mirror have been created expressly to cash in on the Markle sparkle. These sites are effectively online stores devoted to all things Meghan, selling and shipping with just a few clicks, and in the case of MeghansMirror.com, using the same e-commerce site, RewardsStyle, as The Tig in its heyday.

The editor of Meghan's Mirror, Christine Ross, explained that Meghan's popularity was because her style was relatable to the everyday woman.

Ironically, when she was running her own website, Meghan was getting a share of the pie. Now she doesn't earn a penny, though the rewards are much greater.

This total head-to-foot commercialization of a royal princess is a far cry from the days when a bored Buckingham Palace press officer would grudgingly hand out a piece of paper describing what the Princess of Wales was wearing that day – and, if you were lucky, giving the name of the designer. During the 1980s, Diana rarely wore High Street, preferring designers like Arabella Pollen, Victor Edelstein, who made the famous John Travolta dress, and later, in her years of independence, the unfussy creations of Catherine Walker. When she did occasionally step out in a High Street brand, such as an elephant-themed ensemble from the upmarket German fashion chain Escada, she faced criticism from the fashion elite.

Even if online shopping had been available in the Diana years, the cost and exclusivity of her clothing would have prevented her adoring female fans from dressing like the late princess. Of course, for years, copies of royal dresses have been run up cheaply and quickly. When Wallis Simpson was married in June 1937, for example, she was furious to learn that her carefully crafted wedding dress, by the American designer Mainbocher, was copied and on sale within hours of the wedding pictures being released. In those days 'cheap' was a relative term, and even the designer knock-offs were beyond most budgets.

In her own quiet way Kate Middleton began the fashion revolution in the House of Windsor by deliberately wearing accessible and affordable clothes, mixing these with high-end designer labels. The Reiss brand, for example, was a regular staple. She was the first proletarian princess – the palace and the High Street working in harmony, her styles and choices imitated from Maidenhead to Madison Avenue. 'Catherine is stylish in affordable clothes and accessories,' noted Reiss brand director Andy Rogers.

Meghan has taken it a stage further, using the semiology of fashion to focus on little-known ethical brands. It was an interest she had long before she met Prince Harry. At the 2014 One Young World conference, for example, Meghan made a point of befriending Ali Hewson, wife of U2's Bono, because she wanted to learn more about her ethical clothing line and make-up lines, Edun and Nude.

Ironically, when Meghan did dress like a princess, wearing a £56,000 gown by the London-based Ralph & Russo for her formal engagement portraits, she was criticized for her extravagance. First in line was her half-sister Samantha, who wondered how she could spend so much on a dress when her father Tom Senior was supposedly in need of a helping financial hand. Meghan was discovering, as Diana and Kate had before her, that whatever you choose to wear, someone always has a better idea. The stunning black-and-white photographs taken by fashion photographer Alexi Lubomirski for the engagement at Frogmore House – the royal burial ground inside Windsor Castle – were a reminder of the charm and appeal exerted by this couple. 'Meghan's sheer glamour marries Hollywood to the House of Windsor', declared the normally sober London *Times*. As Lubomirski commented: 'I cannot help but smile when I look at the photos that we took of them, such was their happiness together.'

While the royal family were not manning the checkout tills, they had approved the sale, at gift shops in Kensington Palace, Sandringham and Buckingham Palace, of mugs, gold-plated spoons, bookmarks, notepads and postcards all adorned with the smiling image of Meghan and Harry. When about a thousand £20 ($27) ceramic mugs commemorating the engagement went on sale following the announcement, they were sold out within twenty-four hours. Every hotel and guest house in the vicinity of Windsor Castle was booked up long before the May wedding, while the English tourism board was expecting a huge influx of visitors – around 350,000 extra tourists came to Britain during the royal wedding of William and Catherine. If visitors could not get a decent view of the happy couple, there would be plenty of professional Harry and Meghan lookalikes to take their place, for a fee.

As for other happy couples, online wedding planner Bridebook reported that enquiries for castles and honeymoons in Botswana had risen dramatically, while sales of diamond engagement rings à la Markle had gone up by a third. Bridebook.com chief executive Hamish Shephard told IBTimes UK: 'Meghan and Harry's nuptials will boost both the wedding industry and the British economy. We're expecting a huge increase.'

Overall, the London *Times* reckoned that the royal family would contribute £1.8 billion to the British economy during 2018. Of that total, valuation consultancy Brand Finance estimated that the royal wedding could be worth £1 billion to the economy and, post-Brexit, help improve Britain's relationship with the United States. Chief Executive of Brand Finance, David Haigh, told Reuters: 'The last royal wedding had an electrifying effect on people's attitude to the monarchy and Britain, and this will impact even more because it has taken things to a global level with Harry marrying a glamorous American.'

❖

Away from these frothy financial figures, on 1 December, a week after the engagement announcement, Meghan had her first introduction to her new world when she travelled to Nottingham, meeting and greeting members of the public during an official royal engagement. It was just like walking along the red carpet, except colder, wetter, and with no red carpet.

Unlike Kate, the Duchess of Cambridge, whose first engagement was christening an offshore lifeboat at a modest ceremony in Anglesey, North Wales, Meghan was thrown in at the deep end, thousands of people waiting for hours under chill, leaden skies for a glimpse of the Hollywood princess. Though the focus was on a visit to a centre linked to the World AIDS Day charity, everyone wanted to see the bride-to-be. She looked a tad nervous, as well she might, and Harry frequently put his arm around her and whispered encouragement in her ear. Introducing herself as Meghan, she quickly got used to the English default conversation, chatting about the weather. (In LA it's the freeway traffic.) She thanked people for waiting in the cold, accepted sweets, hugs, kisses, comparisons to Princess

Diana, and flowers, but declined selfies – the royal bride-in-waiting was learning fast.

Inside the AIDS centre they met with victims and organizers, Meghan impressing with her natural empathy. HIV sufferer Chris O'Hanlon, of Positively UK, a charity which helps people recently diagnosed with the disease, found the couple easy to talk to, sincere and attentive. His verdict: 'Not only will she make a good addition to the royal family, she will make an excellent ambassador to any of the causes she puts her heart and mind to.'

The royal couple went on to watch a hip hop opera, where Harry told a fellow ginger-headed man that being with Meghan was 'Great, unbelievable.' They left Nottingham folk all aquiver. Complimenting Meghan on her 'charm and ease', columnist Jan Moir cooed, 'What an impressive debut. Meghan Markle was not born to be a princess, but she moves with ease in her brave new world.'

With internet searches for Meghan Markle outstripping those for the recently released iPhone 8, it seemed that everyone wanted to dial into the charismatic Ms Markle, including the Queen, her family and her staff. Prince Harry made an edited YouTube version of her show *Suits* to set before the Queen and Prince Philip so that they could understand more clearly what their grandson saw in her. The monarch was impressed enough to waive long-standing rules that only the royal family gather at Sandringham for Christmas. She extended an invitation for Harry's fiancée to join the clan. It was an acknowledgement of the changing times, as the couple had effectively been living together for more than a year. 'Queen bends the Yules for Meghan', punned the *Sun* headline.

The first stage of Meghan's Christmas royal progress was to join the Queen and Prince Harry for the annual Christmas staff party at Windsor Castle. Hundreds of footmen, maids, butlers and gardeners jostled for position to snatch a brief chat with Meghan, who worked her way slowly around the room. One guest said, 'She asked everyone their name and what they did – she was a natural.'

No sooner had she met the staff than Harry was driving her to Buckingham Palace where, on 20 December, the extended royal family – all seventy of them – gathered for lunch. Though it is a family affair, it is still a royal family affair and there is a whole hierarchy to follow of who bows to whom and who curtsies to whom. Meghan, for instance, had to curtsy to her future sister-in-law, the Duchess of Cambridge, and also to the Countess of Wessex, as Prince Edward was in the room. (Interestingly, custom dictates that if he had been absent Meghan would not have had to flex her knees.) Diana's brother Charles Spencer recalled that on one occasion there was so much bowing and curtsying he ended up bowing to a bemedalled footman.

For a girl from California where casual is king and the average American bows to no man, this occasion must have been perplexing, not to say a little troubling. Here she was, a standard bearer for gender equality, curtsying to all and sundry. Of course everyone was dying to meet the new arrival, so along with curtsying, it was a frenzy of handshaking and brief introductions: 'How do you do' and 'So pleased to meet you.'

When they were seated for lunch, Meghan found herself between her future father-in-law, Prince Charles, and Peter

Phillips, an events organizer and only son of the Princess Royal. They pulled crackers together, then Meghan put on a paper crown and joined the others reading out corny jokes as they tucked into turkey and all the trimmings.

A royal source was quoted in the *Daily Mail* as saying, 'She was obviously a bit nervous at first but she soon relaxed with Prince Harry's help as he introduced her to everyone and then she really enjoyed it.'

The lunch, however, is destined to be remembered for all the wrong reasons, as Meghan's near-neighbour, Princess Michael of Kent, who lives at apartment 10 in Kensington Palace just across from Nottingham Cottage, arrived at Buckingham Palace sporting a blackamoor brooch, a piece of sixteenth-century Venetian jewellery that is now considered racist for its depiction of slaves. As Meghan is bi-racial and this was her first encounter with the wider royal family, Princess Michael's decision was considered particularly offensive. The seventy-three-year-old princess apologized profusely and promised not to wear the brooch again.

'The brooch was a gift and has been worn many times before,' a representative for Princess Michael said in a statement. 'Princess Michael is very sorry and distressed that it has caused offence.'

Princess Michael, whose husband is a cousin of the Queen and whose father was a member of Hitler's Nazi Party, is no stranger to racial controversy. When she was at a New York restaurant in 2004 she had a bust-up with a group of African-American diners, reportedly telling them to 'go back to the colonies'. In order to restore her reputation, she gave an extraordinary TV interview in which she described passing herself off as a 'half-caste African' in her youth to experience life among these 'adorable special people' as she travelled around South Africa and Mozambique.

But Meghan had more to worry about than her new neighbour's crass behaviour. Her beloved rescue dog Guy had broken both his back legs in an accident. Though the beagle mix was on the mend after receiving treatment from TV 'Super Vet' Professor Noel Fitzpatrick at his Surrey clinic, it meant she left Guy behind to recuperate when, on Christmas Eve, she and Harry drove to Sandringham to spend Christmas with the royal family.

Though there were enough bedrooms in the majestic pile – Sandringham has 270 rooms – Meghan and Harry accepted William and Catherine's invitation to stay with them at their newly renovated country home, Anmer Hall. It was more relaxed, the 'Fab Four', as they have now been dubbed, becoming closer with every passing day.

Though it was fresh and exciting for Meghan, Christmas at Sandringham has a regular soothing rhythm, like one of the many grandfather clocks that dominate the corridors. On Christmas Eve, following afternoon tea, the royal family open their presents, German style. Then it's church on Christmas Day morning, the main house for lunch, and following that everyone watches the Queen's Christmas broadcast. Boxing Day, the day after Christmas, is a pheasant shoot on the estate's flat acres.

❖

At four o'clock on Christmas Eve, all the family gathered in the wood-panelled drawing room for the Queen's favourite meal of the day, afternoon tea. Small sandwiches, home-baked scones, muffins and cakes were on offer, along with Earl Grey tea and the Queen's special Indian blend.

After a short rest, they all came together again in the white drawing room at six o'clock to open the presents, which were laid out on cloth-covered trestle tables, with a name-card marking each family member's pile of goodies.

Princess Margaret's ex-husband Lord Snowdon once described the scene as 'total uproar' as everyone tore open their gifts. The royal adults don't buy expensive presents but rather joke items or whimsical gifts. One year, Harry gave the Queen a shower cap with the printed phrase 'Ain't life a bitch' on it. Another year he gave her a singing Big Mouth Billy Bass, which now has pride of place on the piano in her Balmoral study. In her day, Diana was once given a pair of false bosoms, while Princess Anne received a monogrammed door mat. One report suggested that Meghan got into the zany spirit, giving the Queen a singing hamster, which, apparently, the corgis eyed dolefully.

Once the merriment had subsided the family headed back to their bedrooms to dress for dinner – long dresses for the ladies, black tie for the men. At eight o'clock on the dot the family gather once more for pre-dinner drinks. The Queen arrives at 8.15 for her evening tipple, a dry Martini.

The Duchess of York once recalled: 'Christmas can be exhausting, not least because you sometimes change seven times in twenty-four hours. You never let the Queen beat you down for dinner, end of story – to come in any later would be unimaginably disrespectful.'

This Christmas Eve the banquet consisted of Norfolk shrimps, Sandringham estate lamb, and a pudding of Tarte Tartin. During their starters, the family pulled another round of their bespoke crackers decorated with silver or gold crowns. Like everyone except the Queen, Meghan crowned herself with the paper hat.

On Christmas Day, Meghan enjoyed a light breakfast with Harry, William and Kate at Anmer Hall as George and Charlotte excitedly opened their main presents.

Then it was over to the Big House for the walk to the nearby church of St Mary Magdalene. This year the Queen, age finally getting the better of her, arrived by car, accompanied by the Duchess of Cornwall.

Warned beforehand about the biting Norfolk winds, Meghan dressed stylishly but warmly in a Sentaler cream baby alpaca wool wrap coat, suede boots and a brown beret-style hat. The 3,000-strong crowd, some of whom had been waiting in the freezing conditions for hours, cheered as Meghan, Harry, William and Catherine walked by. Meghan smiled, waved and even playfully pointed her tongue out.

As luck would have it, the best photograph of the day was taken, not by a professional cameraman, but by single mother Karen Anvil, whose picture of the royal quartet easily paid for her own Christmas.

When they came out of church, it was time for Meghan's first public curtsy as the Queen walked back to her chauffeur-driven Bentley.

For the first time, Meghan looked visibly nervous, clinging on to her fiancé's arm as she dropped a wobbly bob, a rictus grin on her face. A smiling Kate – a seasoned veteran of such occasions – showed how it should be done, dropping the perfect relaxed curtsy.

Then it was time to thank those who had waited for so long. The most that well-wishers could hope for was a handshake and a brief 'Happy Christmas'.

A few, though, went further to win a moment in the royal sun. Among the crowd were a large number of Americans, some from a nearby US Air Force base. Student Michael Metz from Wisconsin used the occasion to propose to his Texan girlfriend Ashley Millican, the crowd cheering as Michael went down on one knee. When Harry and Meghan heard about their betrothal, they offered their congratulations. 'It was amazing, like a fairy tale,' said Michael.

Back at the main house the royal family sat down for the traditional Christmas meal, the bountiful repast eaten within ninety minutes so that the family could watch the Queen's Christmas broadcast at three o'clock sharp. This year, Meghan got an oblique shout-out when the Queen mentioned welcoming new arrivals into the family.

In the evening the television is turned off and the royal family play traditional games such as charades. The Queen is an excellent mimic, particularly of political figures, including several American presidents, whom she has met over the years.

On Boxing Day the royal men lead the guns out to the fields, where hundreds of pheasants, specifically reared for this sport, are slaughtered. William and Harry love shooting – Princess

Diana called her boys 'the killer Wales' – and enjoy spending the day outdoors in field sports. Not this year. For the first time, Harry left his guns in their cases. Perhaps he had already had his fill. He had been shooting in early December, flying to Germany for a weekend of boar hunting with a group of pals, the shooting party organized by German aristocrat Franz Albrecht Oettingen-Spielberg – known as The Boar Terminator.

However, his absence from the fields of Sandringham was noted widely among the press – 'Gun-der the thumb already?' one asked.

At least Harry had an excuse. He had to be in London to prepare for his stint as the guest editor of the *Today* programme, the flagship BBC morning radio show. He had been given a clear editorial palette, deciding to highlight causes close to his heart, notably youth violence, mental health, social media in society, the armed forces, conservation and the Commonwealth. He had lined up a number of big hitters, namely his father Prince Charles, who called Harry 'my darling boy' and discussed the 'untold horrors' caused by climate change, and the former American president Barack Obama, whom he had interviewed at the Invictus Games in September in the Fairmont Hotel, Toronto.

Before the interview began, a clearly relaxed Obama jokingly asked if he should speak with a British accent. He also wondered if he should speak faster than usual, because he was a 'slow speaker'.

The prince replied, 'No, no not at all. But if you start using long pauses between the answers you're probably going to get the face.'

When Mr Obama asked to see 'the face', Prince Harry gave him a stern look. 'I don't want to see that face!' retorted a laughing Obama.

The conversation covered topics including Obama's memories of the day he left office and his hopes for his post-presidential life, including his plans to focus on cultivating the next generation of leaders through the Obama Foundation. With an oblique swipe at the man who took his job, Mr Obama said that irresponsible use of social media was distorting the public's understanding of complex issues.

In a quick-fire round of questions he was asked which programme he preferred, *The Good Wife* or *Suits*. The ex-president replied, '*Suits*, obviously.'

A whimsical piece in *The Times* caught the mood of the broadcast. 'The man who was once naughty Harry, drunken Harry, Boujis Harry, has left behind the fleshpots. Now he is Saint Harry who spends his time toiling among the needy and making outreach radio in which he speaks to those others ignore. The injured. The depressed. The Prince of Wales.'

By great fortune, the Radio Four presenters had backed their way into a scoop, Harry's engagement having been announced long after they had arranged for his stint as a guest editor. The news angle was the upcoming nuptials.

Boxer Anthony Joshua, who was interviewed by the prince, offered to be his best man, while presenter Sarah Montague quizzed Harry about Meghan's first Christmas with 'the Firm'. 'It was fantastic, she really enjoyed it,' he said. 'We had great fun staying with my brother and sister-in-law and running around with the kids. I think we've got one of the biggest families that

I know of, and every family is complex as well. She has done an absolutely amazing job.'

So far so endearing. As the interview wound down he remarked, 'She's getting in there and I suppose it's the family she's never had.'

Cue foot in mouth. Prince Philip would be proud.

14

Invitation to a Wedding

Retired Army captain Prince Henry of Wales walked straight into a fusillade of criticism when he told the world that the Windsors were the family that Meghan Markle never had.

The Markles galloped straight into action, Meghan's half-sister Samantha leading the charge. 'Actually she has a large family who were always there with her and for her,' she thundered. 'Our household was very normal, and when dad and Doria divorced, we all made it so it was like she had two houses.'

For once her brother, Tom Junior, who generally had little time for his elder sister, went into battle on her side.

'My father will be extremely hurt. He dedicated the majority of his time and everything to her. He made sure that she had what she needed to be successful and get to where she's at today.' As far as the pundits were concerned, Harry 'dropped a clanger', a 'howler' by commenting on the family set-up of his future in-laws. In his defence, he was basing his account on that presented to him by his fiancée. When she was growing up, she felt little sense of family – after all, her parents separated when she was only two. That was her truth, no matter what others believed.

Within days the plotting and in-fighting among the Markle clan suggested a family at war. Samantha continued to tout her upcoming book, *The Diary of Princess Pushy's Sister*, tearfully appearing on television to ask for Meghan's forgiveness and speaking of her hope that she would be invited to the wedding. In the end, Samantha was invited to the wedding, Meghan's half-sister calling a truce with the future duchess. She even changed the name of her book, calling it *The Tale of Two Sisters*.

Samantha also firmly dismissed suggestions that her retiring father would not be speaking at the wedding. 'He should not be deprived of the right that fathers have to give a proud speech at the wedding. A father speaking at a wedding is not patriarchy, it's poetic justice.'

Finally, the man at the centre of so much speculation, Meghan's elusive father, Tom Markle Senior, was tracked down to his Mexican hideaway by an enterprising British tabloid reporter. Though he accepted a congratulatory bottle of champagne, the retired lighting director gave little in the way of illumination as to his plans. He expressed himself 'pleased and delighted' with the news of his daughter's engagement, later describing Harry as a 'gentleman'. In the months before the wedding there was much speculation about whether Meghan's father would even attend his daughter's nuptials. A shy man to the point of reclusive it was thought that his personality and his health issues – he had a dodgy knee that makes walking painful – would preclude him from the big day. As his son Tom Junior told me: 'My father worships the ground Meghan walks on. I know how proud he will be to take her arm and walk her down the aisle. But I also know how terrified he will be. If he doesn't go he will regret it for the rest of his life. He has to know that he is not just representing his family, he is representing America.'

However, Tom Senior made it clear that he wanted to walk his daughter down the aisle and with two months to go before the May wedding the retired lighting director was going for fittings for a morning suit.

Meghan herself was also very careful of her privacy – even with members of her family. Several months before, for example, Meghan had given her father her new mobile number, which he had quite innocently passed on to Samantha. In turn, she sent Meghan a text saying that it had been years since they had spoken, but if she wanted to resume the connection she would be happy to advise and guide her. Meghan was unhappy that her new phone number was being passed around and complained to her mother who in turn contacted her ex-husband and told him never to give out Meghan's private telephone number again. 'Well, she is her sister,' replied Tom Senior.

Meanwhile Samantha's estranged brother Tom was finding all the media scrutiny difficult to bear. His girlfriend Darlene ended up in jail overnight after an overly boisterous, boozy New Year's Eve celebration at their Oregon home, the second time since Meghan and Harry's relationship went public that police had made an arrest at his house. Previously he was arrested in January 2017 for the 'unlawful use of a weapon and menacing'. The charges were dropped. Tom later told me that he suspected that a member of his own family had sold the story to the press. As he admitted, 'All this attention has been really hard on the family.'

The ghosts from Meghan's past kept arriving to haunt her. A warring family was one thing, a former husband out for his pound of flesh was quite another. She was less than thrilled to learn that her ex-husband Trevor Engelson had sold a pilot comedy drama to Fox TV, which he was slated to produce, based on the idea of a recently divorced man whose wife has married into the royal family. The comedy conflict focuses on the estranged couple bickering over access to their children. He had the idea when he was discussing his chequered love life with fellow producer Dan Farah.

Whether or not the show is ever broadcast, Meghan will have to get used to being made fun of. She has already been introduced as a character in the no-holds-barred Channel Four comedy *The Windsors*. Kathryn Drysdale plays her as a relentless name-dropper, while Harry is so dumb he cannot even read. And talking of dumb, the US cable network Lifetime announced that it would release *Harry and Meghan: The Royal Love Story* just before the wedding. Their previous offering, entitled *William and Kate: The Movie*, which they produced in 2011, was described by the *Guardian* newspaper as 'toe-curlingly, teeth-furringly, pillow-bitingly ghastly'.

What was no laughing matter was the decision by Meghan's lifelong friend Ninaki Priddy, who was her maid of honour at her first wedding, to sell her photograph albums and story to the highest bidder, receiving a six-figure sum for her memories. Given the longevity of their relationship, Meghan may have expected rather more loyalty. Unlike Ms Priddy and other members of the Markle family, her mother remained a publicly silent but supportive presence, advising on and discussing the details of the wedding with her daughter.

❖

Indeed, Meghan and Harry had to tune out what she calls 'the noise' and focus on the job in hand – organizing their wedding. Unlike her first marriage, which she left largely in the hands of a wedding organizer in Jamaica, Meghan wanted to control every detail, the big day reflecting what their spokesman described as the 'fun, laughter and love' of their 'fairy tale'.

First item on the agenda was the guest list. It was going to prove trickier than either of them expected. The first indications were when Harry was asked if his friends, former President and First Lady, Barack and Michelle Obama were getting a stiff white envelope. He was uncharacteristically evasive, saying that nothing had been decided.

The elephant careering around the royal chapel was Donald Trump. When he was a Republican candidate, Meghan had made her disdain for him perfectly clear, telling talk-show host Larry Wilmore in May 2016 that she would stay in Canada if he were elected. Her then-publicist Ken Sunshine is a significant figure in the Democrat party and she spoke about electing Hillary Clinton as the first female president.

Six weeks later, Prince Harry entered her life and her political world went smartly onto the backburner – though after their second date together she still registered her disappointment when Britain voted to leave the European Union, posting an Instagram snap of the famous placard 'If EU leave me now, you take away the biggest part of me.' Fast forward to February 2017 when a story appeared in *US Weekly* magazine, supposedly revealing that Harry was not a fan of President Trump. Not by a long chalk.

The source went further, suggesting that Harry thought Trump was 'terrifying' and a 'threat to human rights'. He supposedly called on the same words reportedly used by Trump's former Secretary of State Rex Tillerson to describe the President of the United States: 'a moron'.

While Kensington Palace refused to comment on anonymously sourced stories, alarm bells were ringing in Whitehall. By now, every diplomat in the world knows that Trump is a narcissist who bears a grudge. With Britain, though, at the time in a state of post-Brexit paralysis, Prime Minister Theresa May needed all the help she could get to land trade deals, and North America was a prime target.

The last thing she wanted was a popular prince taking pot shots at the president. Not that he seems to have noticed. When Trump was asked by Piers Morgan in a TV interview in January about the royal couple, he said he wasn't aware if he had been invited to the wedding but wished the couple well. When Piers helpfully reminded him that Meghan was not a fan, Meghan having accused Trump of being a 'divisive misogynist', Trump seemed unruffled: 'Well, I still hope they are happy.'

Closer to home there were other difficult decisions about whom to invite. While Meghan's own family is fractured, there are also rifts in the royal family that the wedding may help to heal. The Duchess of York, who is divorced from Harry's uncle Prince Andrew, was not invited to the wedding of Prince William and Catherine Middleton. She later confessed to Oprah Winfrey that the snub left her feeling 'so totally worthless'. A palace source indicated that this time around, Sarah Ferguson will indeed be going to the wedding of the year. 'Harry and Meghan have total control over who goes to the wedding and there was never an issue at the palace about Sarah being invited,' noted a palace official.

The thorny issue of the guest list – St George's Chapel can accommodate 800 – was just one of the items on their wedding agenda. As they had chosen the day of the FA Cup football final to plight their troth, they had to ensure that William, as both President of the Football Association and Harry's best man, was able to attend the nuptials before driving to Wembley Stadium in north London, where he would be meeting the teams and presenting the trophy.

Once that logistical headache was resolved, the couple went to Monaco, flying economy to see in the New Year with friends. Then Harry flew alone to Botswana as part of his work for the Rhino Conservation charity, leaving Meghan at Nottingham Cottage with her friend Jessica Mulroney, the professional wedding planner flying in from Toronto to help with arrangements. They had loads of ideas to discuss. As the wedding represents the symbolic union of two nations, there was debate about how best to integrate the red, white and blue of the Union flag and the Stars and Stripes. Naturally Meghan wanted it to be classy – her favourite word – not cheesy. The flowers in the chapel, her dress and even the tiara she will borrow from the Queen's collection are all ways of symbolizing the theme of two nations united.

When Meghan visited the chapel and looked around the magnificent medieval building, after pinching herself, she'd have been forgiven for perhaps wondering what it would be like to have her Emmy-winning father in charge of the lighting for the TV broadcast. With an expected audience of two billion, it would have been the biggest gig of his career – and no doubt he would have preferred to have a behind-the-scenes role. What would he have thought about his Valley Girl daughter getting her own coat of arms? Fancy that.

One concern was the aircraft noise. With so many aircraft taking off and landing at nearby Heathrow Airport, the world's busiest, Meghan worried that the billions at home wouldn't be able to hear the service. As many an American tourist has wondered, why on earth did they build Windsor Castle so near to Heathrow? During the big day, would air traffic control at least divert aircraft onto a different flight path so that everyone could hear her say 'I do'? The Civil Aviation Authority answered in the affirmative, agreeing to move all flights away from Windsor for 'security and safety' reasons.

Meghan certainly wouldn't be saying the traditional 'love, honour and obey', as did the Duchess of York when she became Prince Andrew's wife and Sophie Rhys-Jones when she married Prince Edward. She will follow the lead of Diana and Kate, who promised to 'love, comfort, honour and keep' her royal spouse.

Decisions, decisions, decisions. The couple wanted to surprise their family and friends with 'quirky and imaginative' elements. The Middleton sisters had led the way; in 2011 Catherine installed a posh ice-cream van and burger stalls at Buckingham Palace for her evening reception, while her sister Pippa brought in table-tennis tables for her nuptials. She played a match with tennis star Roger Federer, who then took on Catherine, William and Harry.

As fun as all this was, the centrepiece for the last great royal wedding for a generation would be Meghan's wedding dress. Like every bride, royal or not, she wanted to keep the wedding dress secret, only unveiling the unique creation on the big day. With a royal bride, the chosen couturier goes to extraordinary lengths to keep the design and fabric under wraps. Sarah Burton, who designed Kate's wedding dress, put up net curtains in her studio, changed the door code and banned cleaners from the building. Other royal couturiers have burned samples and shredded pencil drawings to leave no clue for the beady-eyed. For Meghan's wedding dress, the bookies' favourite was the Queen's designer, Stewart Parvin, who made the wedding dress for Zara Phillips, daughter of the Princess Royal. Other runners and riders included Erdem Moralıoğlu, Roland Mouret, Victoria Beckham and, of course, Stella McCartney.

In anticipation of Meghan's final appearance on *Suits* and the royal wedding hoopla, *Suits* producers released a trailer for the climax of season seven which featured Meghan in a wedding dress. After all the twists and turns of their relationship, Meghan's character Rachel Zane was about to marry her on-screen lover, Mike Ross. This was indeed art imitating life, the show's producers hoping that the ratings would be as happy and glorious as Meghan's real-life affair.

While the world eagerly sought scraps of wedding information, this time Meghan wasn't giving out any clues on her social media platforms as she had during the very early days of her royal romance. She had already closed her blog The Tig the previous March, but in January 2018 she went further, closing all her social media platforms – Instagram, Twitter and Facebook – and removing all her pictures and comments.

During their lifetime she had accumulated a substantial fan club, with well over a million followers on Instagram, 350,000 on Twitter and 800,000 likes on her Facebook page. Her decision to end them outraged her fans, who began a petition to have the sites reinstated. The petition, which was started by Sabrina A., who also runs the website meghanmaven.com, argued that by shutting down these accounts the royal family was cutting off the chance to reach an entirely new audience, especially as the royal family's website attracted more than a million extra hits once Meghan joined the fold.

She has a point. After all, Princess Beatrice, the Duchess of York's eldest daughter, has a Twitter account, and other European royals, notably Princess Charlene of Monaco and Princess Madeleine of Sweden, have their personal sites on social media. Then there is that other American princess, formerly Sarah Butler, now Princess Zeid of Jordan, who has her own Twitter account, which focuses on worthy topics such as global learning, refugee relief and disaster philanthropy.

In recent months, information regarding Meghan and Prince Harry has been shared through Kensington Palace and official royal family accounts. Eventually, Meghan may want her own vehicle to promote her work and chosen causes. Her fans argue that it should be launched via her existing base. I was told that inside the palace there is debate about this issue; those officials who are in favour of individual websites for members of the royal family are conscious that they can't get 'too far ahead of the Queen' on this matter.

If she still had access to her social media accounts she would have no doubt had a few choice words to say about the controversial decision by Simon Dudley, leader of the borough council that is home to Windsor Castle, to ask the police to ensure that 'aggressive' homeless beggars were removed from the castle surroundings before the big day.

His comments were described as inappropriate and there were calls for his dismissal. Ironically, the row broke out in early January just as Meghan was getting down to wedding details with Jessica Mulroney. As Meghan's first-ever charity commitment was to the homeless in downtown LA when she was a teenager, and as Jessica is co-founder of the Shoebox project, which has so far donated 91,000 boxes of toiletries to homeless women living in shelters, there was no need for a hotline to Kensington Palace to gauge the reaction. Moreover, as both Prince William and his late mother are and were patrons of Centrepoint, the charity for homeless youth, the council leader could not have picked a target more likely to arouse regal ire.

While the row rumbled on, Meghan and Harry made their second joint official visit, the couple touring the social enterprise radio station Reprezent 107.3 FM in Brixton, south London, home to many of the capital's African and Caribbean communities. As the excited crowd chanted, 'We love you', Meghan smiled, waved and blew kisses. When the noise reached a ragged crescendo, she coyly put her hand in front of her mouth.

During her tour of the station, which trains hundreds of young people every year in media and related skills, the gender-equality campaigner singled out presenter YV Shells, asking the twenty-four-year-old if he was the guy who supported women DJs, empowering women and creating a space that is not so male-driven. 'I think that's incredible,' she said.

Inevitably attention focused on what she was wearing – a £45 bell sleeve black wool jumper, a staple from the mid-market Marks & Spencer clothing chain. It was a marked contrast to the £56,000 dress she wore for her engagement portrait.

On a walkabout outside, she met with American students Jennifer Martinez and Millicent Sasu from Baltimore. Jennifer approved of the American import: 'She's black, she's white, she's an actress, she's American. She brings a bit of everything and has so many different qualities. She brings so much to the table.'

Not everyone thought so. During her time on the TV reality show, *Celebrity Big Brother*, former member of Parliament Ann Widdecombe described her as 'trouble', saying that she was worried about the 'background' and 'attitude' of Harry's fiancée. Matters got uglier as racist remarks made by the girlfriend of Henry Bolton, leader of the pro-Brexit UK Independence Party, were made public.

In a series of text messages, glamour model Jo Marney told a friend that Meghan would 'taint' the royal family with 'her seed' and pave the way for a 'black king'. She went on to say that she would never have sex with 'a negro' because they are 'ugly'. Many of the party's front-bench spokesmen walked out in protest when Bolton refused to quit.

He was eventually ousted after a vote by the party's shrinking membership. The vote took place before the alarming revelation in February that a letter containing a white powder and a racist letter was sent to Meghan and Prince Harry at Kensington Palace. While the white powder was deemed harmless, it brought back memories of the anthrax scares in America a week after the 9/11 attack in 2001 when various senators and others were sent the deadly powder through the mail by, it was believed, an American bio-defence scientist. This domestic terrorism left five dead and seventeen others affected by the anthrax spores; it proved so alarming that it enabled future mischief makers to cause chaos and disruption for the price of a postage stamp.

The incident, which was officially treated as a race hate crime, was a further example, if any more were needed, that racial prejudice is still a potent issue in multi-racial Britain. These sensitive subjects of race and colour were also issues that concerned those who wondered what happened inside the royal palaces once the cameras and microphones are switched off.

The answer is perhaps surprising: class rather than colour is the great divider. Though the Duchess of Cambridge now seems part of the royal wallpaper, it wasn't always the case. She has faced far more prejudice from those on the inside, the first commoner for 400 years set to be queen, than the bi-racial Californian. Since first meeting William at St Andrews University in Scotland, Kate was seen by royal courtiers simply as the girl who encouraged him to stay on when he had a well-publicized wobble in the first semester. She was viewed as a perfectly pleasant middle-class girl who, at some point, would marry someone of her own class when she had finished her degree. When casual friendship morphed into romance it is safe to say that royal courtiers were stunned. 'She got in under the wire,' said one.

Once she started moving among William's circle of aristocratic friends, she faced snide remarks and out-and-out bigotry. The focus was on her mother, who was raised in a council house in Southall and once worked as an air stewardess. 'Doors to manual', was the cry of William's snooty pals. It didn't help Catherine that, in the early days, William was sending mixed messages about her. His ambivalence gave others the chance to criticize and snipe. Not so Harry. From the get-go he was certain that Meghan was the one. No ifs or buts. It has left no room for anyone inside the palace to raise an eyebrow at his choice of bride – commoner or not. It is fair to say that eyebrows have remained studiously unraised. The lead has been taken from the top and that lead has been entirely positive.

Indeed, even though she has only been officially engaged since November 2017, it is as if she has always been part of the family. Meghan has only made a handful of public appearances, but she is well on the way to being accepted as a bona fide National Treasure. By the time she travelled to Wales a week after her visit to south London, she was well into her stride, the slight reticence that had characterized her first couple of engagements replaced by a relaxed manner and a willingness to have fun, to go with the flow.

During their walkabout at Cardiff Castle – where Meghan exhibited spot-on sartorial diplomacy by sporting black jeans from the small Welsh brand Hiut Denim – Meghan described herself as a 'super-lucky woman' and even joked with two fans that the Welsh city would be a 'fun' location for a hen party. Unlike on her first outing, she felt confident enough to pose for selfies, signed an autograph for one star-struck schoolgirl and described her husband-to-be as a 'feminist'. She was even presented with a wooden Welsh love spoon as an early wedding gift.

Meghan-mania reached fever pitch by the time she and Harry arrived at Star Hub community leisure centre in the economically deprived area of Tremorfa. Meghan was soon surrounded by youngsters desperate to meet her. They were given their cue by Harry, who told them, 'Let's all give Meghan a group hug!'

Her visit was a triumph, with even tabloid cynics going all misty-eyed about her performance. 'Centuries of royal tradition melted away as the US actress brought the warmth of modern celebrity to adoring crowds,' opined the *Sun*'s Jack Royston.

After the Cardiff visit, Harry took Meghan on a short drive to meet the other woman in his life, his former nanny and companion, 'Tiggy' Legge-Bourke, who had mentored the princes following Diana's divorce and subsequent death. For Meghan, it was a chance to get to know and understand the woman who had such a striking impact on the upbringing of the man she was due to marry.

Though she would never meet Harry's mother, reminders of her influence and presence were everywhere. Meghan's first evening appearance was at Goldsmiths' Hall in the City of London, which, by extraordinary coincidence, was where Lady Diana Spencer also undertook her first evening engagement in the run-up to her wedding at St Paul's Cathedral.

A generation on, and now Diana's youngest son was taking his own bride-to-be there. They were guests of honour at the Endeavour Fund Awards, set up by Harry's Royal Foundation, to celebrate and honour the achievements of wounded, injured and sick servicemen and women who have taken part in remarkable sporting challenges over the last year. A veteran of awards ceremonies, Meghan was cool and poised, unfazed when the envelope containing the winner of the award 'celebrating excellence' went missing for a few seconds while her co-presenter hunted for the errant piece of paper. 'I am truly privileged to be here,' she told a specially invited audience of former service personnel and their families. Unlike Diana, who arrived for her first evening engagement in a low-cut dress that she almost spilled out of when she got out of the car, Meghan plumped for a sleekly sophisticated Alexander McQueen trouser suit. The nineteen-year-old Diana would have surely been in awe of such confident self-assurance – in some ways, the groomed and camera-ready Ms Markle was the woman Diana always strove to become.

Yet much also connects them. Both women shared a humanitarian mission, albeit on a vastly different scale, both were charismatic and glamorous, and both recognized that they were invested with a power to do good in the world.

However, when Diana broke through the barriers of class and ethnicity on both sides of the Atlantic, her appeal as a celebrity lay as much in her vulnerability as in her star status. She was all the more attractive because of that sensitivity, especially to women with unhappy marriages. Her social work, visiting those in hospices on their last lonely journey, was therapeutic, as healing for her as it was for those she comforted.

The word vulnerable does not immediately spring to mind when assessing Ms Markle's many splendid qualities. Empathetic certainly, but also self-possessed, sophisticated and poised, equally at home on a podium making a speech or on a photoshoot. She is a flag bearer for a new generation of confident, assertive women, determined to kick through the glass ceiling.

❖

Time and again Meghan has proved herself a team player, embracing her new family and her new country with enthusiasm.

This California girl may inwardly wince at the idea of bending the knee, and may miss all those opportunities to take stylized selfies and rage at the near impossibility of finding a ripe avocado or a decent hot yoga studio in central London, but she will survive and thrive. She will struggle over the pronunciation of Derby, Leicester and Torquay, learn that Brits prefer to sneer than do sincere, and discover that irony is not a device with which to press your designer shirts. She will learn, sometimes painfully, that while we share the same mother tongue, the British and Americans are very different people.

Her presence inside the royal family is a challenge and an opportunity.

Long before Prince Harry transformed her life, Meghan had articulated what was effectively her manifesto for her future life. Following a visit to Rwanda she wrote, in her now defunct blog, The Tig: 'My life shifts from refugee camps to red carpets, I choose them both because these worlds can, in fact, coexist. I've never wanted to be a lady who lunches – I've always wanted to be a woman who works. And this type of work is what feeds my soul and fuels my purpose.'

For all that, her very presence inside the royal family will make the monarchy seem more inclusive and relevant to multicultural Britain, even as the nation struggles to come to terms with diversity in a post-Brexit world.

The image of the Queen and Meghan's mother, Doria Ragland, an African-American, standing outside St George's Chapel together, will be a symbolic moment; one the descendant of a slave, the other the longest-serving monarch in British history. Meghan, who has already proved herself to be an immensely popular choice of bride, will complement her husband and the august institution she has married into, bringing a freshness, diversity and warmth to the chilly corridors of Buckingham Palace.

Her many fans and admirers are eager to watch the next episode of her great royal adventure. With her smarts, sophistication, beauty and talent, Meghan represents the American Dream of having it all, achieving her success by dint of hard work and ability. Her life intersected with Prince Harry's at a point where he had proven himself worthy of respect, in spite of, not because of, the privileges bestowed upon him by his birth and heritage. While they may have come from different countries, backgrounds and cultures, their union is undoubtedly the crowning symbolic achievement of the special relationship between a monarchy and a republic.

PICTURE CREDITS

PLATE SECTION ONE

Page 1: MEGA (top); MEGA (bottom)

Page 2: Mail on Sunday / Solo Syndication (top); Mail on Sunday / Solo Syndication (bottom)

Page 3: Mail on Sunday / Solo Syndication (top); Mail on Sunday / Solo Syndication (bottom)

Page 4: Splash News (top); Splash News (bottom)

Page 5: The Sun / News Licensing (top); Splash News (bottom)

Page 6: © John Dlugolecki / Contact Press Images (top, left); © John Dlugolecki / Contact Press Images (top, right); Splash News (bottom)

Page 7: © Vicki Conrad / Contact Press Images (top, left); © John Dlugolecki / Contact Press Images (top, right); © John Dlugolecki / Contact Press Images (bottom)

Page 8: Splash News (top); © John Dlugolecki / Contact Press Images (bottom)

Page 9: Courtesy of Emmanuel Eulalia (top); Courtesy of Emmanuel Eulalia (bottom, left); Courtesy of Emmanuel Eulalia (bottom, right)

Page 10: Courtesy of Emmanuel Eulalia (top); © John Dlugolecki / Contact Press Images (bottom)

Page 11: © John Dlugolecki / Contact Press Images (top); Splash News (bottom)

Page 12: Splash News (top); © Tameka Jacobs (bottom)

Page 13: Splash News (top); Splash News (bottom)

Page 14: Moviestore / REX / Shutterstock (top); Frank Ockenfels / Dutch Oven / Kobal / REX / Shutterstock (bottom)

Page 15: Dutch Oven / Kobal / REX / Shutterstock

Page 16: Startraks Photo / REX / Shutterstock (top); Birdie Thompson / AdMedia / Sipa USA / REX / Shutterstock (bottom)

PLATE SECTION TWO

Page 1: Mail on Sunday / Solo Syndication (top); Splash News (bottom)

Page 2: MediaPunch / REX / Shutterstock (top); Alpha Press (bottom)

Page 3: Mike McGregor / Getty Images for Cantor Fitzgerald (top); DOD Photo / Alamy (bottom)

Page 4: DOD Photo / Alamy (top); Clodagh Kilcoyne / Getty Images (bottom)

Page 5: Pictorial Press Ltd / Alamy (top); Ben Rosser / BFAnyc.com / REX / Shutterstock (bottom)

Page 6: Nicholas Hunt / Getty Images

Page 7: The Sun / News Licensing

Page 8: Karwai Tang / WireImage / Getty Images

Page 9: WENN Ltd / Alamy (top); World Vision / Splash (bottom)

Page 10: Evan Agostini / Invision / AP / REX / Shutterstock (long portrait) (top); Photograph by Mark Stewart, Camera Press London (bottom)

Page 11: Karwai Tang / WireImage / Getty Images (top); Chris Jackson / Getty Images for the Invictus Games Foundation (bottom)

Page 12: Facundo Arrizabalaga / EPA-EFE / REX / Shutterstock (top); WENN Ltd / Alamy (bottom)

Page 13: Chris Jackson / Getty Images

Page 14–15: Photograph by Paul John Bayfield, Camera Press London

Page 16: Dominic Lipinski / AFP / Getty Images (top); Chris Jackson / AP / REX / Shutterstock (Royal Foundation Forum) (bottom)

INDEX